Books by Madeleine Kamman

Dinner Against the Clock

Dinner Against the Clock

MADELEINE KAMMAN

Atheneum 1973 *New York*

To my sisters—and brothers—in liberation

Introduction

This volume does not pretend to be the definitive book on quick cookery, for there is actually no quick cookery, there are only methods of cookery that allow one to prepare certain foods in a relatively short time.

After a little over a decade of what truly can be called an awakening to the world of fine foods, America remains divided in its culinary habits. Rural America still uses its own homemade and home-grown products, and being more isolated from cosmopolitan influences, has yet to experience desire to experiment with new foods. The Atlantic and Pacific coasts, on the contrary, are widely open to the influences of Europe and the Far East, and are both more adventurous and more snobbish in their food habits. Quite a few European and Far Eastern dishes have become part of the daily diet, to the point that quiche Lorraine, moo goo gai pan, and tempura have become or are about to become bores.

Even in the more sophisticated parts of American society, there are differences. Some will forever just admire, copy, and cook recipes, and find joy in the innumerable books written by authors with varying degrees of knowledge of food preparation, trusting the final taste of their daily or festive meals to someone else's taste buds. Others, on the contrary, seem more interested in creating their own blends and flavors, and understanding in depth what they are doing in the kitchen.

I have had the privilege of seeing many of these kitchen adventurers stream through my cooking school and enjoy themselves thoroughly as they saw a meal being improvised in a matter of forty minutes. This book is dedicated to them, to all the young women and men who have been let out of their homes without the slightest idea of how to go about preparing a decent simple meal, and to those not-so-young men and women who, having felt the need to finally get into the kitchen themselves, have ended up as my captive audience—and most of whom have gradually become enthusiastic, sometimes passionate, quick cooks.

Ideally, schools and teachers should coach their students to think out how best to apply newly acquired knowledge. The role of an honest cooking teacher is not only to show how to cook so-and-so's gastronomic masterpiece, but also to point out and explain in depth what techniques and principles so-and-so has applied to build his/her recipe, and to bring the student to understand that the very same technique can be applied to multiple other combinations of ingredients.

This method of teaching cooking is not a gimmick; I have used it for over twelve years now, and the results have exceeded my best hopes. I will grant, for sure, that learning sheer technique does not appear to be what makes cooking a joy, but my experience has proved that only those persons who are willing to learn and understand techniques and general cooking principles in depth ever end up being real cooks, as opposed to mere recipe copiers. I have, as a culinary translator, worked for years on many a recipe written by the greatest names of the French culinary world, and there is no doubt that those who show the greatest genius at the stove have, besides the innate talents of a natural cook, the most vast technical culinary culture. There is absolutely no doubt that cooking is an art, which, like playing a musical instrument, needs to be mastered.

Besides the matter of technique, there remains the matter of balancing seasonings, and this will always remain dependent on the cook's personal taste and palate. In this book I want to impose nothing; the plain, simple recipes I have included are meant to be examples of what can be done with a basic technique, and the seasonings and flavors can by all means be changed by the cook. It is my fervent wish that, having mastered the basic techniques of quicker cookery and having learned how to get organized, the novice cook will after a while relegate this book to a shelf and continue on his or her own merry way to a personal style.

I have organized the book so it can be used as a manual. Key recipes explain briefly the quickest traditional methods to be followed to cook soups, sauces, meats and fish, eggs, vegetables, and desserts. In the chapters covering main dishes—eggs, meat, poultry, and fish—the key recipe is followed by proposed dinner menus, each menu containing: (1) a recipe for the main course, that recipe being an application of the technique featured in the key recipe; (2) the order in which the steps for preparing the whole dinner can be executed. This kind of organization will force the cook to do some homework, giving him or her a chance to become a thinking cook, rather than remaining a life-long slave to a recipe.

Throughout, I have provided short tables that indicate the amounts of ingredients to use in serving from two to six persons. And, to make the book more usable until you feel more ready to improvise, the formula used in professional kitchens to enlarge an already existing recipe can be found, with an example of how to use it, on page 200.

I would like to emphasize that the preparation times indicated on menus and recipes are bound to vary both with individual temperament and experience. The first time you try something may seem to take a lot longer than the time indicated, but as you gain experience and gather speed you will be soon spending only as much time as is indicated in the book.

Now some general notes:

I express regrets that not everyone will be willing, or will find the time, to make stock; this item truly makes the difference between just a dish and a very good dish, and I feel compelled to mention here that if you use canned broth or bouillon cubes, you should under no circumstances expect the results you would obtain with the homemade veal stock described on page 11. And although I have indicated margarine as an alternative for butter, I will never consider that the first can at any time replace the second; my personal source of polyunsaturated oil will remain a bottle of natural corn or sunflower oil rather than a stick of margarine.

One implement that one might expect to find in a quick cookery book has been eliminated from this one. That implement is the pressure cooker, this writer's point of view being that foods cooked in a pressure cooker taste, to say the least, different.

Radically eliminated also are the preprocessed and prepackaged items that ruin the taste of good honest food; the use of cans is a rarity, and "pussycat food" casseroles are nowhere to be found. And while ideas for grain dishes have been adopted from the "natural cooks" clan—and so has its wise use of honey as a replacement for refined sugar—this is an everyday cookbook for everyday cooks, which also wants to demonstrate that, between the prepackaged, preprocessed, and precooked way and the natural foods way, there is a reasonable path accessible to all.

Madeleine Kamman

Newton Centre, Massachusetts
December 1972

Contents

Dinner Against the Clock

CHAPTER I

Generalities

EQUIPMENT

Working people often live in small apartments or houses, and the size
of their kitchens, as much as the time they dedicate to cooking, limits
the volume of their cooking equipment. The following implements,
however, are indispensable, and should be in your cupboard:

1 large frying pan or skillet
1 electric frying pan
1 electric deep-fryer
1 four-cup saucepan, preferably of enameled cast iron
1 six-cup saucepan, preferably of enameled cast iron
1 four-quart boiling pot
1 French omelet pan, which can also be used as a crêpe pan
2 wooden spoons
2 rubber spatulas, one small, one large
2 small sauce whisks
1 hand electric mixer
1 blender

3

1 pair of tongs
1 two-quart baking dish
1 9-inch pie plate
1 9-inch cake pan
1 large jelly-roll pan
1 long metal spatula
1 slotted spoon
1 set of measuring cups for dry ingredients
1 four-cup-capacity measuring cup
1 paring knife (Sabatier or Henckels)
1 all-purpose chef's knife, with seven- or eight-inch blade (Sabatier or Henckels)
1 chopping board
1 automatic vegetable chopper (optional, see page 21)
1 corkscrew
1 strainer
1 colander
1 highball glass to use as a pestle in mashing potatoes

SHOPPING

Even if you have only a little time to dedicate to the systematic reading of newspapers, try to tear off and put aside the food pages of the Wednesday and Thursday editions of newspapers, and before you go shopping, take a minute to study what is on sale.

To make your shopping easier, set aside time once a week to plan what you intend to prepare each night for dinner, first checking to see what is still present in your larder before buying new ingredients. Make a shopping list, and if at all possible, get used to shopping in the very same market every week so you can go to the shelves without the slightest hesitation and know where to find each ingredient. Go to a different market only if it offers an excellent sale on a particular cut of meat.

For busy people, the best time to shop is on Thursday and Friday after dinner—shelves are filled and the store is less crowded than on Saturday.

BASIC INGREDIENTS

Natural Foods and Organic Foods

If you know the difference between natural foods and organic foods, you are less likely to lose money.

A natural food is one that is free of any additive of any kind, such as artificial colors and flavors, emulsifiers, and preservatives. The word "organic" is confusing, for anything that contains a carbon molecule should really be called organic—such as a diamond, for example. But in today's terminology an organic food is one that has been grown in a soil fertilized by organic matter and/or natural mineral fertilizers.

Among the many foods sold both on special shelves of supermarkets and in health food stores, many are hoaxes. Here are a few pointers that may be useful:

BREADS   Breads made with whole-grain, unbleached flour and without vegetable shortening are available in health food stores and also in supermarkets under at least two well-known commercial labels. The prices of the commercial natural breads sold in supermarkets are less extravagant that those of breads sold in health food stores.

CEREALS   Even supermarkets carry whole-grain cereals at reasonable prices. The best are unsweetened and contain neither artificial colorings nor flavorings. Read the labels.

FLOUR   Stone-ground flours offered for sale in health food stores are the best, since they have been ground "cool" and their heat-sensitive nutrients have been well preserved—but they must be stored in the refrigerator. Commercial unbleached and enriched flour is, on the other hand, quite acceptable, nutritionally speaking, and costs about one-third less than the stone-ground flour.

SUGAR   So-called raw unrefined sugar is the biggest hoax of all. In point of fact this sugar is not raw, and it contains only traces more of essential minerals than white sugar. The true nutritious substitutes for sugar are honey and unsulfured blackstrap molasses.

SALT There is no benefit in using sea salt. Sea salt should ideally consist only of what is left after sea water has evaporated, and it should be unrefined. But the sea water it is extracted from is so very dirty that the salt must be refined for purposes of cleaning it. The refining disposes of all the minerals, so that sea salt is not any better, nutritionally speaking, than any other iodized supermarket salt.

PASTA AND RICE Whole-grain pasta and brown rice may both be purchased in health food stores, and are worth the price asked for them.

HONEY Honey is organic whether sold in a supermarket or in a health food store, because any bee feeding on a sprayed flower would immediately die of poisoning. But the chances are that honeys sold in health food stores will come from bees feeding only on unsprayed flowers, not on sugar water, and from bees that have never been treated with sulfa drugs when sick. In any case, health food store honeys taste better than supermarket honeys.

YOGURT Buy plain yogurt made with whole milk; even supermarkets carry it under several labels at reasonable prices.

VEGETABLES AND FRUIT There are at least ten times more so-called organic vegetables sold than are actually grown. True, organically grown vegetables taste better than the supermarket vegetables, but the nutritional value is identical.

Most fruit sold in supermarkets is waxed with a paraffin coating that does not wash off, so the fruit should, ideally, be peeled. If you like to eat unpeeled fruit, go to the health food store and buy unsprayed, uncoated, organically grown fruit; but be prepared to spend a great deal of money for it—and make sure that the store owner is honest.

DAIRY PRODUCTS

MILK AND CHEESE Milk is too often discarded from the diet in young adulthood. Even if you do not like milk, you need its calcium and phosphorus. If you object to drinking plain milk, add it to your tea, coffee, or soup. The comparative caloric values of milk are the following per eight-ounce cup:

> Whole milk: 148 to 159 calories
> Plain skim milk: 82 calories
> Fortified skim milk: 127 to 137 calories

If you have a delicate stomach, you may want to drink whole or plain skim milk, which is easier to digest than fortified skim milk. If your resistance to milk is total, eat ice milk, or better, yogurt and/or cheese, plain or in your food. Cheddar, Parmesan, and Swiss contain the largest amounts of calcium and phosphorus. One ounce of each provides about the same amount of calcium and phosphorus as one cup of whole or skim milk. The best cheese is natural. Avoid any processed type that contains all kinds of chemicals beneficial neither to your diet nor to your taste buds.

CREAMS If you use cream, expect the following types to produce the following amount of calories per tablespoon:

> Heavy cream: 50 calories
> Light cream: 28 to 37 calories
> Half-and-half: 20 calories
> Commercial sour cream: about 15 calories

The best taste and texture for food prepared with cream is obtained with heavy cream. To limit weight problems, use heavy cream only for special occasions. Light cream or half-and-half may be used on a more regular basis. Yogurt, with 8.5 calories per tablespoon, is an excellent replacement for sour cream.

Fats and Oils

VEGETABLE SHORTENING Vegetable shortening has only one virtue—it is cheap. It does not taste good, it is highly saturated and cholesterol producing, and plainly not good for the daily diet. The same remarks apply to lard.

OILS Do not, for the sake of economy, buy a very large amount of oil at once; oil oxidates fast and loses freshness. There are a variety of good polyunsaturated oils to choose from, and the best of these are corn, soybean, and sunflower. Corn and soybean oils are the cheapest when bought in supermarkets. When bought in health food stores they are more expensive, because they do not contain artificial antioxidants. Sunflower oil is to be found almost exclusively in health food stores. It is delicious, but quite expensive. Safflower oil, the most polyunsaturated of all oils, has one very bad drawback—it turns rancid very quickly. If you use it, buy very small bottles and renew your supply often. Use cottonseed oil only if eating pesticides doesn't bother you, for cottonfields are heavily sprayed by farmers.

Olive oil is monosaturated only. It is the best-tasting salad oil and gives the best results for dishes of Mediterranean style or origin, but if you are concerned with cholesterol, you may omit it, for it will not benefit you in a dietary way. All oils produce from 120 to 128 calories per tablespoon.

MARGARINES Watch margarines carefully. Check their list of contents; the first ingredient should be "liquid corn oil." If it is not, the margarine is not polyunsaturated and there is very little benefit in using it. Margarine, like butter, is made of about 80 percent fat and 20 percent liquids or added solids (which burn in the pan when you pan-fry). Margarine, like butter, produces 100 calories per tablespoon.

BUTTER Butter is generally salted because in colonial America it was salted for preservation and the American palate has remained used to its taste. Many cheap salted butters are rancid. Unsalted butter has every chance of being fresher than salted butter, but once in a while whey fermentation will have started in a shipment and the butter will smell rancid even through its wrappers. Do not hesitate to smell the butter you intend to buy.

Although expensive for everyday use, butter is the tastiest pan-frying fat. Unclarified, butter burns fast and the food appears pitted with burned milk solids; clarified, it fries as cleanly as oil. And while you may think clarified butter is a luxury item to be reserved for elaborate cooking, it is a good idea to know how to make it and to keep a small jar of it frozen. It can transform a pan-fried chicken cutlet or fish fillet into a dish fit for company.

CLARIFIED BUTTER

Melt at least ½ cup of butter over medium heat. Turn the heat off and let stand 15 minutes. Skim off the top crust and spoon the liquid butter-fat into a small jar, discarding the whey at the bottom of the pan.

GENERAL NOTES ON FATS AND OILS For your everyday diet; you may want to use the following guidelines:

For a completely unsaturated diet, use exclusively the best grade of polyunsaturated oil of your choice. (You may use polyunsaturated margarine if you do not mind all the chemicals added to it.)

For a regular diet, use half butter and half polyunsaturated oil.

For problem budgets, the best all-around cooking fat is a polyunsaturated oil. Pure corn oil bought in a supermarket, for example, costs a little over a cent per tablespoon, while for the same amount of a polyunsaturated margarine you may well pay one and one half times as much.

MEAT, POULTRY AND FISH

If you live in a small apartment and have a small refrigerator, it may be smarter to shop for meats twice rather than once a week. Shopping thriftily is useless if you do not store the meat you buy properly. First and foremost, remove all tight plastic wrappers on all types of meat. Anaerobic bacteria develop under the wrappers and cause rapid spoilage in chicken, veal and pork; the same spoilage develops less rapidly in lamb and beef, but it still takes place and discolors the meat very unpleasantly. The following directions can safely be observed for the categories of meats listed below:

BEEF AND LAMB Cuts of beef and lamb can wait in a refrigerator for a week to 10 days without spoiling. Larger roasts and thick steaks will discolor, shrink, and dehydrate but gain in tenderness and flavor.

Store the pieces of meat on a cake rack placed over a jelly roll pan and extremely loosely covered by a small tent of foil, open at each end.

VEAL AND PORK   Cuts of veal and pork may wait 72 hours, loosely wrapped, before being used. Ground veal and pork should be used on the day purchased.

CHICKEN   Parts may wait up to 4 days before being used if kept loosely wrapped. Whole chickens will also keep that long if the bag of giblets is removed from the cavity.

VARIETY MEATS   Variety meats will wait only 24 hours in the refrigerator, loosely covered.

FISH   Fish bought in a supermarket must be consumed on the day purchased, while fish bought in a specialized fish market may wait 1 day, loosely covered.

GENERAL NOTES ON BUYING AND STORING   Organize your meat consumption. Should you buy the meats listed below on a Saturday, it would be best to use them on the days listed below:

> Fish: Saturday
> Calf's liver: Sunday
> Veal: Monday
> Chicken: Tuesday
> Pork: Freeze on Saturday, defrost
>   on Tuesday, and cook on Wednesday
> Lamb: Thursday
> Beef: Friday

Wrap meats before freezing, first in waxed paper and then in heavy-duty foil. Do not defrost meats on the kitchen counter but in the refrigerator. Small pieces will defrost in 24 to 36 hours, small roasts in 2 to 3 days, larger roasts in 4 days. There will be only a very small loss of natural juices.

BROTHS AND STOCKS

It is too bad that the making of broth will not be considered by everyone in quick everyday cookery.

While quick "natural and organic" cooks will have to consider making their own broth, "regular" cooks will have canned broth or even bouillon cubes to resort to. It is advisable when using bouillon cubes to choose the least salty of all. Try successively each brand available at the beginning of your cooking career and settle on the brand that adapts best to your personal taste. Imported bouillon cubes are likely to be less salty than domestic ones.

It is recommended that you use semisolid meat extracts sold in jars only to reinforce finished sauces rather than diluted in water for a broth. When you do use them, do so very sparingly. Start with a baby pea-sized amount on the tip of a teaspoon and add more only if necessary. Whatever the instructions of the manufacturers, never use a half or a whole teaspoon at once—you will ruin the dish you are preparing.

If you think that for quick entertaining you need a good stock—an expensive cut of meat truly deserves better than canned broth or cubes—you can obtain a very fast stock by using the following recipe. To prevent excess heating of the kitchen, make the stock after you have done your dinner dishes and before you go to bed, while you are, dare I suggest, relaxing.

GOOD BASIC STOCK FOR EXPENSIVE MEAT COOKERY
(*white or red*)

YIELD: ABOUT 6 CUPS

3 pounds veal breast, cut in small chunks
1 pound chicken wings
2 quarts cold water
2 small carrots

2 large onions, each stuck with 1 clove
2 large leeks or 4 scallions
1 2-inch piece of celery rib
1 bouquet garni (page 12)
1½ teaspoons salt

The butcher will gladly saw the veal breast in chunks for you. Put them and the chicken wings in your 4-quart stock pot. Cover with cold water and bring to a boil. Skim; add all the vegetables, herbs, and salt, and let simmer, uncovered, for 2½ hours. Strain and chill overnight. Degrease when the broth is cold and the fat solidified. Store in a 1-cup mason jar and store any unused amount in the freezer, if freezer space is available.

To use the stock for red meats and browned veal, color the stock artificially with a bottled coloring such as Gravy Master. The flavor of veal is most adaptable to all meats, red or white, including game birds and venison.

Spices, Herbs, and Aromatics

Although it is more often used in long cooking procedures, such as boiling and braising, than in quick everyday food, it is good to know that a little bundle of parsley enclosing 1 bay leaf and ¼ teaspoon of dried thyme is called a "bouquet garni." It is not, if one wants it to release its full flavor, to be enclosed in cheesecloth.

Make a place in your cupboard for the following collection of herbs and spices and use them. You will be surprised how they will transform humdrum food into a joy;

Bay leaves	Summer savory leaves
Chervil leaves	Basil leaves
Tarragon leaves	Nutmeg, whole
Marjoram leaves	Cloves, whole or ground
Rosemary leaves	Thyme leaves
Oregano flowers	Ground coriander
Mint leaves	Ground cinnamon

Note that there are two kinds of bay leaves; use half as much of the California bay leaf as you would of the Turkish bay leaf.

Parsley is plentiful enough so that you can find and use it fresh year round. It takes only a few seconds to chop it yourself. When you do so, stop chopping as soon as the parsley juices start coloring the board green.

A mixture called "Provençal herbs" is very much in use in modern French cuisine. You can make a mixture of those yourself, mixing and crumbling well:

1 tablespoon each dried thyme, chervil, tarragon, and marjoram
1 teaspoon each dried oregano and summer savory
½ teaspoon each dried rosemary and mint
2 bay leaves (or 1, if California)

Store the mixture in a small jar, and keep it tightly closed.

The best aromatics (onions, carrots, leeks) are chopped fresh by holding your chef's knife firmly on the chopping board without extending your index finger over the blade, and by sliding the blade back and forth on the board, cutting through the vegetables. If you are truly in a mad rush, do not hesitate to use frozen chopped onions, but take great care to sauté them well to evaporate all their excess moisture.

TOMATO PASTE

No more cans of tomato paste left to die on the refrigerator shelf! As soon as you have used the initial amount you need, measure tablespoons of the remainder into ice-cube trays and freeze. Then store the frozen lumps in a small plastic container. Keep frozen and use as needed.

BREAD CRUMBS AND GRATED CHEESE

Make bread crumbs in the blender with leftover Italian bread, using the crust for dry crumbs and the center for fresh crumbs. Store in half-cup jars in the freezer if you have enough freezer space. These crumbs are better than the packaged type, which, while requiring no work, are tasteless.

You may also make whole-wheat and rye crumbs using the same method. For additional nutrition, all bread crumbs may be blended with some wheat germ.

Grate a large amount of cheese; freeze it in small jars and defrost whatever amount you need when you need it.

WINES AND SPIRITS

Do not hesitate to use a bit of wine or spirits in your everyday cooking. It will pep up your food. Even if you are not normally an alcohol user, you may still use alcoholic beverages in cooking, since the cooking heat evaporates the alcohol.

For everyday use, buy honest table wines from California. An opened bottle of white wine, recorked, may be kept a few days in the refrigerator. Although dry vermouth never really replaces white wine, you may consider using it in quick cookery if you do not have any white wine on hand.

Red wine does not keep as well as white wine. Either drink the remainder of the bottle you are using, or pour it into a smaller bottle, which must be recorked carefully. Buying a half bottle of wine may very well be your solution if you plan to use the wine exclusively in your cooking.

Adding any amount of uncooked table wine to a finished dish will make it harsh and unpalatable, so take great care in reducing the wine at least by half. The only wines you may add uncooked, but in very small quantities, to a finished dish are those of the fortified type, such as sherry, Madeira, port, and Marsala.

If a recipe calls for brandy and you have none, replace it by whatever whiskey is in your cupboard. Scotch or bourbon are fine spirits, perfectly able to substitute for brandy or Cognac.

Flambéing means heating spirits in a small pot, lighting them, and pouring them flaming over a meat. It gives the meat additional flavor and burns off the alcohol in the spirits.

CHAPTER II

About Your Dinner Menu

A BALANCED DIET AND YOUR DINNER MENU

To obtain all the vitamins and minerals you need, your daily diet must include:

2 eight-ounce cups of milk or equivalent (cheese, yogurt, ice milk)

2 three-ounce servings of meat, fish, poultry, eggs, nuts, or legumes

2 servings of ½ cup each cooked or 1 cup each raw vegetables

2 servings of fruit per day (1 apple or pear or 1 cup of berries per day, plus 1 orange is an ideal combination); fruit juice may replace fruit

4 servings of bread or cereals per day (A good combination would be ¾ cup cooked cereals or 1 cup dry cereals for breakfast, 2 slices of good nutritious bread for a lunch sandwich, and ½ cup rice, noodles, or spaghetti for dinner.)

To keep your weight down, eat small, well-balanced meals; limit your intake of sugar; *positively never eat between meals*; and exercise as much as you can.

To keep your cholesterol level down, make sure that your total daily intake of fats and oils always includes 2 *tablespoons of polyunsaturated oil*. Eat more fish (with the exception of salmon and shellfish) and chicken than any other meat product.

Your efficiency at work and your enjoyment of life after work depend much on your nutrition. If you eat too much you will be irritable because you will put weight on. If you do not eat enough, you will be irritable because of subtle, creeping malnutrition.

Build your dinner menu in accordance with what you ate for breakfast and lunch. If you had bacon and eggs for breakfast and a high-protein sandwich for lunch, look for light meats, such as fish or chicken, for dinner; but if both breakfast and lunch have been light in protein and fats, use a red meat for dinner.

The best way to keep in shape is never to skip a meal; in our modern society, however, this isn't always possible. If you must skip a meal, then, try to make it the evening meal that you skip, for you will not expend energy while you are sleeping.

To obtain the full benefit of the vitamins contained in your food, cook a fresh dinner every day. Leftovers may save time, but they lose their vitamin content on the refrigerator shelf.

COOKING DINNER

The key to speed is organization. Let us look at a simple dinner menu and examine the order in which its different elements should be prepared for the sake of maximum efficiency:

> Garlic soup
> Wiener schnitzel
> Paprika salad
> Grapefruit with raspberry sauce

Study the menu and find the one element that requires the most time to prepare, or that will require chilling. In this menu the dessert requires time, for the raspberries have to defrost. To do this quickly, immerse the solidly frozen box of fruit in a bowl of hot water and let it soak while you prepare the second most time-consuming dish, which is the soup.

Bring the soup water or broth to a boil. Crush the unpeeled garlic cloves and add them to the boiling water. Let simmer happily. Toast the bread slices, put them in the soup bowls, and sprinkle them with some grated cheese.

Go back to the raspberries; drain off most of the canning syrup, pour the remainder of the contents of the box in the blender, and puree. Peel and slice the grapefruit. Put the slices in a dish and pour the raspberry puree over. Chill. (When you become more experienced you will even find a few minutes to strain the fruit so you do not have to eat all those seeds.)

The salad and the meat are now left for you to prepare. Wash the lettuce, tear the leaves in bite-sized pieces, roll them in a terry towel and keep them refrigerated until you are ready to eat. Make the salad dressing directly in the salad bowl.

Preheat your electric frying pan. Beat an egg with a pinch of salt and pepper and a drop of oil and water. Put a large piece of waxed paper on your table or counter top. In its left corner put a small heap of flour, in its middle the bowl with the beaten egg and in its right corner a heap of bread crumbs. Flour the veal cutlets, brush them with egg, then coat them with crumbs. Put the first side of the cutlets on in the pan to brown while you strain the soup into your bowls; their second side will cook while you eat the soup, and they will come fresh and crisp to your plate.

If you are totally inexperienced, the first time you attempt a dinner of this type alone you probably will end up thinking this cookbook author is crazy, and you'll hate yourself because you will be slow and it will take you a bit of time to do "all that." But remember that everything comes with practice, and after a month or so, the preparation time for a tasty dinner made of exclusively fresh ingredients will be reduced to a maximum of forty-five minutes.

Things will be easier if you can divide the work. We are in the last third of the twentieth century, and young men with working wives and a tendency to relax while she is doing the kitchen work are becoming a rarity. If you work together with someone, dinner will be ready in twenty-five minutes, even if both of you are novices; all you have to do is divide the preparation. On the next day exchange your chores so that neither of you ends up being a specialist on meats or vegetables, but so that each of you will be able to take over completely, should the other be sick or busy elsewhere.

In the same spirit, you may want to wash the dishes together; it takes the distress out of having to face them alone after a long day of tense work. Whatever your internal organization, make sure that the work is divided fairly—this will keep your household relaxed and happy.

For a company dinner, please *plan*; sit down, study your menu, make your shopping list, and remain—at all times—*organized*. Panic and a last-minute scramble for missing ingredients are your worst enemy. And note that all the ingredients required for the making of a company dinner should, with the exception of perishable fish, be in your refrigerator at least thirty-six hours before you start preparing the dinner.

DINNER SUGGESTIONS

You will find the following everyday dinner menu suggestions (serving 2) on the pages indicated:

Omelet dinners (pages 44–47)
Poached and molded egg dinners (pages 47–51)
Soufflé and roulade dinners (pages 52–59)
Quiche dinners (pages 60–66)
Broiled steak dinners (pages 74–77)
Chipped steak dinners (pages 83–86)
Pan-fried steak dinners (pages 78–82)
Pan-fried veal dinners
   Breaded (pages 97–100)
   Without Breading (pages 92–96)
Sautéed veal dinners (pages 104–106)
Broiled pork dinners (pages 118–120)
Sautéed pork dinners (pages 110–112)
Cured pork (boiled ham, etc.) dinners (pages 123–125)
Pan-fried pork dinners (pages 115–116)

Roast lamb dinner (page 133)
Broiled lamb dinners (pages 150–153)
Pan-fried lamb dinners (pages 137–139)
Sautéed lamb dinners (pages 142–143)
Variety meat dinners (pages 156–164)
Roast and casserole-roasted chicken dinners (pages 168–174)
Whole poached chicken dinners (pages 181–182)
Broiled chicken dinners (pages 176–178)
Pan-fried chicken cutlet dinners (pages 187–190)
Oven-poached chicken cutlet dinners (pages 194–196)
Sautéed chicken leg dinners (pages 199–203)
Oven-poached fish dinners (pages 207–209)
Court-bouillon poached fish dinners (pages 212–214)
Pan-fried fish dinners (pages 217–219)
Broiled fish dinners (pages 221–223)
Baked fish dinners (pages 225–229)
Pan-fried shrimp dinner (page 231)
Pan-fried scallop dinner (page 234)
Broiled scallop dinner (page 236)
Steamed mussel and clam dinners (pages 241–243)

You will find the following company dinner menu suggestions (serving 6) on the pages indicated.

Roulade dinner (polyunsaturated) (page 58)
Quiche dinner (page 65)
Pan-roasted beef dinner (page 70)
Pan-fried steak dinner (page 81)
Veal stew dinner (page 88)
Pan-fried veal dinners (pages 101–102)
Sautéed veal dinner (page 107)
Sautéed pork dinner (page 113)
Pan-fried pork dinner (page 116)
Broiled pork dinner (page 121)
Boiled ham dinner (page 125)
Roast lamb dinner (page 129, 131, 134)
Stewed lamb dinner (page 146)
Broiled lamb dinner (page 153)

Pan-fried lamb dinner (page 140)
Sautéed lamb dinner (page 144)
Roast chicken dinner (page 170)
Whole poached chicken dinner (page 183)
Broiled chicken dinner (page 178)
Pan-fried chicken dinner (page 191)
Oven-poached chicken cutlet dinner (page 196)
Sautéed chicken leg dinner (page 203)
Oven-poached fish dinner (page 209)
Court-bouillon poached dinner (page 215)
Crabmeat dinner (page 239)

RECIPES AND PROPORTIONS

Although this book contains charts giving proportions for basic preparations for one to six persons, the reader may want to know how to increase a recipe designed for two persons to serve a larger number. This can be done very easily by applying the following formula:

$$\frac{\text{Required number of portions}}{\text{Number of portions the existing recipe is for}} = ?$$

? × each ingredient = the required amount of each ingredient

For example, in the recipe for watercress soup on page 23, if you want to increase the number of persons to be served from two to six:

$$\frac{6}{2} = 3$$

Watercress: 1 bunch × 3 = 3 bunches
Water: 2¼ cups × 3 = 6¾ cups
Potatoes: 2 × 3 = 6
Sour cream: 2 tablespoons × 3 = 6 tablespoons

All you now have to do is follow the directions given in the recipe, using the new measurements.

Quick Soups

C ANNED and dried soups have become part of our civilization. Their main drawback is their uniformly tired taste. They all contain a bit too much MSG and salt, and their vegetables, pasta, and rice lack freshness and crispness.

A good soup with a fresh, clean taste can be obtained in an average of thirty minutes without overheating a small kitchen. Useful implements for this are a mechanical vegetable cutter (among these Vegomatic dices, Feemster slices, and Mouli-Julienne cuts in the thin strips known as "julienne"), a food mill, and a blender.

OLD-FASHIONED VEGETABLE SOUPS

Use water and fresh or frozen vegetables. Fresh vegetables taste better; frozen vegetables are faster since they are already cleaned, pared, and blanched.

BASIC PROPORTIONS FOR VEGETABLE SOUPS

No. of Servings	Water	Vegetables	Butter	or	Cream
1	1¼ cups	¾ cup	1½ tsp.		1 T.
2	2¼ cups	1½ cups	1 T.		2 T.
3	3½ cups	2¼ cups	1½ T.		3 T.
4	4⅔ cups	3 cups	2 T.		¼ cup
5	5⅔ cups	3¾ cups	2½ T.		5 T.
6	6½ cups	4½ cups	3 T.		6 T.

KEY RECIPE: Bring the water to a boil. Add the julienned or coarsely chopped vegetables, half of which should be potatoes, salt and pepper, and bring to a second boil. Cook, uncovered, 20 to 30 minutes on medium heat. If desired, strain through a food mill. Reheat well and enrich with butter or cream of your choice— only if you wish, and if your diet allows it. Correct the seasoning.

FRESH TOMATO SOUP

SERVINGS: 2

PREPARATION TIME: 35 MINUTES

3 large tomatoes
2¼ cups water
2 medium potatoes, peeled and coarsely diced

½ teaspoon dried basil
Salt and pepper
1 tablespoon butter or 2 tablespoons cream of your choice (optional)

Squeeze the seeds and water out of the tomatoes, then follow the key recipe (above), adding all the ingredients except the butter or cream to the boiling water. Bring back to a boil, then simmer for 25 minutes. Strain through a food mill. Add butter or cream, if desired, and correct the seasoning.

LEEK AND POTATO SOUP

SERVINGS: 2

PREPARATION TIME: 35 MINUTES

2 leeks, green part included
2¼ cups water
2 medium potatoes, peeled and diced
Salt and pepper

1 tablespoon butter or 2 tablespoons cream of your choice (optional)
1 teaspoon fresh or frozen chopped chives

Cut the leeks in ½-inch chunks and wash very carefully. Then follow the key recipe (page 22), adding all the ingredients except the butter or cream and chives to the boiling water. Bring back to a boil, then simmer 25 minutes. Straining through a food mill is desirable. Add butter or cream if desired. Correct the seasoning and garnish the finished soup with chives.

VARIATIONS: Instead of leeks, you may use 2 large onions or 1 whole bunch of scallions.

WATERCRESS SOUP

SERVINGS: 2

PREPARATION TIME: 30 MINUTES

1 bunch watercress
2¼ cups water
2 medium potatoes, peeled and coarsely diced

Salt and pepper
2 tablespoons sour cream or plain unflavored yogurt

Wash the watercress very carefully and cut off the large stems. Then follow the key recipe (page 22), adding all the ingredients except the cream or yogurt to the boiling water. Cook 20 minutes. Straining through a food mill is desirable. Add the cream or yogurt and correct the seasoning.

VARIATION: Instead of watercress, you may use a large bunch of flat-leafed parsley leaves and one garlic clove, crushed but unpeeled.

BOSTON LETTUCE OR ESCAROLE SOUP

SERVINGS: 2

PREPARATION TIME: 40 MINUTES

1 small head Boston lettuce or escarole
2 slices Canadian bacon
2¼ cups water

2 medium potatoes, peeled and coarsely diced
Salt and pepper
4 teaspoons grated mild Cheddar cheese

Wash the lettuce and cut it in fine strips. Dice the bacon small, then follow the key recipe (page 22), adding all the ingredients to the boiling water except the cheese. Cook for 30 minutes, then strain though a food mill and reheat. Put the grated cheese into soup plates and pour the soup over the cheese.

GREEN BEAN SOUP

SERVINGS: 2

PREPARATION TIME: 30 MINUTES

2¼ cups water
1 ten-ounce package frozen French-style green beans
2 small potatoes, diced small

½ teaspoon dried basil
Salt and pepper
4 teaspoons freshly grated Parmesan cheese

Add all the ingredients to the boiling water except the cheese, and cook 20 minutes. Strain through a food mill, then reheat well. Put the grated cheese into soup plates, then pour the soup over the cheese.

JULIENNE OF CARROT SOUP

SERVINGS: 2

PREPARATION TIME: 30 TO 40 MINUTES

2 small carrots, peeled
2¼ cups water
2 tablespoons white or brown rice
Large pinch of grated nutmeg

Salt and pepper
2 tablespoons sour cream or yogurt
    or 1 tablespoon lemon juice
1 tablespoon chopped parsley

Using a vegetable chopper or grater, cut or grate the peeled carrots in julienne. Then, follow the key recipe (page 22), adding all ingredients to the boiling water except the sour cream, yogurt, or lemon juice and parsley. Simmer 20 minutes with the white rice or 30 minutes with the brown rice. Add cream, yogurt or lemon juice and correct seasoning. Add parsley.

QUICK MINESTRONE

SERVINGS: 6

PREPARATION TIME: 45 MINUTES

3 tablespoons olive oil
6 slices Canadian bacon, diced small
3 tablespoons chopped parsley tops
3 cloves garlic, crushed
6½ cups water or broth of your
    choice
1 ten-ounce package frozen mixed
    vegetables

1 rib celery, diced
1 small unpeeled zucchini, diced
2 teaspoons dried basil
Salt and pepper
3 tablespoons soup pasta
6 tablespoons grated Parmesan
    cheese

Heat the olive oil and sauté the bacon, parsley, and garlic in it for 3 to 4 minutes. Add the water or broth and bring to a boil. Add all the vegetables and the basil. Cook 25 minutes, on medium heat, then add the pasta, and simmer 10 minutes more. Ladle into bowls and sprinkle each bowl with a tablespoon of cheese.

CLEAR SOUPS

A clear soup is one made with a large amount of bouillon or stock and garnished with a small amount of varied ingredients. It will be one hundred percent good nutritionally speaking only if you use fat-free homemade broth. Made with a processed liquid base, it should be considered more as an emergency filler and/or a warmer. A good clear soup should be made exclusively with homemade stock, but in quick cookery, many cooks will consider using instead a canned broth, the cooking water of vegetables from a previous meal, or even bouillon cubes diluted in water. If you are a convinced natural and organic foods cook, you will have to make the quick broth below.

QUICK BROTH

YIELD: 1 quart

PREPARATION TIME: 1½ HOURS

3 cups chopped or ground lean meat (chicken, veal, or beef, or a mixture of any or each)
2 tablespoons oil of your choice
5 cups cold water
2 carrots
2 large onions
2 cloves
2 large leeks
Small bouquet garni
1 teaspoon salt
3 peppercorns

Brown the ground meat lightly in the hot oil, then cover with the water. Bring to a boil very slowly and add the vegetables and seasonings. Skim, then simmer for 1 hour. Strain carefully. The stock is now ready to use.

To cut the monotony of that basic eight-ounce cup of bouillon, add any garnish you like; it will enliven a processed broth, make it more nutritious and a lot more interesting tastewise.

The addition of a bit of wine, strong aromatics, or vegetables will be a great help against the monosodium glutamate, the taste leveler and uniformizer of nearly all canned and processed products. Remember that clear soups made with canned broth or cubes will barely need any additional salt.

KEY RECIPE: If the soup is not garnished with a slight thickener and does not have to simmer, use 1 cup of bouillon per person.

If the soup contains a slight thickener, use 1¼ cups of bouillon per person to allow for absorption. Simmer, uncovered, while the thickener is cooking.

The usual thickeners for clear soup are farina or semolina, pastina, rice. Allow, per person, 1¼ tablespoons farina or semolina, 1 tablespoon pastina, or 1 tablespoon white or brown rice.

It is a good idea to replace toasted bread by unflavored Melba toast or whole-grain crackers; both are light and do not absorb as much liquid; use 1 Melba toast or cracker per person.

SHERRY SOUP

SERVINGS: 2

PREPARATION TIME: 15 MINUTES

2½ cups chicken bouillon of your choice
3 tablespoons farina or semolina
2 egg yolks

2 tablespoons dry sherry
Pepper
Salt (optional)

Bring the bouillon to a boil. Add the farina or semolina, stirring until the boil returns. Simmer about 7 minutes, then turn off the heat. Mix the egg yolks and sherry in a small bowl. Gradually add half of the soup to the egg mixture, then pour it back into the soup pot. Reheat without boiling, then add ground pepper, and salt only if needed.

VARIATIONS: You may use Madeira or port instead of sherry.

LEMON SOUP

SERVINGS: 2

PREPARATION TIME: 15 MINUTES

2½ cups chicken bouillon of your choice
2 tablespoons tiny soup noodles

2 egg yolks
Juice of 1 lemon
Salt and pepper

Bring the broth to a boil and add the pasta, stirring until the boil returns. Simmer 7 to 8 minutes. Turn off the heat. Mix the egg yolks and lemon juice in a small bowl. Gradually add half of the hot soup to the egg mixture, then pour it back into the soup pot. Reheat well, but do not boil. Correct the seasoning; the presence of lemon juice will probably necessitate the addition of more salt.

CHEESE SOUP

SERVINGS: 2

PREPARATION TIME: 15 MINUTES

2½ cups beef bouillon of your choice
¼ cup dry white wine
1 good pinch grated nutmeg

2 Melba toast rounds or whole-grain crackers
¼ cup grated Swiss cheese

Bring the bouillon, wine, and nutmeg to a boil, then simmer 10 minutes. Put one toast round in each soup bowl and sprinkle with half the cheese. Pour half of the hot bouillon into each bowl and sprinkle with the remainder of the cheese.

ZUCCHINI SOUP

SERVINGS: 2

PREPARATION TIME: 15 MINUTES

2 cups chicken bouillon of your choice

1 good pinch Provençal herbs (page 12) or dried basil

1 small unpeeled zucchini, grated

Salt and pepper

Grated Parmesan cheese

Bring the chicken bouillon to a boil. Add the herbs and zucchini and bring back to a boil. Simmer 7 to 8 minutes, then correct the seasoning and add cheese to taste.

GARLIC SOUP

SERVINGS: 2

PREPARATION TIME: 30 MINUTES

2½ cups beef bouillon of your choice

3 large cloves garlic, peeled and crushed

2 Melba toast rounds or whole-grain crackers

2 teaspoons olive oil

2 tablespoons grated Swiss, Parmesan, or mozzarella cheese

Bring the bouillon to a boil. Add the 3 garlic cloves and simmer together for 20 minutes. Place each toast round or cracker in a soup bowl. Sprinkle each with 1 teaspoon of olive oil and 1 tablespoon of cheese. Strain half of the bouillon into each bowl.

QUICK FISH SOUP

SERVINGS: 6

PREPARATION TIME: 45 MINUTES

The fish market will be happy to give you the fish heads and bones. Discard the skins.

3 to 4 pounds heads and bones of sole, flounder, whiting, or ocean perch
¾ cup dry white wine
3 cups each cold water and cold clam juice
Salt and pepper
1 carrot, thickly sliced
3 onions, thickly sliced
6 large cloves garlic, peeled and crushed

1 tablespoon tomato paste
1 bouquet garni (page 12)
1 teaspoon each saffron and Provençal herbs (page 12)
1 piece orange rind the size of a dime
½ teaspoon fennel seeds
6 Melba toast rounds
6 tablespoons Parmesan cheese

Place the fish bones in a 4-quart boiling pot. Add all the ingredients except the saffron, herbs, fennel seeds, orange rind, toast rounds and cheese. Bring to a boil, cook on medium-high heat for 20 minutes. Add the saffron, herbs, fennel seeds, and orange rind. Simmer another 15 minutes.

Place a Melba toast round in each bowl and strain the soup over. Sprinkle each with a tablespoon of Parmesan cheese.

CREAM SOUPS

Fresh cream soups with a true taste of fresh vegetable and not too much starch can be obtained in just a few minutes with the help of a blender.

As cooking liquid for the vegetables, you may use either plain water, the cooking water of vegetables from a previous meal, the broth of your choice, or bouillon cubes dissolved in water. The cream or milk may be any of the following listed here in decreasing calorie content: heavy cream, medium cream, light cream, half-and-half, whole milk, fortified skim milk, skim milk.

For best taste and texture, use any of the creams; for an exceptional company dinner, use heavy cream. For a reasonable taste and best all-around nutritional value use whole milk; for stringent diets, use skim milk.

As a thickener use cornstarch or potato starch.

KEY RECIPE: Bring the liquid of your choice to a boil. Add the coarsely chopped vegetables and bring back to a boil, adding salt, if needed, and pepper. Simmer 20 minutes, or until the vegetables fall apart. Puree in the blender. To thicken, mix the potato starch with the cream or milk you have chosen to obtain a slurry, then stir into the simmering puree until the soup boils again and thickens. Correct the seasoning.

BASIC PROPORTIONS FOR CREAM SOUPS

No. of servings	Bouillon or water	Vegetables	Potato starch	Cream or milk
1	1½ cups	½ cup	2¼ tsp.	¼ cup
2	2½ cups	1 cup	1½ T.	½ cup
3	3⅓ cups	1½ cups	2 T.	¾ cup
4	4½ cups	2 cups	3 T.	1 cup
5	5¾ cups	2½ cups	3½ T.	1¼ cups
6	6¼ cups	3 cups	4 T.	1½ cups

CREAM OF SPINACH SOUP

SERVINGS: 2

PREPARATION TIME: 20 MINUTES

2½ cups water, vegetable cooking water, or broth of your choice
1 ten-ounce box frozen spinach
⅛ teaspoon grated nutmeg
Salt and pepper

1½ tablespoons potato starch
½ cup milk or cream of your choice
1 hard-boiled egg, chopped (optional)

Bring the water to a boil, add the frozen spinach. Bring to a second boil, add the seasonings, and simmer only 5 minutes. (The soup may or may not be blended, according to personal taste, before being thickened.) Follow key recipe for thickening. When serving, garnish the top of the soup with the chopped hard-boiled egg, if desired.

CREAM OF BROCCOLI SOUP

SERVINGS: 2

PREPARATION TIME: 25 MINUTES

2½ cups water, vegetable cooking water, or chicken broth of your choice
1 cup fresh chopped broccoli, packed firm

Salt and pepper
1½ tablespoons potato starch
½ cup cream or milk of your choice
1 tablespoon toasted sesame seeds

Follow the key recipe (page 31). Toast the sesame seeds and garnish the soup with them.

VARIATION: Use the same amount of cauliflower instead of broccoli and garnish with chopped chives.

CREAM OF DILL SOUP

SERVINGS: 2

PREPARATION TIME: 20 MINUTES

2 cups chicken broth or bouillon of
    your choice or 1 cup each water
    and clam juice
1 cup chopped fresh dill

Salt and pepper
1½ tablespoons potato starch
½ cup milk or cream of your choice
Juice of 1 lemon

Follow the key recipe (page 31), simmering the dill weed in the broth for 10 minutes. Correct the seasoning carefully after thickening and adding the lemon juice; the soup will probably need more salt.

CREAM OF MUSHROOM SOUP

SERVINGS: 6

PREPARATION TIME: 30 MINUTES

In this recipe less liquid is needed because the mushrooms render a lot of moisture.

1 pound fresh mushrooms
2 tablespoons butter
Salt and pepper
6 cups chicken bouillon or broth of
    your choice
2 shallots, finely chopped

¼ cup potato starch
3 egg yolks
1 cup heavy cream
3 tablespoons dry Madeira, sherry,
    or port

Chop the mushrooms coarsely. Sauté the mushrooms in the butter, adding salt and pepper, until their juices have rendered. Bring the bouillon to a boil, add the mushrooms and shallots, and simmer for 10 minutes. Mix the potato starch, egg yolks, and cream and add, stirring, to the simmering soup to thicken it. Add the wine and correct the seasoning.

CHAPTER IV

Sauces in Quicker Cookery

From a strictly nutritional point of view, it would be wise to keep sauces to a minimum in quick everyday cookery. But a quick and uncomplicated sauce or gravy can truly make the difference between a humdrum dish and a varied, interesting, and palate-pleasing one.

THE WHITE SAUCE FAMILY

A basic white sauce is made with either a roux or a slurry. The liquid is milk, cream, chicken broth, or clam juice (the last being used for fish dishes), or even the cooking liquid from vegetables. The quality and texture of a white sauce made with milk or cream depends on the quality of the milk or cream used. Heavy and light cream are lovely and delicious, but too rich for everyday use. Evaporated milk gives a white sauce with a texture identical to that of a sauce made of heavy cream, but requires adequate spicing to mask the all-too-evident "cooked milk" taste. Regular milk is the best all-around white sauce material; skim milk requires additional flavoring and results in a sauce

34

lacking body, but remains the best material for cholesterol-restricted diets.

A roux-thickened sauce tastes better than a slurry-thickened one, but it is richer.

A slurry-thickened sauce is prepared faster than a roux-thickened one; it is blander, not as rich, and when made with skim milk, the best for cholesterol-restricted diets.

To obtain an all-purpose, medium-thick white sauce, use the following proportions of starch to liquid:

BASIC PROPORTIONS FOR MEDIUM-THICK WHITE SAUCE

Servings	Liquid	Butter-flour roux	Cornstarch	Potato starch	Arrowroot
1	½ cup	1 T. each	2½ tsps.	1 tsp.	1 tsp.
2	1 cup	2 T. each	5 tsps.	2 tsps.	2 tsps.
3	1½ cups	3 T. each	2½ T.	1 T.	1 T.
4	2 cups	4 T. each	3 T. + 1 tsp.	4 tsps.	4 tsps.
5	2½ cups	5 T. each	4 T. + ½ tsp.	5 tsps.	5 tsps.
6	3 cups	6 T. each	5 T.	2 T.	2 T.

KEY RECIPE: *White sauce made with a roux* (flour cooked in a fat or oil): Cook the flour in very warm butter, margarine, or oil for 2 to 3 minutes, stirring with the whisk. Whisk in the scalded liquid and bring back to a boil, stirring, to thicken. Season.

White sauce made with a slurry (corn or potato starch or arrowroot dissolved in cold liquid): Dilute the starch with one-quarter of the cold liquid. Bring the remaining three-quarters of the liquid to a boil, turn down to a simmer, and stir in the slurry; the sauce will thicken immediately. (Make sure that it reboils.) Season.

You may vary the taste of a basic white sauce with the addition of any type of spice or herb while it cooks. But if you want an onion sauce, sauté the chopped onion in some butter or oil first, or the milk will curdle.

If you wish to flavor a white sauce with tomato, add tomato paste exclusively, blending some of the sauce into the paste first, then blending the tomato mixture back into the bulk of the sauce. This will prevent curdling.

THE TOMATO SAUCE FAMILY

QUICK YEAR-ROUND TOMATO SAUCE
SERVINGS: 6 (2 CUPS)

PREPARATION TIME: 45 MINUTES

The purpose of recooking canned tomatoes with their sauce is to give the sauce more flavor and to temper its relatively sharp acidity. This all-purpose mixture is far superior to plain canned tomato sauce, and does not require any special care while cooking. Any amount not used can be frozen.

1 tablespoon oil of your choice
2 tablespoons chopped fresh or frozen onions
1 large can peeled Italian plum to-matoes
1 small clove garlic, peeled and mashed
Small bouquet garni (see page 12)
½ teaspoon dried basil, well crumbled (optional)
Salt and pepper

Heat the oil well, then add the onions and sauté until golden. Add the tomatoes with their canning water, garlic, bouquet garni, and dried basil, salt (if needed) and pepper. Bring to a boil and simmer 35 to 40 minutes. Puree in the blender.

QUICK SUMMER MARINARA SAUCE

SERVINGS: 2

PREPARATION TIME: 5 MINUTES

For full flavor, prepare this sauce fresh as needed; the cooking time is, so to speak, negligible. For larger quantities, count 2 small tomatoes per person and use only 1 large clove of garlic per each 6 persons. Great on scrambled eggs and on omelets; livens up plain rice and noodles.

3 large sun-ripened tomatoes
1 tablespoon olive oil or other oil of
    your choice
½ small clove garlic, peeled and
    mashed

1 tablespoon chopped fresh parsley
1 fresh basil leaf, scissored
Salt and pepper

Scald and peel the tomatoes, then cut them in ¼-inch slices. Heat the oil, add the tomatoes, garlic, parsley, basil, salt and pepper and toss on high heat for 3 to 4 minutes.

THE BROWN GRAVIES

The making of a regular brown sauce is not even to be considered in everyday cookery—it is too time-consuming.

To make a very fast and delicious sauce for meats, use the meat juices at the bottom of the cooking pan.

First, discard the cooking oil or fat, then dissolve the caramelized cooking juices with water, wine, or a broth of your choice—or a mixture of any of these. You may add any herb or spice you like as a flavoring. This procedure is called "deglazing."

From then on, you can follow any of these three procedures:

1. Serve the plain deglazing liquid well reduced and seasoned.

2. Make a gravy by using a larger amount of deglazing liquid and what is known as a "beurre manié" as thickener. A beurre manié is a mixture of 1 tablespoon butter—or margarine, if need be—and 1

tablespoon flour. Whisked into 1 cup of simmering liquid, it will thicken it instantly. A beurre manié may be replaced by a slurry of cold liquid and potato starch, in which case the proportion of starch to use is 1¼ teaspoons per cup of liquid.

3. Reduce the deglazing liquid to a very small amount and whisk in, off the heat, 1 tablespoon of fresh butter per person. This butter sauce tastes best, but it is very rich, and you may want to keep it for quick-cookery entertaining.

COMPOUND BUTTERS

A compound butter is plain butter mixed with flavoring ingredients. You can flavor butter, salted or unsalted, and use it to pep up broiled meats, fresh vegetables, pasta, and rice.

To make 1 or 2 tablespoons of any compound butter, mash the butter with the fresh or dried and well-crumbled herbs of your choice; add salt, if needed, and pepper.

If you have freezer space, whip ½ cup butter, flavor it with the herbs or aromatics of your choice, reshape it into a bar or cake, and freeze it. Cut the frozen butter into 8 one-tablespoon chunks or 16 half-tablespoon chunks. Keep frozen in a well-sealed small jar and use at your discretion.

HEAVY CREAM AS A SAUCE

By letting 1 cup of heavy cream, a pinch each of salt, pepper, and herbs and aromatics of your choice cook slowly for 30 minutes, you will obtain a very smooth, fine, and rich sauce, which requires no other care than an occasional stirring. But be careful—this sauce is extra rich, and should probably be reserved for quick-cookery entertaining. Any onion-family member can be added, but it must be precooked first and added just before serving or the sauce will curdle.

Adapt the taste of your sauce to the food you are serving; for example, tarragon will adapt well with chicken cutlets, while dill will blend very well with salmon or any other fish.

THE HOLLANDAISE FAMILY

The wisest approach to a rich butter sauce of the hollandaise type is to keep it for an occasional treat and make it with the only fat it should really be made of—butter. But it may be useful to know that hollandaise sauce, and all the related sauces, may be made with melted first-quality, unsalted margarine, warmed corn or sunflower oil, or even olive oil. The heavier the oil, the stronger the acid base of the sauce should be.

Hollandaise and all its related sauces—béarnaise, mousseline sauce, and so on—are made according to the following principle: egg yolks are poached in a small amount of very acid and well-seasoned liquid, then melted unsalted butter or, as mentioned above, margarine or even oil is whisked into the foamy egg yolk. In quick cookery this is best done by using the blender and the following proportions.

BASIC PROPORTIONS FOR HOLLANDAISE

2 servings	*3–4 servings*	*5–6 servings*
2 egg yolks	3 egg yolks	4 egg yolks
2 T. boiling water	3 T. boiling water	¼ cup boiling water
1 T. lemon juice	2 T. lemon juice	3 T. lemon juice
Salt and pepper	Salt and pepper	Salt and pepper
½ cup melted unsalted butter, margarine, or even oil	¾ cup melted unsalted butter, margarine, or even oil	1 cup melted unsalted butter, margarine, or even oil

KEY RECIPE: Place the egg yolks, boiling water, lemon juice, salt, and pepper in the blender container. Turn the blender, on high speed, off and on for 45 seconds. Then turn the blender down to medium speed and add the warm melted fat or oil of your choice in a thin, regular stream, but not too slowly. (If you add the butter too slowly, the sauce will be very compact; if you add it too fast, it will separate. If you stay in between the sauce will be just right, light and fluffy.)

Use hollandaise on fish, asparagus, cauliflower, and broccoli. To make sauces related to hollandaise:

MOUSSELINE SAUCE

Make a basic hollandaise according to the key recipe above. Put 1½ teaspoons heavy cream per serving in a small bowl, whip it, and fold it into the basic hollandaise.

Use mousseline sauce on fish, asparagus, cauliflower, and broccoli.

MALTAISE SAUCE

In the key recipe for hollandaise (page 39) replace the water with boiling orange juice and add a bit of orange rind to the fruit juices and egg yolks. Then follow the key recipe.

Maltaise sauce is a special treat for fresh asparagus.

BÉARNAISE SAUCE

Béarnaise sauce is so popular with all broiled meat and all broiled and poached fish that it would be a shame not to prepare it because its acid base requires a bit of time-consuming chopping and cooking. This drawback can be overcome by preparing the acid base of béarnaise sauce in bulk, according to the directions below, and keeping it in a well-sealed jar in the refrigerator. The mixture improves with age.

YIELD: 1¼ CUPS SAUCE BASE OR 16 SERVINGS

PREPARATION TIME: 30 MINUTES

2 cups dry white wine
⅔ cup wine vinegar
1 large onion, finely chopped
5 shallots, finely chopped
1 bay leaf, crushed
½ teaspoon dried thyme

1 tablespoon dried chervil
1 tablespoon dried tarragon
2 tablespoons chopped fresh parsley
2 teaspoons salt
½ teaspoon white pepper

Combine all the ingredients. Bring the mixture to a boil, then simmer until only 1¼ cups of the mixture are left. Store the unstrained mixture in a well-sealed jar in the refrigerator.

To make a quick béarnaise sauce, use the following proportions:

BASIC PROPORTIONS FOR QUICK BÉARNAISE

2 servings	*3–4 servings*	*5–6 servings*
2 T. acid base	3 T. acid base	¼ cup acid base
2 egg yolks	3 egg yolks	4 egg yolks
½ cup melted un- salted butter or margarine	¾ cup melted un- salted butter or margarine	1 cup melted unsalted butter or marga- rine
½ tsp. each revived chervil and tarra- gon	¾ tsp. each revived chervil and tarra- gon	1 tsp. each revived chervil and tarra- gon
1 tsp. chopped fresh parsley	1½ tsp. chopped fresh parsley	2 tsp. chopped fresh parsley

Strain the amount of base you need into a small pan, heat it, and pour it into the blender container. Proceed from then on as you would for a basic hollandaise (page 39). Add to the finished sauce a mixture of dried tarragon and chervil revived in a tiny bit of boiling water, and the parsley.

MAYONNAISE

Please, bid forever good-bye to the poison that is mayonnaise bought in a jar. You can prepare a jar of your own tasty and healthy mayonnaise in the blender in record time. Blender mayonnaise, well refrigerated, will keep 1 week, but it *does not freeze*.

YIELD: 1¼ CUPS OR 20 ONE-TABLESPOON SERVINGS

PREPARATION TIME: 5 MINUTES

1 whole egg
1½ teaspoons wine vinegar
⅓ teaspoon salt
¼ teaspoon white pepper

1 teaspoon English or prepared Dijon mustard
1 cup oil of your choice
1 to 2 tablespoons lemon juice
1 tablespoon boiling water (optional)

Put all the ingredients except ¾ cup of the oil, the lemon juice, and the boiling water in the blender container. Blend on medium speed, then, still blending, add the remainder of the oil in a steady stream and lemon to suit your personal taste.

If the sauce is to be stored more than one day, blend in 1 tablespoon of boiling water. Store in a tightly sealed jar in the refrigerator.

VARIATIONS: The variations of mayonnaise are manifold. You can add chopped fresh herbs of your choice, capers, or tomato paste to the basic recipe and create a new sauce every time; just let your personal taste and imagination guide you.

POLYUNSATURATED MAYONNAISE

For fat-controlled, cholesterol-restricted diets:

YIELD: 1¼ CUPS OR 20 ONE-TABLESPOON SERVINGS

PREPARATION TIME: 5 MINUTES

1 egg white
2 tablespoons skim milk
1 teaspoon prepared Dijon mustard
2 drops yellow food coloring

1 tablespoon lemon juice
⅓ teaspoon salt
¼ teaspoon white pepper
1 cup polyunsaturated oil of your choice

Put the egg white, skim milk, mustard, food coloring, lemon juice, salt, pepper, and ¼ cup of the oil in the blender container and blend on medium speed. Still blending, pour the remainder of the oil in a steady stream at the center of the trough. The sauce will thicken like true mayonnaise.

VINAIGRETTE-TYPE SALAD DRESSINGS

See the chapter on salads, pages 246–251.

CHAPTER V

Eggs for a Quick Dinner

I N O U R Anglo-Saxon country, eggs are more or less reserved for lunch and breakfast, but in continental Europe, they are very often used at dinner time—poached, in French omelets, or in soufflés and roulades. Eggs for dinner are perfect whenever your breakfast has consisted mostly of cereals and/or bread. They should, however, be considered carefully by those who have high cholesterol problems and have to reduce their egg intake to three or four per week.

OMELETS

Have a small pan that you reserve exclusively for omelets. Before you use it for the first time, wash it of all industrial grease, then fill it with oil and bring the oil to the smoking point. Let the pan stand overnight. In the morning, pour off the oil, which you may reuse, and wipe the pan dry.

KEY RECIPE: Since an omelet for one person takes 15 seconds to cook, do not hesitate to prepare individual omelets for each person, using the following ingredients:

2 large eggs
1 tablespoon water
Large pinch of salt

Small pinch of pepper
1 tablespoon butter or other cooking fat or oil of your choice

Put the omelet pan on to heat, and while it is heating beat well with a fork, but no more than 30 strokes, the eggs, water, salt, and pepper. Place the butter or oil of your choice in the pan and make sure that it sizzles. (You cannot use margarine here; it would burn.) Coat the pan well with the butter or oil by tilting it and swirling the butter or oil around the bottom.

Add the egg batter. Shake the pan back and forth on the burner with your left hand while you stir the batter in a circle with a fork held in your right hand. As soon as the egg curd looks cooked but still shiny, lift the pan at a 45-degree angle and push the cooked egg with your fork to the front of the pan, building a neat little bunch. (While you do this, the handle should be toward you and the egg should be in line with the handle but on the other side of the pan.) Now, turn the pan by 90 degrees so that the handle of the pan is facing to the right. Put your right hand, palm up, under the handle of the pan, close your hand on the handle, and tilt the omelet pan upside down over a plate to invert the omelet. Its top will appear smooth and shiny.

If you want to fill the omelet, put the filling at the center of the flat omelet, then fold the flaps on either side over the filling and invert the omelet as described above.

SUGGESTED FILLINGS FOR OMELETS

If you are preparing several omelets, prepare the filling for all the omelets at once, separating it on a plate in as many little heaps as you will have individual omelets. Fill each omelet with one heap of filling.

Use per omelet:

1 tablespoon shredded cheese of your choice

1 tablespoon chopped ham mixed with 2 teaspoons each shredded cheese and chopped parsley

The chopped white part of 1 small leek and 2 chopped mushrooms, presautéed in butter or the oil of your choice

Chopped fresh herbs (mix the herbs into the batter, using 1 tablespoon per omelet)

1 slice Nova Scotia salmon

2 tablespoons cooked shrimp, marinated in a few drops of soy sauce

1 small green pepper and 1 small tomato, presautéed in butter or oil

About 10 tiny bread croutons, presautéed in butter or oil

¼ avocado mashed with a pea-sized piece of garlic and 1 tablespoon chopped parsley, a squeeze of lemon juice, salt, and pepper (Sprinkle a pinch of curry in the pan before cooking the omelet.)

1 rasher of bacon, rendered and crumbled

1 small potato, diced and presautéed in butter

2 tablespoons cooked asparagus tips or pieces

2 tablespoons tuna mixed with a pea-sized nugget of anchovy paste

SUGGESTED EVERYDAY DINNER MENU

Fresh tomato soup (page 22)
WALNUT AND CHEESE OMELET
Romaine and cucumber salad (page 252)
Grapefruit in raspberry sauce (page 273)

SERVINGS: 2

APPROXIMATE TOTAL PREPARATION TIME: 1 HOUR

WALNUT AND CHEESE OMELET

SERVINGS: 2

PREPARATION TIME: 10 MINUTES

4 eggs
2 tablespoons water
Large pinch of salt
Small pinch of pepper

2 tablespoons butter or oil of your
choice
2 tablespoons each chopped walnuts
and cheese

Follow the key recipe for omelets (page 45), adding the chopped walnuts to the batter. Make the omelets individually and sprinkle half of the cheese on each omelet before rolling it and inverting it on a plate.

ORDER OF DINNER PREPARATION:

1. Defrost the box of raspberries in a bowl of hot water.
2. Peel and pare the soup vegetables. Start cooking the soup.
3. Puree the raspberries; peel and slice the grapefruit; pour the puree over the grapefruit slices and chill.
4. Clean and prepare the romaine and cucumbers; make the dressing. Chill separately.
5. Strain the soup. Keep warm.
6. Prepare batter for the omelets, each in a separate bowl; chop the walnuts and grate the cheese.
7. Serve the soup.
8. Make the omelets and toss the salad; serve both.
9. Serve the dessert.

POACHED AND MOLDED EGGS

Either poached or molded eggs can be used to make a very pleasant dinner. Since they are light, they can be garnished with a variety of fresh vegetables, and/or served with a starchy vegetable and a salad. Let your imagination go for the vegetable garnishes.

KEY RECIPE: *For poaching eggs:* Use extremely fresh eggs (Grade AA); you may poach as many as 4 at a time. Butter or oil lightly the bottom of a 9-inch skillet. Add cold water to a depth of 2½ inches. Bring to a boil, add 2 tablespoons vinegar and 1 tablespoon salt and lower the heat to a simmer. Break each egg into its own cup, then slide into the bath of water. Let the eggs cook 3½ minutes. Remove them to a bowl of warm water, then drain and serve. The total preparation time is 8 minutes.

For molded eggs: Preheat the oven to 375° F. Use any Grade A egg. Butter, grease, or oil a custard cup. Break the egg into the cup and salt and pepper lightly. Bring water to a depth of 1½ inches to a boil in a flameproof baking dish. Bake the eggs in this hot water bath 12 to 14 minutes, depending on their size. Unmold on a small piece of toast. The total preparation time is 15 minutes.

SUGGESTED EVERYDAY DINNER MENU I

EGGS NAPOLI
Spaghetti with basil and Parmesan (page 269)
Boston lettuce and sliced fennel salad (page 252)
Fresh fruit

SERVINGS: 2

APPROXIMATE TOTAL PREPARATION TIME: 1 HOUR

EGGS NAPOLI

SERVINGS: 2

PREPARATION TIME: 20 MINUTES

2 tablespoons butter or oil
1 onion, finely chopped
2 large tomatoes, peeled if desired
⅓ very small garlic clove, peeled
  and mashed

Large pinch of oregano
A few fennel seeds
Salt and pepper
1 tablespoon chopped fresh parsley
4 poached eggs (see key recipe,
  page 48)

Heat the butter or oil well and sauté the onions until golden. Add the tomatoes, sliced in slices ⅓ inch thick. Fry 3 minutes on one side, then turn over. Salt and pepper them and sprinkle them with the garlic, oregano, fennel seeds, and parsley, well mixed. Pile the tomato slices onto 2 plates and top each portion with 2 poached eggs.

ORDER OF DINNER PREPARATION:

1. Prepare the salad greens and dressing. Chill separately.
2. Bring water to a boil for the spaghetti and eggs in two separate pans.
3. Cook the spaghetti and poach the eggs simultaneously.
4. Transfer the poached eggs to warm water bath.
5. Drain the spaghetti and season with basil and butter. Keep warm.
6. Cook the vegetable garnish for the egg dish.
7. Serve the egg dish and the spaghetti.
8. Toss the salad in the dressing; serve.
9. Serve the fresh fruit.

SUGGESTED EVERYDAY DINNER MENU II

BERLINER EIER
Boiled green beans in lemon and parsley butter (page 255)
Camembert and French bread
Fresh pears

SERVINGS: 2

APPROXIMATE TOTAL PREPARATION TIME: 40 TO 50 MINUTES

BERLINER EIER

SERVINGS: 2

PREPARATION TIME: 25 MINUTES

1 tablespoon butter or oil
2 large onions, sliced
Salt and pepper
1 teaspoon prepared Dijon or
Düsseldorf mustard

2 pumpernickel toast points
4 molded eggs (see key recipe, page 48)
1 tablespoon chopped fresh parsley

Heat the butter or oil well. Add the onion slices and toss 1 minute on high heat, then add salt and pepper and cover the pan. Let steam until the onions are tender, then blend in the mustard. Place each toast point on a plate and spread half of the onion mixture on each of them. Top with 2 eggs per plate and sprinkle with the chopped parsley.

ORDER OF DINNER PREPARATION:

1. String the green beans if applicable, then cook and drain them.
2. Slice and cook the onions for the egg dish; prepare the toast points.
3. Mold and bake the eggs.
4. Toss the green beans in their lemon butter.
5. Assemble the egg dish on the serving plates.
6. Serve the eggs and vegetable.
7. Serve the cheese and fruit.

SUGGESTED EVERYDAY DINNER MENU III

SWISS EGGS
Tomato and julienne of green pepper salad (page 252)
Sliced oranges in Grand Marnier (page 272)

SERVINGS: 2

APPROXIMATE TOTAL PREPARATION TIME: 50 MINUTES

SWISS EGGS

SERVINGS: 2

PREPARATION TIME: 25 MINUTES

2 tablespoons butter or oil of your choice
½ pound mushrooms, sliced
Salt and pepper
⅓ clove garlic, peeled and mashed
1 tablespoon chopped fresh parsley
2 toast points

2 slices boiled ham
4 poached eggs (see key recipe, page 48)
¼ cup grated Swiss cheese
2 tablespoons milk of your choice
½ teaspoon paprika
1 teaspoon prepared Dijon mustard

Heat the butter or oil well; add the mushrooms, salt and pepper, garlic, and parsley. Continue sautéing until the moisture has completely evaporated. Place the toast points in two flameproof dishes. Top each with a slice of ham, half the mushrooms, and 2 poached eggs. Mix the Swiss cheese, milk, paprika, and mustard and put one-fourth of the mixture onto each egg. Pass under the broiler for 1 to 2 minutes, just to melt the cheese.

ORDER OF DINNER PREPARATION:

1. Peel and slice the oranges; sprinkle them with Grand Marnier and chill.
2. Slice tomatoes; cut pepper into julienne; prepare the dressing. Chill the salad and dressing separately.

3. Sauté the mushrooms; prepare the toast points and topping for the eggs. Keep warm.

4. Poach the eggs; put the mushrooms and eggs on the toast points, top with the topping, and broil 1 to 2 minutes.

5. Mix the salad while the egg topping broils.

6. Serve the eggs and salad.

7. Serve the oranges.

SOUFFLÉS AND ROULADES

Soufflés

Soufflés are wildly overrated culinary preparations, which in truth present neither the difficulties nor the time involvement they are reputed to.

A soufflé is made of two parts:

1. A base, which is mostly a thick white sauce flavored with herbs, cheese, or blended with a blender-made puree of raw meat or fish.

2. Beaten egg whites, which are folded into the base. They make the soufflé rise when the air they contain dilates in the warmth of the oven. They must be stiff enough to carry the weight of a raw egg in its shell. If the soufflé batter appears heavy, do not hesitate to beat an additional egg white and fold it into the batter.

BASIC PROPORTIONS FOR SAVORY SOUFFLÉS

No. of servings	Milk	Potato starch	Separated eggs or plain egg whites	Dish size	Baking Time at 325° F.
1	¼ cup	1½ tsp.	2	2-cup	20 min.
2	½ cup	1 T.	3	3-cup	25 min.
3–4	1 cup	2 T.	4	6-cup	30 min.
5–6	1½ cups	3 T.	6	8-cup	40 min.

KEY RECIPE: Mix the milk of your choice and the starch in a large saucepan. Bring to a boil, stirring, to thicken. Add flavoring or garnish and egg yolks, one by one, if used. Add salt and pepper. Beat the egg whites until they can carry the weight of a raw egg in its shell. Mix one quarter of their volume into the base —*this is a must, and should never be forgotten*— then fold in the remainder, as follows:

Do not turn the spatula handle in your hand while you fold, but hold it very steady. Cut down at a right angle into the base to the bottom of the bowl, bringing the base over the whites while you turn the bowl from left to right with your left hand. Fold until very well homogenized; no traces of egg white should be visible in the batter.

Butter or grease a baking dish, which may be any circular ovenproof dish (the straighter the sides the better for the texture of the soufflé, because of even heat penetration). Turn the soufflé mixture into the dish, filling it to within ½ inch of the rim, never higher. Bake on the lowest rack of a 325° F. oven, using a hot water bath only if you desire a soft bottom and soft sides to the soufflé.

You may freeze any soufflé before baking it. That means that you can make a larger amount of batter at once, bake some of it and mold and freeze the remainder and use it later. Use a Corningware casserole. Put the solidly frozen soufflé to bake for twice as long as you would bake a nonfrozen soufflé batter, and at the same temperature. The preparation time of a soufflé batter is in the vicinity of ten minutes.

ROULADES

Roulades are flat soufflés with a base made of white sauce or simply egg yolks mixed with a bit of flour. After folding the whites into the base of a roulade, turn it into a jelly-roll pan lined with buttered waxed paper. If there is not enough batter to fill the jelly-roll pan, make the roulade as long as the batter will stretch in the pan, and as thick as the pan is deep. Small roulades for 2 persons may be cooked in a frying pan on a stove burner as one would a huge pancake. It should then be cooked 3 to 4 minutes on each side in some butter or oil.

Cooked roulades may be filled with meat, fish, shellfish, vegetables, or cheese. The key recipe sequence is the same as for soufflés.

POLYUNSATURATED SOUFFLÉS AND ROULADES

Enriched polyunsaturated soufflés and roulades can easily be obtained by making a base with soy flour and skim milk or fat-free chicken broth. The base is tastier with broth, but whatever the liquid used in the batter, it should be highly seasoned and flavored with an herb to temper the rather strong beany taste of the soy flour.

BASIC PROPORTIONS FOR POLYUNSATURATED SOUFFLÉS AND ROULADES

Servings	Soy flour	Skim milk or broth	Egg whites	Dish size	Baking time at 325° F.
1–2	¼ cup	⅓ cup	2	2-cup	15–20 min.
3–4	½ cup	¾ cup	3	3-cup	20–25 min.
5–6	⅔ cup	1 cup	5	6-cup	30–35 min.

SUGGESTED EVERYDAY DINNER MENU I

SOUFFLÉ ZERMATT
Green bean salad (page 252)
Strawberry ice (page 285)

SERVINGS: 2

APPROXIMATE TOTAL PREPARATION TIME: 50 MINUTES

SOUFFLÉ ZERMATT

SERVINGS: 2

PREPARATION TIME: 35 MINUTES

½ cup milk of your choice
1 tablespoon potato starch
2 tablespoons chopped raw ham
  (prosciutto type)
¼ cup chopped Swiss cheese
2 tablespoons chopped fresh parsley

2 eggs, separated
Salt and pepper
1½ tablespoons fat or 1 tablespoon
  oil of your choice to grease the
  mold

Mix the milk and starch and bring to a boil, stirring constantly. Add the ham, Swiss cheese, parsley, egg yolks, salt, and pepper. Beat the egg whites, and fold into the base as indicated in the key recipe (page 52). Bake in a greased 3- to 4-cup soufflé dish for 25 minutes at 325° F.

ORDER OF DINNER PREPARATION:

1. Prepare the soufflé batter and put the soufflé in to bake.
2. String and clean the green beans; boil them, drain them, and cool them under cold water.
3. Make the salad dressing, toss the beans in dressing.
4. Remove the bag of frozen berries from freezer to room temperature.
5. Remove the soufflé from the oven and serve with the bean salad.
6. Blend the semidefrosted berries with as much sugar or honey as you like to obtain soft fruit ice.
7. Serve the dessert.

SUGGESTED EVERYDAY DINNER MENU II

LIEDERKRANZ AND WALNUT SOUFFLÉ
Cauliflower, watercress, and tomato salad (page 252)
Honeydew melon in Marsala (page 272)

SERVINGS: 2

APPROXIMATE TOTAL PREPARATION TIME: 50 MINUTES

LIEDERKRANZ AND WALNUT SOUFFLÉ
SERVINGS: 2

PREPARATION TIME: 35 MINUTES

½ cup milk of your choice
1 tablespoon potato starch
2 ounces Liederkranz cheese, diced large
2 tablespoons chopped English walnuts

Salt and pepper
2 eggs, separated
1½ tablespoons fat or 1 tablespoon oil of your choice to grease the mold

Mix the milk and starch in a large saucepan. Bring to a boil, stirring to thicken. Add the diced Liederkranz, chopped walnuts, salt and pepper, and the egg yolks. Then beat the egg whites and fold into the base, following the key recipe (page 52). Turn into a buttered or greased 3-cup dish and bake for 25 to 30 minutes in a 325° F. oven.

ORDER OF DINNER PREPARATION:

1. Peel and slice or dice the melon and steep in Marsala. Chill.
2. Prepare the soufflé batter. Put the soufflé in to bake.
3. Peel the cauliflower; wash and trim the watercress, slice the tomatoes.
4. Make salad dressing; toss the salad and dressing.
5. Serve the soufflé and the salad.
6. Serve the melon.

SUGGESTED EVERYDAY DINNER MENU III

RICOTTA ROULADE
Boston letttuce and sliced fennel salad (page 252)
Refreshed nectarines (page 276)

SERVINGS: 2

APPROXIMATE TOTAL PREPARATION TIME: 50 MINUTES

RICOTTA ROULADE

SERVINGS: 2

PREPARATION TIME: 20 MINUTES

2 eggs, separated
1 tablespoon flour
¼ cup chopped raw fresh spinach
Salt and pepper
2 tablespoons butter, or fat or oil of
    your choice

⅔ cup very fresh ricotta cheese
3 tablespoons grated Parmesan
    cheese
½ cup tomato sauce of your choice

Beat the egg yolks until almost white and foamy. Blend in the flour, spinach, salt, and pepper. Beat the egg whites and fold them into the base, following the key recipe. Heat half the butter or oil in a 9-inch frying pan. Pour the batter into the pan and let cook until the bottom is golden. Slide onto a plate, add the remainder of the fat to the pan only if necessary, and invert the uncooked side of the roulade back into the frying pan. Cook another 3 to 4 minutes. Meanwhile, mix the ricotta with the Parmesan in a small pan and heat gently, adding salt and pepper if necessary. Spread the ricotta filling on the roulade, roll, and serve with the tomato sauce.

ORDER OF DINNER PREPARATION:

1. Refresh the nectarines; peel the kiwi, add the liqueur, and chill.
2. Clean the Boston lettuce and slice the fennel; make the dressing and chill both vegetables and dressing separately.

3. Heat the tomato sauce.

4. Make the roulade and cook the first side.

5. Make the ricotta filling.

6. Turn the roulade over, finish cooking it, and roll it around the ricotta filling.

7. Toss the salad in its dressing.

8. Serve the roulade and the salad.

9. Serve the nectarine dessert.

SUGGESTED COMPANY DINNER MENU

Zucchini soup (page 29)
MUSHROOM ROULADE
Belgian endive salad (page 252)
Tarte aux fraises (pages 301–303)

SUGGESTED WINE: French Beaujolais or California Gamay Beaujolais

SERVINGS: 6

APPROXIMATE TOTAL PREPARATION TIME: 1½ HOURS

MUSHROOM ROULADE

SERVINGS: 6

PREPARATION TIME: 45 MINUTES

⅔ cup soy flour
1 cup fat-free chicken broth
Salt and pepper
2 tablespoons polyunsaturated oil
1 pound mushrooms, finely chopped

1 clove garlic, finely chopped
¼ cup chopped fresh parsley
6 egg whites
¾ pound raw boneless white meat
  of chicken

Mix the soy flour and broth in a large saucepan and bring to a boil, to thicken. Add salt and pepper. Heat 1 tablespoon of the oil in a frying pan. Sauté the chopped mushrooms on high heat with a bit of salt and pepper until dry and brown, then add the garlic and 2½ tablespoons of the chopped parsley. Mix the mushrooms into the soy base. Beat the egg whites and fold them into the base, following the key recipe (page 52). Turn into a jelly-roll pan lined with baking or waxed paper, evenly rubbed with the remaining tablespoon of oil. Bake for 15 to 20 minutes at 325° F.

While the roulade bakes, cut the chicken into ⅓-inch strips. Heat the remaining tablespoon of oil and sauté the strips for 2 minutes on high heat. (They will be cooked.) Add salt, pepper, and the remaining garlic and parsley and toss well.

Spread the chicken mixture on the cooked roulade and roll to enclose the filling. Using a long, flat spatula, transfer the roulade to a dish.

ORDER OF DINNER PREPARATION:

1. Calculate the proportions for the zucchini soup to serve 6. (See formula page 20.)

2. Make the pastry shell for the strawberry tart, using the polyunsaturated pastry on page 301 and an 8- or 9-inch pie plate.

3. Make the custard filling, using the polyunsaturated recipe on page 303. Wash and hull the strawberries.

4. Prepare the endives and the dressing for the salad. Chill separately.

5. Prepare and cook the zucchini soup.

6. Make the soy flour base for the roulade.

7. Sauté the mushrooms for the roulade.

8. Finish the roulade and put it in to bake.

9. Serve the soup while the roulade bakes.

10. Remove the soup plates and sauté the chicken strips.

11. Roll the filling in the roulade.

12. Serve the roulade; while your guests help themselves, toss and serve the endive salad.

13. Put the pie together: turn the custard into the shell, put the berries on top of the custard, and sprinkle with confectioners' sugar.

14. Serve the dessert.

QUICHES

A quiche makes a complete and delicious main course. Everything is there: starches, too much fat alas, protein, and calcium. There is so much of everything that all you need with it is a very green salad and a piece of fresh fruit.

A quiche is a pie shell filled with meat, cheese, vegetables, or a combination of any of these, on which a custard is poured. The pie is then baked until both pastry and custard are set. Quiches are one of the staples of Germanic cookery, and they can be found made with meat or fruit in the eastern provinces of France, the western and southern provinces of Germany, and all of Switzerland.

For your quiches, invest in a 3½-inch individual French tin *single-bottomed* pie plate, in an 8- or 9-inch French china pie plate, in an 8- or 9-inch dull aluminum pie plate or a 9-inch Corningware pie plate. All other plates will cook the bottom unevenly and result in a soggy bottom, especially the French tin plates with detachable bottoms.

QUICHE PASTRY

Butter is the very best for the taste of a pastry, and polyunsaturated margarine and oil the best for the future of your blood vessels. You can use either of the three or a 50-50 blend of butter and margarine. If you use margarine, let it sit for 15 minutes in the freezer before making the pastry; the shell will be flakier. Below are basic proportion tables and key recipes for pastry as made with butter and/or margarine and polyunsaturated oil.

BASIC PROPORTIONS FOR PASTRY MADE WITH BUTTER OR MARGARINE

2 servings	*4 servings*	*6 servings*
2 3½″ pie plates	1 8″ pie plate	1 9″ pie plate
½ cup sifted flour	⅔ cup sifted flour	1 cup sifted flour
3 T. butter or semi-frozen margarine	¼ cup butter or semi-frozen margarine	6 T. butter or semi-frozen margarine
¼ tsp. salt	⅓ tsp. salt	½ tsp. salt
1½ T. water	2 T. water	3 T. water

BASIC PROPORTIONS FOR PASTRY MADE WITH POLYUNSATURATED OIL

2 servings	*4 servings*	*6 servings*
2 3½″ pie plates	1 8″ pie plate	1 9″ pie plate
½ cup sifted flour	⅔ cup sifted flour	1 cup sifted flour
6¼ tsp. sunflower oil *	3 T. sunflower oil *	4½ T. sunflower oil *
¼ tsp. salt	⅓ tsp. salt	½ tsp. salt
4 tsp. water	1¾ T. water	2⅔ T. water

* Any oil may be used. Sunflower is indicated here because it is delicious and highly polyunsaturated.

KEY RECIPE: For pastry made with butter or margarine: Make a well in the flour. Add the butter, cut in coarse cubes, the salt, and the water. Mix all the ingredients with your fingertips; a ball will form. Bit by bit, push the dough 6 inches ahead of you on a board or the counter top to flatten the butter between the layers of flour and water paste. Gather into a ball and repeat the same flattening a second time. Gather the dough into a ball, shape it into a flat ½-inch cake and refrigerate it for 15 minutes. Although it will still be a bit soft, the dough can be used after this short rest in the refrigerator.

For pastry made with polyunsaturated oil: Mix flour, oil, salt, and water and gather into a ball. Flatten into a cake ½-inch thick and refrigerate 15 minutes. Roll out between two sheets of waxed paper.

You may make a large amount of pastry at once; separate it into small portions and freeze. (See the proportions and directions given on page 301.)

FILLING FOR QUICHES

To make a quiche filling you may use light cream, whole milk, or skim milk. Heavy cream produces a too-tough custard and should be reserved for a custard made only with egg yolks.

BASIC PROPORTIONS FOR QUICHE FILLINGS

2 servings	4 servings	6 servings
2 3½" pie plates	1 8" pie plate	1 9" pie plate
⅔ cup light cream or milk	1⅓ cup light cream or milk	2 cups light cream or milk
1 egg	2 eggs	3 eggs
¼ tsp. salt	⅓ tsp. salt	½ tsp. salt
Small pinch pepper	Large pinch pepper	¼ tsp. ground pepper

ASSEMBLING AND BAKING QUICHES

KEY RECIPE: Roll the pastry out to a thickness of ⅛ inch. Line the greased pie plate with it and crimp the edge with the tines of a fork. Put the meat, cheese, or vegetable garnish on the bottom of the pie crust. Mix eggs, milk, salt, and pepper with a fork until well mixed but not liquid, and pour over the garnish.

Bake in a 375° F. oven, first half of the baking time on the bottom rack of the oven, second half on the top rack. For a 3½-inch pie plate, bake 20 to 25 minutes; for an 8-inch pie plate, bake 30 to 35 minutes; for a 9-inch pie plate, bake 35 to 40 minutes.

If you have a freezer and space, prepare more than one quiche at a time and keep the unused one unbaked and frozen. Bake at the usual temperature one and one half times the regular cooking time.

SUGGESTED EVERYDAY MENU I

TOMATO-ZUCCHINI WAEHE
Escarole and bacon salad (page 252)
Raw apple mousse (page 279)

SERVINGS: 2

APPROXIMATE TOTAL PREPARATION TIME: 1 HOUR 15 MINUTES

This quiche recipe comes from southern Switzerland.

TOMATO-ZUCCHINI WAEHE

SERVINGS: 2

PREPARATION TIME: 45 TO 50 MINUTES

Pastry of your choice for 2 (pages 60–61)
1 teaspoon anchovy paste
1 small tomato, sliced
1 small zucchini
1 teaspoon dried basil
2 tablespoons grated Parmesan cheese
½ cup milk of your choice or light cream
1 egg
Salt and pepper

Roll the pastry out to a thickness of ⅛ inch and fit into two 3½-inch individual pie plates. Brush ½ teaspoon anchovy paste on the bottom of each shell, then add half of the tomato slices and 4 ⅛-inch thick slices of zucchini to each. Sprinkle with the dried basil and the Parmesan cheese. Beat the milk, egg, salt, and pepper and pour over the vegetables. Bake in a 375° F. oven for 10 minutes on the bottom rack, 10 to 15 minutes on the top rack.

ORDER OF DINNER PREPARATION:

1. If you have some pastry frozen, take one recipe of pastry made with ½ cup flour out of the freezer, or make the pastry with ½ cup flour. Let it rest.
2. Make the apple mousse.
3. Prepare the elements of the quiche filling, both liquid and solid.
4. Assemble the quiche and put it in to bake.
5. While the pie bakes, prepare the salad and make the dressing.
6. Serve the quiche and salad.
7. Serve the apple mousse.

SUGGESTED EVERYDAY DINNER MENU II

HAMBURGER QUICHE
Romaine, walnut and leek salad (page 251)
Blueberry yogurt (page 276)

SERVINGS: 2

APPROXIMATE TOTAL PREPARATION TIME: 1 HOUR 15 MINUTES

HAMBURGER QUICHE

SERVINGS: 2

PREPARATION TIME: 45 MINUTES

Pastry of your choice for 2 (pages 60–61)
¼ pound ground beef
¼ cup small-curd cottage cheese

1 tiny white onion, grated
¼ teaspoon rubbed sage
1 egg, beaten
Salt and pepper

Roll out the pastry to a thickness of ⅛ inch and fit into 2 3½-inch individual pie plates. Crumble the ground beef into a preheated frying pan and pan-fry on high heat until the meat has rendered all its fat. Drain the fat off carefully. Mix the hamburger, cottage cheese, grated onion, and sage and blend in the beaten egg, salt, and pepper. Pour half of the mixture into each shell and bake in a 375° F. oven, 10 minutes on the bottom rack and 10 to 15 more minutes on the top rack.

ORDER OF DINNER PREPARATION:

1. Defrost frozen pastry if you have some, or make pastry with ½ cup flour. Let it rest.
2. Pan-fry the hamburger to extract its excess fat, then make the filling for the quiche.
3. Put the quiche together and put it in to bake.

4. Prepare the salad greens, chop the walnuts, and make the salad dressing.

5. Mix washed blueberries with plain yogurt.

6. Toss the salad and serve with the quiche.

7. Serve the blueberry yogurt.

SUGGESTED COMPANY DINNER MENU

Quick minestrone (page 25)
SALÉE AUX NOIX
Iceberg lettuce and romaine salad with mint dressing (page 252)
Bûche Ardéchoise (page 312)

SUGGESTED WINE: Swiss Dézaley, Fendant, or Neuchâtel

SERVINGS: 6

APPROXIMATE TOTAL PREPARATION TIME: 2 HOURS

SALÉE AUX NOIX

SERVINGS: 6

PREPARATION TIME: 1 HOUR

Pastry:	*Filling:*
1¼ cups sifted flour	1 tablespoon butter
¼ cup finely ground walnuts	⅓ cup chopped walnuts
9 tablespoons butter	1¼ cups grated Gruyère cheese
1 teaspoon salt	2 eggs
3 to 4½ tablespoons water	¼ cup flour
	2 cups light cream
	¼ teaspoon grated nutmeg
	Salt and pepper

Make the pastry, following the instructions given in the key recipe (page 61), taking care to mix the ground walnuts into the flour. Use the tablespoon of butter to butter a 9-inch china pie plate. Mix the chopped walnuts and 1 cup of the grated Gruyère. Mix the eggs and flour, blend in the cream, then add the nutmeg, salt, and pepper.

Roll out the pastry to a thickness of ⅛ inch and fit it into the plate, building a very high fluted edge. Sprinkle the mixture of Gruyère and walnuts on the bottom of the pan and strain the cream over the cheese. Bake in a 375° F. oven for 20 minutes on the bottom rack of the oven. Sprinkle the remaining ¼ cup grated Gruyère on top of the hot custard. Finish baking the pie, 20 minutes on the top rack of the oven.

ORDER OF DINNER PREPARATION:

Spread the work over 2 days or evenings:

DAY ONE:

1. Prepare the pie crust and keep it refrigerated overnight.

2. Bake the cake completely, fill it, ice it and keep it well refrigerated overnight.

DAY TWO:

1. Cook the minestrone.

2. Clean the salad greens and prepare the salad dressing. Chill each separately.

3. Assemble the quiche and put it in to bake.

4. Serve the minestrone while the quiche finishes baking.

5. Serve the quiche, and toss the salad at the table while your guests help themselves.

6. Serve the cake.

CHAPTER VI

Beef for a Quick Dinner

B E EXTREMELY careful of the grade of beef you are buying. The best grade is "choice" because it is not too fat for everyday use. Occasionally, for a special evening, go to a butcher shop and buy a small roast or steaks graded "prime"; you will notice the large marbling of fat running in between the meat fibers.

You may purchase a roast or steaks of any grade or cut as much as one week ahead of time and keep it refrigerated, on a small cake rack, very loosely covered with foil. But hamburger should preferably be bought, ground, and eaten on the same day as purchased. (When you buy hamburger meat already ground and packaged, you will find that the inside of the block of meat is redder than the outside. This is called "bloom." The brown discoloration disappears as soon as the meat is unwrapped and exposed to the outside air again.)

In the everyday cookery of beef, avoid long cooking procedures such as braising, pot roasting or even the cooking of a large oven roast; they are too time-consuming for everyday food. The technique that consists of cooking a stew "the night before" or "early in the morning" is fallacious, for you will end up working longer than you should anyhow.

67

Keep long cooking procedures for the weekends, when you will have time to enjoy them and dedicate to them the time they deserve.

One exception to this rule is beef marinated overnight. Beef (small roasts or steaks) marinated in wine or brandy acquires additional flavor, but remember the following points carefully:

1. Start marinating at least the night before.

2. Before you cook the meat, wipe it completely dry or it will not sear properly.

3. *Never marinate ground beef.* If you do, it will lose all its natural juices.

4. If you broil a marinated steak, do not baste it with its marinade while it broils; no sooner will the meat be sealed with the broiler heat, than it will be unsealed with the moisture of the marinade. To use the marinade, reduce it over high heat, and after adding a bit of butter, use it as a sauce on the steak.

BEEF FOR QUICK ROASTING

Choose from the following cuts in decreasing order of cost:

> Tenderloin and sirloin strip
> Rib
> Sirloin tip, rump, and eye of the round
> Shoulder (so-called London broil)

KEY RECIPE: *For oven roasting:* You may roast a small piece of beef weighing about 3 pounds very quickly if you use a well-preheated 400° F. oven. For a rare roast, count 20 minutes cooking time for the first pound and 15 additional minutes for each additional pound. But mind this important exception: *a 3-pound piece of tenderloin will be ready in a total cooking time of 25 to 30 minutes.*

Salt and pepper the meat during the last 10 minutes of roasting, and let the meat rest 15 minutes before carving it. If you like your beef medium rare, roast a 3-pound roast for a whole hour and then let it rest for another 10 to 15 minutes. With this concentrated roasting method, there is almost no gravy, but the meat is succulent. On such a small piece of meat the shrinkage is not excessive.

For pan roasting: This method is particularly well adapted to small pieces of fat-free tenderloin, 2-inch-thick rib or strip steaks, and 1½- to 2-inch-thick shoulder London broils, for a total of 1½ to 2 pounds.

Heat 3 tablespoons oil of your choice in a pot just large enough to contain the piece of meat (a 2-quart enameled cast-iron oval braising pan is ideal). Sear the piece of meat on rather high heat and on all sides; do not salt or pepper the meat before searing it.

Turn the heat down to medium and continue turning the piece of meat every 5 minutes, keeping the pot uncovered at all times and taking into account the fact that a 2-pound roast will be cooked rare in 30 to 35 minutes, medium rare in about 40.

Salt and pepper the meat during the last 10 minutes of cooking. There will be some meat juices caramelized at the bottom of the pot; discard the fat and dissolve those caramelized juices with ¾ cup of beef broth or a mixture of wine and broth.

SUGGESTED COMPANY DINNER MENU

Cream of mushroom soup (page 33)
BEEF ROAST MARJOLAINE
Green beans with garlic and parsley butter (page 255)
Sliced tomato salad (page 252)
Rote Grütze (page 290)

SUGGESTED WINE: Châteauneuf du Pape or California Zinfandel

SERVINGS: 6

APPROXIMATE TOTAL PREPARATION TIME: 2 HOURS

BEEF ROAST MARJOLAINE

SERVINGS: 6

PREPARATION TIME: 45 MINUTES, INCLUDING OVERNIGHT MARINATION

2-pound shoulder roast (London broil)
2 shallots, thinly sliced
1 clove garlic, thinly sliced
1½ cups dry white wine
¼ teaspoon dried marjoram
½ cup beef bouillon of your choice

¼ teaspoon meat extract
1 tablespoon tomato paste
1 tablespoon butter
1½ teaspoons flour
Salt and pepper
2 tablespoons chopped fresh parsley

The night before your party, trim all fat off the piece of beef and put it in a 1-quart baking dish. Mix the sliced shallots and garlic with the wine and marjoram in a saucepan; bring to a boil and simmer 10 minutes, then cool completely. Pour over the meat when cold and let marinate 24 hours, turning the meat once while it marinates (in the morning before you go to work).

Pat the meat very dry with paper towels. Pan-roast the meat as described in the key recipe (page 69). While the meat cooks, reduce the marinade with the vegetables to ¼ cup. When the meat is cooked, deglaze the roasting pan with the marinade, add the broth, meat extract, and tomato paste and simmer together 5 minutes. Make a beurre manié with the butter and flour and thicken the sauce with it. Strain the sauce into a small bowl, correct the seasoning, and add the chopped parsley. Slice the roast in fine slivers across the grain, then spoon the sauce on the slices of beef.

ORDER OF DINNER PREPARATION:

Spread the work over 2 days:

DAY ONE:
1. Marinate the beef roast.
2. Make the fruit pudding dessert. Keep it well chilled.
3. String and clean the green beans. Keep them chilled.

DAY TWO:
1. Make the cream of mushroom soup.
2. Prepare the sliced tomatoes and their dressing.
3. Whip the cream for the dessert decoration and keep it chilled.
4. Put the beef on to cook, and while it roasts serve the soup.
5. Cook the beans; prepare their garlic and parsley butter.
6. Finish the beef sauce and season the beans with their butter.
7. While your guests help themselves to meat and vegetables, season the tomatoes.
8. Serve the salad.
9. Serve the dessert.

BEEFSTEAKS AND HAMBURGER STEAKS

The different beefsteaks you can buy are listed below in decreasing order of cost.

Expensive are:
>Tenderloin steaks
>Sirloin strip steaks, T-bone, Porterhouse steaks

Rib-eye steaks
Club steaks
Rib steaks (the bone is in)
Sirloin (boneless, pin bone, flat bone)

Less expensive are:
Petite steaks (also called "blade" or "chicken" steaks, they are cut from the chuck)
Top round steaks
Tip and sirloin-tip steaks (in steaks or ground)
Shoulder steaks

The best all-round everyday buy is the petite steak; it is very tasty and very juicy. Its drawback is the tough nerve that separates both strips of meat; simply cut your bite-sized pieces on each side of it—do not cut through it.

The cooking procedures indicated below apply to all kinds of steaks or ground meat patties. Follow the key recipe and use any garnish you may wish with the meat: vegetables, melted cheese, flavored butter. Let your imagination go.

A special word for hamburger: Buying ground beef meat nowadays is a tough proposition, because a number of supermarkets have given up the regular denominations of "chuck," "round," and so on to adopt the loose "regular ground," "lean ground," "extra-lean ground" beef. As a result one never knows what cut one is buying. The percentage of fat in the beef is government regulated and mentioned on the package, but you are never sure you are obtaining the particular flavor you are looking for, for the meat you are buying is a mixture of pieces coming from a variety of cuts, which include chuck and round, as well as shank and plate. To circumvent the problem, when you want to purchase hamburger, ask the butcher for a piece of meat in the cut you like and have it ground under your very eyes. It may cost you half a dollar more but you will not see one quarter of the volume of your meat melt in the frying pan or broiler pan. You will know exactly what you are eating and obtain the flavor you like. If you have budget problems, you can stretch hamburger meat by adding eggs, soft regular or whole-grain bread crumbs, or wheat germ to it.

BASIC PROPORTIONS FOR HAMBURGER STRETCHERS

Servings	Meat weight	Eggs	Bread crumbs	Wheat germ
1	3–4 oz.	0 *	1 T.	1½ tsp.
2	5 oz.	1	2 T.	3 tsp.
3	8 oz.	1	6 T.	4½ tsp.
4	11 oz.	2	½ cup	2 T.
5	14 oz.	2	⅔ cup	2½ T.
6	1 lb.	3	¾ cup	3 T.

* If this single portion seems insufficient, poach or fry one egg and top the hamburger steak with it.

BROILED STEAKS, CUBES, OR GROUND MEAT PATTIES

KEY RECIPE: For the benefit of your arteries, trim off all traces of fat surrounding the meat. Also trim off the connective tissues around the steaks—left on the meat, they will curl up and the meat will cook unevenly. *Do not* salt or pepper the steaks; do, however, brush them with a thin film of oil. Set the steaks on a cold broiler tray, then sear them well on one side in the broiler. Salt and pepper the seared side; turn the steaks over and sear the other side.

For steaks or patties ¾ to 1 inch thick: Broil 4 inches from the flame, 5 minutes on the first side, 3 minutes on the second side for rare and 5 minutes on the second side for medium rare.

For steaks 1½ inches thick: Broil 4 inches from the flame 5 minutes on the first side and 4 minutes on the second side, then turn the oven heat down to 350° F. and let cook another 6 minutes for rare and about 10 minutes for medium rare.

For beef cubes on skewers: Cut the meat into 1½-inch cubes. Do not salt and pepper them, but roll them in oil, skewer them, and broil 4 minutes on each side, 4 inches from the flame.

The most classic accompaniment to broiled beef is the béarnaise sauce on page 40. But it is rich for every day, and you may want to keep this for a company dinner.

Try rubbing ½ to 1 tablespoon of cold, plain, fresh, unsalted butter on the surface of each cooked steak—this is a treat. You may become a bit more fancy with the butter and use ½ to 1 tablespoon of a compound butter (see page 38).

SUGGESTED EVERYDAY DINNER MENU I

BROILED STEAKS WITH ANCHOVY BUTTER
Saffron- and basil-flavored rice pilaf (page 263)
Grated carrot salad (page 252)
Fresh fruit

SERVINGS: 2

APPROXIMATE TOTAL PREPARATION TIME: 50 MINUTES

BROILED STEAKS WITH ANCHOVY BUTTER
SERVINGS: 2

PREPARATION TIME: 10 MINUTES

Oil of your choice
2 beefsteaks of your choice
1 tablespoon butter

1½ teaspoons anchovy paste
Pepper

Broil the oil-brushed steaks as indicated in the key recipe (page 73). While the steaks broil, work together on a small plate the butter, anchovy paste, and pepper. Top each broiled steak with half the butter.

ORDER OF DINNER PREPARATION:

1. Prepare the grated carrot salad and dressing.
2. Trim the steaks and brush them with oil. Turn the broiler on; prepare the anchovy butter
3. Put the rice pilaf on to cook.
4. During the last 10 minutes of pilaf cooking time, broil the steaks.

5. Toss the salad and dressing while the steaks broil.
6. Serve the steaks, rice, and salad.
7. Serve the fresh fruit.

SUGGESTED EVERYDAY DINNER MENU II

BROILED STEAK WITH TOMATO-BASIL BUTTER
Boiled potatoes with grated Swiss cheese (page 258)
Romaine, leek, and chopped walnut salad (page 251)
Blender strawberry mousse (page 282)

SERVINGS: 2

APPROXIMATE TOTAL PREPARATION TIME: 45 MINUTES

BROILED STEAKS WITH TOMATO-BASIL BUTTER
SERVINGS: 2

PREPARATION TIME: 10 MINUTES

Oil of your choice
2 beefsteaks of your choice
1 tablespoon butter
1½ teaspoons tomato paste

Salt and pepper
¼ teaspoon finely powdered dried basil

Broil the oil-brushed steaks as indicated in the key recipe (page 73).
On a small plate, and using a fork, whip the butter with tomato paste,
salt, pepper, and finely powdered basil until the mixture is smooth and
homogenous. Top each broiled steak with half the mixture.

ORDER OF DINNER PREPARATION:

1. Make the strawberry mousse. Keep it chilled.
2. Trim the steaks; make the tomato-basil butter.
3. Clean and trim the salad greens, chop the walnuts and the leeks.
Make the salad dressing.

4. Peel the potatoes and start cooking them; grate the Swiss cheese. Turn the broiler on.

5. Drain the potatoes and cover them with the grated cheese. Keep them warm.

6. Broil the steaks; serve the steaks and potatoes.

7. Toss and serve the salad.

8. Serve the dessert.

SUGGESTED EVERYDAY DINNER MENU III

BROILED STEAK WITH BLUE CHEESE AND CARAWAY BUTTER

Buttered steamed brown rice (page 262)
Raw mushroom and spinach salad (page 251)
Orange compote (page 274)

SERVINGS: 2

APPROXIMATE TOTAL PREPARATION TIME: 50 MINUTES TO 1 HOUR

BROILED STEAK WITH BLUE CHEESE AND CARAWAY BUTTER

SERVINGS: 2

PREPARATION TIME: 10 MINUTES

Oil of your choice
2 beefsteaks of your choice
1 tablespoon butter

1½ teaspoons blue cheese
¼ teaspoon crushed caraway seeds

Broil the oil-brushed steaks as indicated in the key recipe (page 73). On a small plate, and using a fork, combine the butter with the blue cheese and the crushed caraway seeds until the mixture is homogenous. Top each broiled steak with half the mixture.

ORDER OF DINNER PREPARATION:

1. Prepare the orange compote. Chill it.
2. Put the rice on to cook.
3. While the rice cooks, prepare the spinach, slice the mushrooms, and make the salad dressing. Turn the broiler on.
4. Trim the steaks and broil them.
5. Make the cheese and caraway butter while the steaks broil.
6. Serve the steaks and rice.
7. Toss the salad and serve.
8. Serve the oranges.

PAN-BROILED AND PAN-FRIED STEAKS

Pan-broiled and pan-fried steaks are cooked according to the same technique, the only difference being the amount of fat used to cook the meat. If the meat is pan broiled the layer of fat must be extremely thin; it is there only to prevent the meat from sticking to the pan. If the steaks are pan fried, the layer of fat should be ⅛-inch deep. In both cases proceed as follows:

KEY RECIPE: Pour oil into a large skillet or electric frying pan and preheat to 425° F., or until the oil starts smoking. Remove the fat and the surrounding connective tissues from the steaks. Do not season them. Sear on one side for 2 to 3 minutes, then turn over, salt and pepper the seared side, and continue cooking until the red meat juices pearl at the surface of the steaks: the steaks are then cooked rare. If you prefer a medium-rare steak, turn the steak over again and continue cooking 2 or 3 more minutes.

To bring some change to everyday humdrum cookery, you may want to build a sauce, using the meat juices caramelized at the bottom of the pan and a bit of water, broth, or wine. Whatever liquid used, let it reduce at least by half to concentrate the flavor, and enrich the sauce with as much butter as diet and budget will let you afford. If you wish the sauce thickened, use a beurre manié of 1 tablespoon each butter and flour per cup of liquid. Remember that 2 to 3 tablespoons of sauce per person is ample enough.

SUGGESTED EVERYDAY DINNER MENU I

BIFTECK À LA CROQUE AU SEL
Noodles with cracked black pepper (page 267)
Belgian endive salad with mustard dressing (page 252)
Fresh sliced pears with Grand Marnier (page 272)

SERVINGS: 2

APPROXIMATE TOTAL PREPARATION TIME: 45 MINUTES

BIFTECK À LA CROQUE AU SEL

SERVINGS: 2

PREPARATION TIME: 10 MINUTES

¼ cup coarse or kosher salt
2 beefsteaks of your choice
Pepper

1 tablespoon fresh, cold, unsalted butter

Heat well a thick-bottomed frying pan or an electric frying pan to 425° F. Add the coarse salt so as to build an even layer of salt ⅛-inch thick on the bottom of the pan. Heat until the salt crystals start jumping. Add the steaks; sear them on one side and let cook 3 minutes. Turn over and let cook until the natural juices pearl at the surface of the meat. Remove to a plate, add pepper, then brush each steak with 1½ teaspoons cold, unsalted butter.

ORDER OF DINNER PREPARATION:

1. Peel and slice the pears; sprinkle with lemon juice, a bit of sugar, and Grand Marnier. Chill.
2. Trim the steaks. Prepare the layer of salt in the frying pan.

3. Prepare the endive salad and dressing. Keep chilled, separately.
4. Put the noodles on to cook.
5. While noodles finish cooking, heat the salt in the frying pan.
6. Cook the steaks.
7. Butter and pepper the noodles. Serve the steaks and noodles.
8. Toss and serve the salad.
9. Serve the dessert.

SUGGESTED EVERYDAY DINNER MENU II

BISTECCA ALLA PIZZAIOLA
Pan-fried zucchini with basil (page 259)
Boston lettuce and sliced fennel salad (page 252)
Flambéed bananas (page 277)

SERVINGS: 2

APPROXIMATE TOTAL PREPARATION TIME: 50 MINUTES

This recipe for tomato-topped beefsteaks comes from Naples.

BISTECCA ALLA PIZZAIOLA
SERVINGS: 2

PREPARATION TIME: 15 MINUTES

2 tablespoons olive oil or oil of your choice
2 beefsteaks of your choice
Salt and pepper
1 small clove garlic, finely chopped

2 small sun-ripened tomatoes, peeled and sliced across in ⅓-inch slices
½ teaspoon dried oregano flowers

Heat the oil and pan-fry the steaks according to the key recipe (page 77). Remove the steaks to a plate. Add the garlic to the pan and sauté 1 minute, then add the tomato slices and fry 3 minutes on each side on very high heat. Sprinkle with the well-crumbled oregano. Serve the steaks topped with the tomatoes.

ORDER OF DINNER PREPARATION:

1. Prepare the salad greens and dressing. Chill separately.
2. Slice the zucchini; slice the tomatoes for the steaks.
3. Pan-fry the zucchini with the basil.
4. Pan-fry steaks and tomatoes.
5. Serve the steaks and zucchini.
6. Toss and serve the salad.
7. Peel the bananas, sauté them in butter, add sugar, add rum, let heat, and flambé. Serve.

SUGGESTED EVERYDAY DINNER MENU III

VANILLE ROSTBRATEN
Spaetzle with poppy seeds and lemon rind (page 269)
Julienne of green pepper salad (page 252)
Cranberry-orange mousse (page 280)

SERVINGS: 2

APPROXIMATE TOTAL PREPARATION TIME: 1 HOUR

This recipe comes from Vienna, where "vanille" is the name of a garlic clove.

VANILLE ROSTBRATEN

SERVINGS: 2

PREPARATION TIME: 15 MINUTES

1 tablespoon oil of your choice
1 large onion, sliced
2 beefsteaks of your choice
¼ cup beef broth or water
Salt and pepper

2 tablespoons chopped fresh parsley
1 clove garlic, finely chopped
1½ tablespoons fresh butter (optional)

Heat the oil in a large frying pan and sauté the sliced onion until golden. Remove the onion to a plate. In the same pan and fat, pan-fry the steaks according to the key recipe (page 77). Remove to a plate when cooked and discard the cooking oil. Return the onions to the pan, add the broth or water, and boil hard for 3 to 4 minutes. Add salt and pepper, the chopped parsley, and garlic and mix well. Turn the heat off and mix in the butter, if used. Correct the seasoning and spoon the sauce over the steaks.

ORDER OF DINNER PREPARATION:

1. Prepare the cranberry-orange mousse. Chill.
2. Prepare the green peppers; prepare and chill the dressing.
3. Make the spaetzle batter; cook the spaetzle.
4. Trim the steaks; slice the onion, chop the garlic and parsley.
5. Sauté the onions; remove to a plate. Pan-fry the steaks.
6. Season the spaetzle with poppy seeds, lemon rind, and butter.
7. Finish the steak sauce.
8. Serve the steak and spaetzle.
9. Toss the salad and serve.
10. Serve the mousse.

SUGGESTED COMPANY DINNER MENU

TOURNEDOS DU LAVANDOU
Small boiled artichokes with tarragon butter (page 254)
Romaine and cucumber salad with olive oil and
    lemon dressing (page 252)
Pesche Emilio (page 296)

SUGGESTED WINE: Côtes du Rhône Red or California Zinfandel

SERVINGS: 6

APPROXIMATE TOTAL PREPARATION TIME: 1½ HOURS

This home-style steak recipe comes from sunny Provence.

TOURNEDOS DU LAVANDOU

SERVINGS: 6

PREPARATION TIME: 30 MINUTES

3 large beefsteak tomatoes
Olive oil
Salt and pepper
Provençal herbs (page 12)
2 each sweet red and green peppers

6 fat-free tenderloin steaks
¼ cup dry white wine
2 tablespoons chopped shallots
⅔ cup tomato sauce of your choice
3 tablespoons butter

Cut the tomatoes in half; remove the seeds and water. Place them in a baking dish, cut side up. Sprinkle with a bit of olive oil, salt, pepper, and Provençal herbs. Set aside.

Preheat the broiler. While it is heating, cut the peppers in fine, ¼-inch-wide strips. Sauté them in 1 tablespoon olive oil until tender but still crisp and brightly colored; while cooking, add salt and pepper and another pinch of Provençal herbs. Remove the cooked peppers to a plate.

Pan-fry the steaks, following the key recipe (page 77), in 2 tablespoons olive oil; at the same time, broil the tomatoes for 5 minutes, 4 inches away from the broiler flame. (Concentrate on the cooking of the steaks and use a timer for the tomatoes.) As soon as the steaks are cooked, set each of them on one half of a broiled tomato. Keep warm.

Discard the cooking oil and deglaze the pan with the white wine; add the shallots and reduce to 1 tablespoon (liquid and solids), then add the tomato sauce and simmer together 3 minutes. Blend the sauce and peppers. Correct the seasoning. Reheat well and blend in the 3 tablespoons of butter. Spoon an equal amount of peppers onto each steak and serve promptly.

ORDER OF DINNER PREPARATION:

1. Make the cold zabaglione, pour over the peaches, and chill.
2. Trim the steaks. Cut tomatoes in halves, season them, put them on broiler pan; cut peppers; chop shallots. Place the wine and tomato sauce in two small containers.
3. Prepare the romaine and cucumbers; prepare the dressing. Chill separately.
4. Boil the artichokes; drain them; season them with tarragon butter.
5. Pan-fry the peppers.
6. Pan-fry the steaks and broil the tomatoes.
7. Make the steak sauce.
8. Serve the steaks and artichokes; while your guests help themselves to meat and vegetables, toss the salad.
9. Serve the salad.
10. Serve the peaches and zabaglione.

CHIPPED STEAKS

If you cut petite (chicken or blade) steaks into 2 strips along the center nerve and then re-cut each strip crosswise into as many $\frac{1}{10}$-inch-thick little slivers as possible, you can prepare some very pleasant dishes that are a great change from just a plain piece of beef.

KEY RECIPE: The meat must be tossed extremely quickly in hot oil, according to the method called "stir-frying" in Chinese cuisine. You may use either a Chinese wok or an electric frying pan preheated to 425°.

The meat may be coated with a starch or left plain for sautéing, and it can be served alone or with a garnish of vegetables.

SUGGESTED EVERYDAY DINNER MENU I
Cheese soup (page 28)
STIR-FRIED BEEF ORIENTAL STYLE
Yogurt ice (page 284)

SERVINGS: 2

APPROXIMATE TOTAL PREPARATION TIME: 1 HOUR

STIR-FRIED BEEF ORIENTAL STYLE

SERVINGS: 2

PREPARATION TIME: 30 MINUTES

2 beefsteaks of your choice, cut in ⅒-x-1-inch slivers
1 tablespoon rice polish or cornstarch
1 tablespoon soy sauce
2 tablespoons vegetable oil of your choice

1 tablespoon sesame seeds
½ cup broccoli, cut in ⅔-inch cubes
½ cup cauliflower, cut in ⅔-inch cubes
Salt and pepper

Mix the beef, rice polish or starch, and soy sauce in a small bowl. If at all possible let stand at room temperature for 15 minutes.

Heat half the oil in the wok or frying pan and add the sesame seeds, to toast them. Then add the vegetables and toss them in the hot oil for 3 to 4 minutes, no more. Push the vegetables to the side of the pan and add the remaining oil and the beef; stir-fry the beef slices for 2 to 3 minutes. Bring the vegetables back into the center of the pan and mix all the ingredients very well, then stir-fry together for another minute. Serve immediately, after correcting the seasoning, if necessary.

ORDER OF DINNER PREPARATION:

1. Prepare the yogurt ice. Store in a shallow pan in the freezer.
2. Prepare the croutons and cheese for the soup; heat the broth.
3. Chip the meat; marinate in starch and soy sauce.

4. Cut the vegetables; prepare the sesame seeds on a small plate.
5. Finish the soup and serve it.
6. Finish the beef dish. Serve it.
7. Serve the yogurt ice.

SUGGESTED EVERYDAY DINNER MENU II

Leek and potato soup (page 23)
GESCHNETZELTES RINDFLEISCH
Grated carrot salad with lemon and olive oil dressing (page 252)
Fresh fruit

SERVINGS: 2

APPROXIMATE TOTAL PREPARATION TIME: 1 HOUR

GESCHNETZELTES RINDFLEISCH

SERVINGS: 2

PREPARATION TIME: 15 MINUTES

This beefsteak dish sauced with cream and Madeira is a favorite in Zurich, Switzerland.

2 tablespoons butter or oil of your choice
2 beefsteaks (preferably strip or blade steak), cut in ¹⁄₁₀-x-1-inch slivers

Salt and pepper
3 tablespoons dry Madeira wine
⅛ teaspoon meat extract
½ teaspoon potato starch
½ cup chilled cream of your choice

Heat the cooking fat or oil well in a frying pan. Add the beef and fry quickly, tossing back and forth until the meat is brown (a matter of a few minutes). Sprinkle the meat with salt and pepper. Remove the meat to a plate and discard the cooking oil. Add the Madeira and meat extract to the pan to deglaze it. Mix the starch with the chilled cream to make a slurry and stir into the hot deglazing liquid; it will thicken almost instantly. Return the meat to the sauce just to reheat it and serve immediately.

ORDER OF DINNER PREPARATION:

1. Prepare the vegetables for the soup. Put the soup on to cook.
2. Grate the carrots; prepare the dressing. Chill both separately.
3. Chip the meat; mix the Madeira with the meat extract; mix the starch and the cream.
4. Strain the soup, if desired. Serve it.
5. Toss the salad.
6. Cook the beef.
7. Serve the beef and salad.
8. Serve the fresh fruit.

CHAPTER VII

Veal for a Quick Dinner

THERE is veal and veal. In a supermarket you will on occasion find true young veal four to fourteen weeks old, but more often you will find only calf fifteen months to one year old. There are two ways of judging the age of the animal: by the size of the loin (kidney) chop and by its color. If the loin chops are small, not much larger than a lamb loin chop, and very pale pink, the meat is veal; if the chop is larger and darker, the meat is calf. True veal is found in fancy butcher shops and should be used for best results in quick-cookery entertaining; calf is fine for an everyday meal.

The supermarket price of choice pieces of veal, such as the rib chop and the loin chop, is generally comparable per pound to that of beef blade steaks, top sirloin or sirloin-tip steaks.

Keep the roasting or pot roasting of veal and calf for the weekend. Both meats need a slow and careful cooking to acquire the right flavor. Do not broil veal—it is too dry.

STEWED VEAL

There is one type of stew that you can make on top of the stove in a relatively short time. You may want to use it for quick-cookery entertaining. A "blanquette" or white veal stew, can be made with any garnish or flavoring you like by using different herbs during the cooking. Use the basic aromatics, meat, and liquid proportions as indicated in the recipe below, but vary the combination of vegetable garnish: with tarragon use artichokes, with nutmeg use mushrooms, and so on. This stew is usable for polyunsaturated diets, provided the egg and cream enrichment are left out of the sauce. The latter will be thinner, but not less tasty.

SUGGESTED COMPANY DINNER MENU

Shrimp salad Fatma (page 250)
BLANQUETTE DE VEAU À LA DANOISE
White rice pilaf (page 261)
Strawberry tart (page 303)

SUGGESTED WINES: Macon-Villages Blanc or California Semillon

SERVINGS: 6

APPROXIMATE TOTAL PREPARATION TIME: 2½ HOURS

This veal stew is a variation on the classic French dish.

BLANQUETTE DE VEAU À LA DANOISE

SERVINGS: 6

PREPARATION TIME: 1 HOUR 15 MINUTES

3 pounds veal shoulder, cubed
3 cups chicken bouillon of your choice or water, enough to cover
Salt and pepper
2 onions, each stuck with 2 cloves
1 carrot, cut in 3-inch chunks
Bouquet garni (page 12)
¼ cup chopped fresh dill or 2 tablespoons dried
3 cucumbers
4 teaspoons potato starch
1 egg yolk (optional)
¼ cup cream (optional)
Lemon juice

Put the veal meat in a 4-quart pot. Add the bouillon to cover and salt and pepper. Bring to a boil, then add the onions stuck with the cloves, the carrot, bouquet garni, and two-thirds of the dill. Simmer 1 hour.

Peel the cucumbers, cut them in half lengthwise, remove the seeds, and cut slantwise into 1-inch chunks. Bring 1 quart of water to a boil, add the cucumbers and blanch 3 minutes. Drain the cucumbers and add them to the meat stew 10 minutes before the end of its cooking time.

Drain the veal and cucumbers into a colander, reserving the cooking liquid. Put the meat and cucumbers in a casserole; keep warm. Put ½ cup of the stock in a measuring cup to cool. Return 1½ cups of cooking liquid to the pot (store any leftover for a soup or for deglazing frying pans) and bring it back to a simmer.

Mix the starch, plus the egg yolk and the cream if used, into the cool stock in the measuring cup. Pour this mixture into the simmering bulk of the stock very gradually, whisking well. Make sure that the sauce reboils or it will not thicken. (Do not hesitate to reboil the sauce—the starch will prevent the egg from curdling.) Correct the seasoning and add lemon juice to suit your taste, then strain the sauce over the meat and sprinkle with the remaining dill.

ORDER OF DINNER PREPARATION:

Spread the work over 2 days.

DAY ONE:

1. Cook the veal stew; do not make the sauce. Cool the meat in its cooking stock. Refrigerate.

2. Make the pastry shell. Cool it and wrap it in foil to preserve freshness.

DAY TWO:

1. Prepare the shrimp salad with only 1 pound of cooked shrimp (this is a first course here).

2. Whip the cream for the tart; keep it chilled. Clean the strawberries.

3. Make the rice pilaf; keep it warm in a low oven, in a hot water bath.

4. Gently reheat the veal stew. Finish and enrich the sauce, if desired.

5. Serve the shrimp salad.

6. Serve the stew and rice.

7. Gently melt the currant jelly for tart

8. Fill tart shell with the cream and berries; lightly brush with currant jelly. Serve.

PAN-FRIED VEAL

You can pan-fry the following rather expensive cuts:

Veal steaks (large ⅓-inch-thick cutlets cut across the whole width of the leg and with the center bone left in)

Veal scallops (¼ inch thick for Italian scaloppine, ⅓-inch thick for French escalopes)

In all cases, completely remove the surrounding fat and connective tissues to prevent curling and uneven cooking.

The veal scallops sold at high prices in a supermarket are always cut in the wrong direction, namely along the grain of the meat. The result is disheartening; the meat curls up, and what should be a succulent little morsel ends up being as tough as shoe leather.

True veal scallops are cut against the grain of the top or sometimes the bottom round of the leg of veal. To obtain true veal scallops, go to a butcher shop of great honesty and ask for a "veal top." You will be given a tight little bundle of meat consisting of one muscle never larger than both your hands put side to side and a maximum of 2½ inches thick.

This piece will be expensive; learn to cut it yourself. No frowns or scowls, please—any intelligent person can learn to cut veal scallops in a matter of minutes. Any honest butcher charging you the usual high price for a veal top will have removed the surrounding membranes. If the membranes are there, get the butcher to remove them for you. Then all you have to do is slice the scallops yourself.

To cut veal scallops use a very sharp all-purpose knife. Push the meat forward and upward with your left hand and cut into slices ¼ inch thick for Italian scaloppine and ⅓ inch thick for French escalopes. Both scaloppine and escalopes should be flattened. Acquire that plain little stainless steel meat bat to be found very easily in Italian markets. Let the bat fall on the meat and slide over it, towards you and parallel to the board. Do not flatten a veal scallop by beating it with a mallet. The mere fact that the meat is cut against the grain makes it tender. Out of one veal top, you will obtain at least 12 scaloppine or 8 escalopes; toward the end of the muscle they will be small.

If you use only part of the slices of meat, separate the remaining ones with sheets of waxed paper, wrap them in foil and freeze them. They will require 24 hours on the bottom shelf of the refrigerator to defrost completely.

VEAL, PAN-FRIED WITHOUT BREADING

KEY RECIPE: Flour the meat if you desire; heat the fat or oil used and sear, on medium high heat, on each side, only until golden. Salt and pepper the meat after searing. (Scaloppine are cooked by the time they are seared on each side; escalopes and steaks will require an additional 3 to 4 minutes on lower heat.) Remove the cooked meat to a plate and keep warm. Discard the cooking fat or oil and deglaze the pan with the liquid of your choice (water, veal or chicken stock, or wine). Reduce the liquid by one-fourth to one-half.

SUGGESTED EVERYDAY DINNER MENU I

Zucchini soup (page 29)
ESCALOPES DE VEAU AU BASILIC
Sliced tomatoes with garlic and parsley vinaigrette (page 252)
Flambéed pears Grand Marnier (page 277)

SERVINGS: 2

APPROXIMATE TOTAL PREPARATION TIME: 1 HOUR

These veal scallops with basil are a popular dish in Provence.

ESCALOPES DE VEAU AU BASILIC

SERVINGS: 2

PREPARATION TIME: 15 MINUTES

1½ tablespoons fat or oil of your choice
4 veal scallops (⅓ inch thick), flattened
Salt and pepper

¼ cup dry white wine
2 tablespoons scissored fresh basil or 1 teaspoon dried, well crumbled
1 tablespoon fresh butter (optional)

Pan-fry the veal scallops according to the key recipe (page 91). Discard the cooking oil or fat and deglaze with the white wine on high heat. Let cook down to 2 tablespoons. Remove from the heat and add the basil. Swirl in the cold butter, if desired. Pour over the meat.

ORDER OF DINNER PREPARATION:

1. Prepare the zucchini soup; put it on to cook.

2. Slice the tomatoes; prepare the vinaigrette with garlic and parsley. Chill both, separately.

3. Cut the pears in half; peel, core, and rub them with lemon. Keep ready to cook.

4. Serve the zucchini soup.

5. Cook the veal scallops while the soup is being eaten.

6. Finish the veal; pour the dressing over the tomatoes. Serve both.

7. Pan-fry the pears in butter; sprinkle with sugar to taste and flambé with Grand Marnier. Serve.

SUGGESTED EVERYDAY DINNER MENU II

SCALOPPINE CON OLIO E LIMONE
Saffron- and basil-flavored rice pilaf (page 263)
Escarole salad with mustard vinaigrette (page 252)
Fruit yogurt (page 276)

SERVINGS: 2

APPROXIMATE TOTAL PREPARATION TIME: 45 MINUTES TO 1 HOUR

Here is one of the multiple preparations for veal scaloppine in Milan.

SCALOPPINE CON OLIO E LIMONE

SERVINGS: 2

PREPARATION TIME: 25 MINUTES

6 scallops (¼ inch thick), flattened
3 tablespoons olive oil of your choice (virgin is best here)

½ teaspoon coarsely grated black pepper
Juice of 1 lemon
Salt

Marinate the veal scallops for 15 minutes in a dressing made of 2 table-spoons olive oil, ½ teaspoon very coarsely ground black pepper, and the juice of 1 lemon. Have the mixture well mixed before you start marinating, and use *no salt* in the marinade.

When you are ready to cook the veal scallops, heat 1 more tablespoon of oil and pan-fry the veal scallops, scraped well of all the marinade. As soon as the scallops are done, discard the cooking oil, and off the heat, add the marinade to the pan. Salt the meat well. Reheat the pan over low heat and roll the veal scallops in the marinade so they are just coated with it. Serve immediately.

ORDER OF DINNER PREPARATION:

1. Marinate the veal scallops in the lemon-oil-pepper mixture.
2. Put the rice pilaf on to cook.
3. Clean the escarole; make the dressing. Chill both separately.
4. Mix the chosen fruit with yogurt. Keep chilled.
5. When the rice is done, cook the scallops.
6. Serve the veal scallops and rice.
7. Toss and serve the salad.
8. Serve the yogurt.

SUGGESTED COMPANY DINNER MENU

Lemon soup (page 28)
SCHNITZEL À LA FRITZ
Broiled tomatoes (page 260)
Boston lettuce and radish salad (page 252)
Crème aux framboises (page 288)

SUGGESTED WINES: Austrian Gumpoldskirschner or California dry Semillon

SERVINGS: 6

APPROXIMATE TOTAL PREPARATION TIME: 2 HOURS

This veal recipe comes from a village on the Austro-Italian border.

SCHNITZEL À LA FRITZ

SERVINGS: 6

PREPARATION TIME: 40 MINUTES

12 eggs
6 tablespoons butter
1 teaspoon anchovy paste
Salt and pepper
3 tablespoons oil of your choice
12 veal scallops (¼ inch thick), flattened

12 small slices prosciutto
½ cup chicken bouillon of your choice
1½ tablespoons scissored fresh basil or 2 teaspoons dried, finely crumbled

Poach the eggs, 3 at a time, according to the instructions given on page 48, and keep them ready in a bowl of fresh, warm, lightly salted water. Cream the butter with the anchovy paste and a bit of pepper, and set aside.

Heat the oil in 2 frying pans and pan-fry the veal scallops, following the instructions given in the key recipe (page 91). As soon as the veal scallops are cooked, top each of them with a small slice of prosciutto. Discard the oil from the frying pans and deglaze each with half the bouillon. Transfer the deglazing of one pan into the other and boil down to about 3 tablespoons. Remove the pan from the heat and whisk in the anchovy butter, then add the basil. Top each veal scallop with an egg and spoon an equal amount of sauce over each portion.

ORDER OF DINNER PREPARATION:

Spread the work over 2 days.

DAY ONE:

1. Make the dessert. Chill as soon as cooled. Chop pistachios and set aside in a small dish.

2. Poach the eggs for the schnitzel topping; put them in lightly salted water and refrigerate.

3. Recalculate the lemon soup recipe for 6 persons (see page 20).

DAY TWO:

1. Make the lemon soup.

2. Cut the tomatoes in half and prepare them for broiling. Keep ready to broil on jelly-roll or roasting pan.

3. Prepare the salad greens and dressing. Chill both separately.

4. Carefully reheat the poached eggs in their water bath.

5. Broil the tomatoes.

6. Cook the veal scallops; top them with the prosciutto and eggs; make the sauce.

7. Serve the tomatoes and the veal dish.

8. While your guests help themselves, toss and serve the salad.

9. Sprinkle the dessert with the chopped pistachios and sugar. Serve.

VEAL, PAN-FRIED WITH BREADING

Both veal steaks and scallops can be breaded before being pan fried, but for pan frying with breading you may want to give a thought to something a bit unusual for most shoppers, the use of veal hamburger. In Europe, the lower cuts of veal are ground and used to make the "frikadellen" of the Germanic countries, the "fricadelles" of the French, and the "polpette" of the Italians, which are either breaded and pan fried or sautéed (page 103).

For good hamburger, buy veal stew, sometimes labeled "cacciatore"; the meat cubes are cut mostly from the shoulder and the largest trimmings from the rib section and legs. You must enrich the hamburger according to the following proportions to obtain a soft, mellow piece of meat, for veal and calf meat are so lean that plain veal hamburger is likely to be quite dry.

If you have too much hamburger, make an additional patty or two and cook them. Veal patties taste delicious cold, and can be used for a high-protein salad or a sandwich. Use the bread crumbs of your choice, although the best taste comes from whole-grain bread. Crumb the bread in a blender before using it or soak it in 1 tablespoon of milk per slice of bread.

BASIC PROPORTIONS FOR PLAIN VEAL HAMBURGER

2 servings	*3–4 servings*	*5–6 servings*
½ lb. ground veal	1 lb. ground veal	1½ lbs. ground veal
1 egg	1 egg	2 eggs
½ slice bread of your choice	1 slice bread of your choice	2 slices bread of your choice
¼ tsp. salt	½ tsp. salt	¾ tsp. salt
Pinch pepper	Large pinch pepper	¼ tsp. pepper

BASIC PROPORTIONS FOR VEAL AND HAM HAMBURGER

2 servings	*3–4 servings*	*5–6 servings*
¼ lb. ground veal	½ lb. ground veal	1 lb. ground veal
2 slices boiled ham, chopped	3 slices boiled ham, chopped	4 slices boiled ham, chopped
1 egg	1 egg	2 eggs
½ slice bread of your choice	1 slice bread of your choice	2 slices bread of your choice
Salt if needed	Salt if needed	Salt if needed
Pinch pepper	Large pinch pepper	¼ tsp. pepper
1 T. chopped parsley	2 T. chopped parsley	¼ cup chopped parsley

For *polyunsaturated diets*, use the plain veal hamburger recipe, omitting the egg yolk.

BREADING For breading veal, use crumbs of your choice, dry or fresh, from white, whole-wheat, or other whole-grain bread. Two slices of day-old bread give between ¾ and 1 cup of bread crumbs. One cup of crumbs will bread 12 veal scallops, 3 veal steaks, and 6 ground veal patties.

For the egg wash, use one of the two given below. Each yields enough for 12 veal scallops, 3 veal steaks, and 6 ground veal patties.

EGG WASH FOR REGULAR DIETS

1 egg

1 teaspoon oil of your choice

1 teaspoon water

Pinch each salt and pepper

EGG WASH FOR LOW CHOLESTEROL DIETS

1 egg white

1 tablespoon water

1 tablespoon polyunsaturated oil

Pinch each salt and pepper

Beat all the ingredients until completely blended. Any leftover wash can be refrigerated and added to a soup, rice, mashed potatoes, or an omelet batter.

KEY RECIPE: Prepare the egg wash. Flour the meat, pat it well to discard excess flour. Brush the egg wash on the first side of the meat with a pastry brush. Invert the egg-brushed side of the meat into the crumbs. Brush the second side with egg wash, crumb it and pat the meat to discard excess crumbs. In a frying pan, heat fat or oil of your choice to a depth of $\frac{1}{10}$ to $\frac{1}{8}$ inch on medium high heat. Cook the meat until golden on both sides, adding salt and pepper only after it is completely cooked.

SUGGESTED EVERYDAY DINNER MENU I

PETER'S SCHNITZEL
Stir-fried green peppers (page 258)
Romaine and cucumber salad with dill dressing (page 252)
Coffee pudding (page 289)

SERVINGS: 2

APPROXIMATE TOTAL PREPARATION TIME: 1 HOUR

This breaded veal dish comes from the kitchen of an Austrian friend.

PETER'S SCHNITZEL

SERVINGS: 2

PREPARATION TIME: 30 MINUTES

1 egg
1 veal steak (⅓ inch thick)
1 tablespoon flour
Egg wash of your choice (page 98)
½ cup bread crumbs of your choice

2 tablespoons fat or oil of your choice
1 tablespoon chopped fresh parsley
Salt and pepper
Lemon juice
4 anchovy fillets

Boil the egg 10 minutes, then cool it fast in cold water. Trim, flour, and bread the veal steak and cook it according to the key recipe (page 98). Chop the egg to obtain a fine yellow and white mixture. Mix it with the chopped parsley. As soon as the meat is done, salt and pepper it, then squeeze lemon juice over it. Put the anchovy fillets on the steak and top with the egg and parsley mixture.

ORDER OF DINNER PREPARATION:

1. Hard-boil the egg for the schnitzel; cool and chop. Chop the parsley.
2. Make the coffee pudding. Chill.
3. Clean and cut the green peppers in slivers; set aside.
4. Clean the romaine and cucumber. Make dressing. Chill all the salad elements separately.
5. Bread the veal steak and pan-fry it.
6. While the veal cooks, stir-fry the peppers.
7. Top the veal steak with the anchovies and egg-parsley mixture.
8. Serve the veal and peppers.
9. Toss and serve the salad.
10. Serve the coffee pudding.

SUGGESTED EVERYDAY DINNER MENU II

POLPETTE AL PREZZEMOLO
Stewed tomatoes (page 260)
Lettuce and avocado salad (page 251)
Refreshed nectarines (page 276)

SERVINGS: 2

APPROXIMATE TOTAL PREPARATION TIME: 1 HOUR

POLPETTE AL PRESSEMOLO

SERVINGS: 2

PREPARATION TIME: 25 MINUTES

Veal and ham hamburger for 2 (page 97)
2 tablespoons flour
Egg wash of your choice (page 98)
½ cup bread crumbs of your choice

3 tablespoons fat or oil of your choice
¼ cup white wine
Salt and pepper
Dash of lemon juice
¼ cup chopped fresh parsley

Shape the ground meat into 4 small patties ⅓ inch thick. Flour, bread, and cook as described in the key recipe (page 98). As soon as the meat is cooked, discard the cooking oil or fat. Add the white wine and cook down to 2 tablespoons; add salt, pepper, a dash of lemon juice, and the parsley. Spoon the sauce onto the patties.

ORDER OF DINNER PREPARATION:

1. Prepare the nectarine dessert. Chill.
2. Prepare the lettuce, avocado, and dressing. Chill separately.
3. Prepare the ground meat; bread the patties.
4. Prepare the tomatoes for stewing.

5. Pan-fry the meat patties and stew the tomatoes simultaneously.
6. Peel the avocado; toss it with the lettuce and dressing.
7. Serve the polpette, tomatoes, and salad.
8. Serve the fruit dessert.

SUGGESTED COMPANY DINNER MENU

Spaghetti with Italian parsley, garlic, and salami (pages 268, 269)
SCALOPPINE MARGHERITA
Artichoke hearts and lemon butter (page 254)
Galliano soufflé (page 297)

SUGGESTED WINE: Soave or Orvieto

SERVINGS: 6

APPROXIMATE TOTAL PREPARATION TIME: 2 HOURS

SCALOPPINE MARGHERITA

SERVINGS: 6

PREPARATION TIME: 45 MINUTES

To prepare this without trepidation, have the remainder of your meal ready. Fry the meat just before serving—it should go from the pan to the plate.

18 veal scallops (¼ inch thick), flattened
¾ cup flour
2 egg yolks
⅓ cup olive oil
Salt and pepper

⅔ cup milk
6 slices prosciutto, cut in julienne strips
Chopped flat-leafed parsley
2 dozen black oil-cured olives, pitted and chopped

Flour the veal scallops. Using ½ cup of the flour, the egg yolks, 1 tablespoon of the olive oil, salt, pepper, and the milk, make a smooth batter. Preheat the remainder of the olive oil in one or two frying pans.

Dip each scallop into the batter and drop it into the hot oil. Cook 3 minutes on each side or until golden.

Put the veal scallops on a plate. Salt and pepper them, sprinkle with the prosciutto, parsley, and olives.

ORDER OF DINNER PREPARATION:

Spread the work over 2 days.

DAY ONE:

1. Make a soufflé for 6 persons, using Galliano as a liqueur (page 297).

2. Turn the finished soufflé into a soufflé dish (preferably Pyroceram) and freeze it.

DAY TWO:

1. Chop the parsley, garlic, and salami to season the spaghetti.

2. Flour the scallops; make the batter for coating the scallops and set aside on a large piece of waxed paper.

3. Cook the artichokes; set aside.

4. Prepare the prosciutto, olives, and parsley to sprinkle on the meat.

5. Cook the spaghetti; season with butter, chopped parsley, garlic and salami. Serve.

6. Remove the soufflé from the freezer. Preheat the oven.

7. Simultaneously, reheat the artichokes in lemon butter and cook the veal scallops. Serve both.

8. Before sitting down to eat your meat course, put the soufflé in to bake (for 25 minutes at 400°, or 35 minutes at 325°).

9. Serve the soufflé.

SAUTÉED VEAL

You may sauté the following cuts:
Moderately expensive:

>Plain veal, or veal and ham, hamburger patties (page 97)
>Veal or calf rib chops
>Veal or calf loin chops

Expensive:

>Veal steaks, trimmed of all fat and cut in thin strips

KEY RECIPE: Remove the tail of the loin chop if you prefer; flour the chops only if you want to. Brown the chops or the strips of meat on all sides, then salt and pepper them.

Veal chops can then be covered for 4 to 6 minutes to let the meat cook through. Deglaze the pan with the liquid of your choice.

Calf chops should cook longer. Add a bit of liquid to the pan (more or less will be needed, depending on the natural juiciness of the meat). Salt and pepper the meat and cook, covered, 20 to 25 minutes, turning the chops once or twice while cooking.

Any herb or spice to flavor the meat should be added before the pan is covered. Any vegetable added as a garnish should be added in the last 10 minutes of cooking of the meat. The meat is done when the tip of a paring knife goes freely in and out of it. Deglaze the pan with more liquid after discarding the fat. (The best deglazing liquid is veal stock, which you will probably not have on an everyday basis, unless you have some of the stock on page 11 frozen. Use any bouillon of your choice, or wine, or even water. Watch bouillon cubes; diluted according to manufacturer's directions they make the outside of the meat too salty. Use twice as much liquid as recommended in the package directions.)

SUGGESTED EVERYDAY DINNER MENU I

VEAL CHOPS COSTA BRAVA
Pan-fried zucchini with chopped parsley (page 259)
Sliced tomato with shallots vinaigrette (page 252)
Natillas y naranjas (page 292)

SERVINGS: 2

APPROXIMATE TOTAL PREPARATION TIME: 50 MINUTES TO 1 HOUR

VEAL CHOPS COSTA BRAVA
SERVINGS: 2

PREPARATION TIME: 40 MINUTES

6 slices (⅛ inch each) Spanish chorizo or Italian pepperoni sausage
2 tablespoons olive oil
1 sweet red onion
1 sweet red pepper, cut in strips ⅓-inch wide

1 sweet green pepper, cut in strips ⅓-inch wide
1 tomato, peeled and seeded
2 calf rib or loin chops
Salt
Dash of cayenne pepper
6 black oil-cured olives, pitted and chopped

Put the sausage slices in a frying pan, and on medium heat, render out the fat. Discard the rendered fat, replace it by 1 tablespoon of the oil, and sauté the peppers, tomato and onion until half tender. Remove to a plate. Add the remaining tablespoon of oil to the pan and brown the chops on both sides. Salt them, then sprinkle with a dash of cayenne pepper. Return the vegetable and sausage mixture to the pan and cook, covered, for 20 minutes. The vegetables should render a lot of moisture, and be overcooked and almost saucelike. Sprinkle with the chopped olives before serving.

ORDER OF DINNER PREPARATION:

1. Prepare the custard for the dessert; slice the oranges. Chill both.
2. Slice the tomatoes for the salad; prepare the vinaigrette dressing with chopped shallots.
3. Slice the zucchini; chop the parsley. Set aside.
4. Prepare and sauté the sausage, onion, peppers, and tomato for the chops; sauté the chops.
5. While the chops cook, pan-fry zucchini very quickly, to keep it crisp.
6. Season the tomatoes with the vinaigrette.
7. Serve the chops, zucchini, and tomatoes.
8. Serve the custard poured over the orange slices.

SUGGESTED EVERYDAY DINNER MENU II

HANNI'S GESCHNETZELTES
Buttered spaetzle (page 267)
Cauliflower, watercress, and radish salad (page 252)
Cantaloupe in port (page 272)

SERVINGS: 2

APPROXIMATE TOTAL PREPARATION TIME: 45 MINUTES

This is a variation on the classic minced sautéed veal so popular in the German-speaking part of Switzerland.

HANNI'S GESCHNETZELTES

SERVINGS: 2

PREPARATION TIME: 25 MINUTES

3 tablespoons butter
1 veal steak, cut in slivers ¼ inch
    thick
Salt

½ teaspoon coarsely cracked black
    pepper
3 tablespoons dry Madeira
1 teaspoon potato starch
½ cup light cream

Heat the butter until the foam starts receding. Gradually add the veal strips and continue sautéing until the meat looks seared. Add salt, the cracked pepper, and the Madeira. Cover the pan and continue cooking, on medium heat, for 12 to 15 minutes. Uncover the pan. Mix the starch and cream and pour into the pan, tossing until the sauce thickens. Correct the seasoning and serve.

ORDER OF DINNER PREPARATION:

1. Peel and dice the melon; sprinkle with port and chill.
2. Prepare the cauliflower, watercress, and radishes; make the salad dressing. Chill separately.
3. Make the spaetzle batter. Let stand.
4. Cut the veal into strips; prepare all the elements for the veal dish.
5. Sauté the veal strips.
6. While they finish cooking, make the spaetzle.
7. Make the sauce for veal. Serve the veal and spaetzle.
8. Serve the salad.
9. Serve the melon.

SUGGESTED COMPANY DINNER MENU

Quick fish soup (page 30)
CÔTES DE VEAU À LA MOUTARDE
Romaine, leek, and walnut salad (page 251)
Narcissa Chamberlain's berry salad with whipped cream (page 273)

SUGGESTED WINE: Hermitage Blanc or California Blanc Fumé
SERVINGS: 6

APPROXIMATE TOTAL PREPARATION TIME: 1½ HOURS

CÔTES DE VEAU À LA MOUTARDE

SERVINGS: 6

PREPARATION TIME: 40 MINUTES

6 large calf rib chops
2 tablespoons oil of your choice
Salt and pepper
½ cup unsalted butter
½ pound mushrooms, sliced
2 tablespoons chopped fresh parsley

¼ cup dry white wine
½ cup veal stock (page 11) or chicken broth of your choice
1 shallot, finely chopped
3 tablespoons prepared Dijon mustard

Trim the chops. Brown them in 2 tablespoons hot oil, then salt and pepper them and remove them to a plate. To the oil in the same pan add 2 tablespoons of the butter and sauté the mushrooms; add salt, pepper, and 1 tablespoon parsley and continue cooking 3 minutes. Return the chops to the pan, cover, and cook 20 minutes, on slow heat, until the meat is tender. Remove the meat and mushrooms to a plate; keep warm. Add the wine, stock, and shallots to the pan and reduce to ¼ cup. Add the mustard, mix well, and on very slow heat, whisk in the remainder of the butter. *Do not boil.* Add the second tablespoon of parsley, then spoon the sauce over the chops.

ORDER OF DINNER PREPARATION:

Spread the preparation over 2 days.

DAY ONE:

1. Make the fish soup; refrigerate it.
2. Make the French bread slices for the soup.

DAY TWO:

1. Clean the berries; macerate them in brandy; whip the cream.
2. Prepare the romaine and leek; chop the walnuts; make the dressing for the salad.
3. Slice the mushrooms and chop the parsley for the chops; assemble all the ingredients for the preparation of the chops.
4. Sauté the chops; finish the sauce.
5. Toss the salad; serve the chops and the salad.
6. Serve the berries and cream.

CHAPTER VIII

Pork for a Quick Dinner

T HE PRICE of pork, compared to that of the red meats, still remains reasonable. Unfortunately, pork is not the meat to eat often if you are a diligent calorie watcher.

Although it should always be well done to prevent the danger of infection by trichinae, pork should really not desiccate in the oven or the pan as it is too often allowed to do. In quick cookery, as for the other types of meats, avoid the roasting or pot roasting of larger pieces and restrict yourself to the use of small flat pieces, such as rib and loin chops and boneless tenderloin steaks, cut to a maximum thickness of ¾ inch and weighing an average of 4 ounces per slice. A good chop is solid, nonmarbled meat surrounded by ½ inch of solid fat. Trim half of the fat away, to leave a thickness of only ⅛ to ¼ inch. To prevent the meat from curling up while cooking, cut small indentations through the tough layer of connective tissue that exists between meat and fat.

SAUTÉED PORK CHOPS AND PORK TENDERLOIN STEAKS

KEY RECIPE: Brown the meat on both sides. Salt and pepper it. Add a bit of liquid and cover the pan. Continue cooking, covered, for 20 to 25 minutes. Turn the meat over once while it cooks, and if necessary add more liquid. The meat is cooked when the tip of a paring knife stuck into the center of each piece comes out freely. If the meat is insufficiently done, it will come out of the pan with the inserted knife.

If you wish to add a vegetable garnish, do so about 10 minutes before the meat is expected to be done; potatoes, though, should be put in the pan as soon as it is covered, since they require 20 minutes to soften.

Watch the liquid you are using. You may use the veal stock given on page 11 if you have some frozen or any bouillon of your choice, water, or even wine. Be very careful of bouillon cubes; use twice as much liquid as required in the package directions, for diluted full strength, they make the outside of the meat very salty.

SUGGESTED EVERYDAY DINNER MENU I

Garlic soup (page 29)
CÔTELETTES DE PORC À LA SAUCE PIQUANTE
Escarole salad with vinaigrette (page 252)
Fresh fruit

SERVINGS: 2

APPROXIMATE TOTAL PREPARATION TIME: 1 HOUR

This is such a popular dish in Paris that it is sold ready made in many "charcuteries," the grandiose French equivalent to this country's delicatessens.

CÔTELETTES DE PORC À LA SAUCE PIQUANTE

SERVINGS: 2

PREPARATION TIME: 45 MINUTES

2 pork chops (¾ inch thick)
2 tablespoons oil of your choice
1 large onion, chopped
Salt and pepper
¼ cup dry white wine

1 teaspoon vinegar
¼ cup tomato sauce of your choice
2 tablespoons finely sliced dill pickle
1 tablespoon butter (optional)

Trim the chops, then brown them on both sides in the oil. Remove them to a plate while you sauté the onion until golden. Return the chops to the pan, placing them on the onions; salt and pepper them, add the wine, and cook, covered, following the key recipe (page 110). As soon as the meat is tender, remove it to a plate; keep it warm. Remove as much of the fat in the pan as possible. Add the vinegar, tomato sauce, pickle slices, a good amount of salt and pepper, and boil hard for 3 to 4 minutes. Remove from the heat and add the butter, if desired. Spoon the sauce over the meat.

ORDER OF DINNER PREPARATION:

1. Put the pork chops on to cook.
2. Prepare the garlic soup; prepare the French bread slices.
3. While the chops and soup cook, clean the salad greens and make the salad dressing.
4. Finish the meat sauce; keep the meat warm in the sauce.
5. Finish and serve the soup.
6. Toss the salad; serve the pork and the salad.
7. Serve the fruit.

SUGGESTED EVERYDAY DINNER MENU II

Parsley soup (page 23)
CÔTES DE PORC DE FLANDRES
Belgian endive salad with mustard dressing (page 252)
Flambéed apples (page 277)

SERVINGS: 2

APPROXIMATE TOTAL PREPARATION TIME: 1 HOUR

CÔTES DE PORC DE FLANDRES

SERVINGS: 2

PREPARATION TIME: 40 MINUTES

A popular way of cooking pork chops in Northern French and Belgian homes.

2 large onions, sliced
2 tablespoons oil of your choice
2 pork chops (¾ inch thick)
Salt and pepper
4 juniper berries, crushed

¼ cup light beer
¼ cup bouillon of your choice or water
1 tablespoon butter (optional)

Sauté the onion slices in 1 tablespoon of the oil until golden. Remove them to a plate. Brown the chops on both sides, then salt and pepper them. Return the onions to the pan, add the juniper berries, and cook, covered, until tender. While the meat cooks, gradually add the beer. When the meat is done, discard the juniper berries. Remove the cooked chops to a plate and degrease the juices in the pan. Add the bouillon or water and let it cook down to 2½ tablespoons. Correct the seasoning of the sauce, add the butter, if desired, and pour over the chops.

ORDER OF DINNER PREPARATION:

1. Start cooking the pork chops.
2. Put the parsley soup on to cook.
3. While chops and soup cook, clean the Belgian endive and prepare the dressing.

4. Peel, core, and slice the apples. Sauté them in a bit of butter or oil of your choice until brown.

5. Strain the soup if desired, then serve it.

6. Finish the pork chops and sauce, and toss the salad. Serve the chops and salad.

7. Reheat the apples with a bit of sugar and flambé with a liqueur of your choice. Serve hot.

SUGGESTED COMPANY DINNER MENU

Lemon soup (page 28)
PORK AND THYME
Romaine, cherry tomatoes, green pepper, marinated olives, and feta
   cheese salad (page 252)
Maraschino-refreshed fruit (page 276)

SUGGESTED WINE: French Beaujolais or California Gamay Beaujolais

SERVINGS: 6

APPROXIMATE TOTAL PREPARATION TIME: 2 HOURS

PORK AND THYME

SERVINGS: 6

PREPARATION TIME: 50 MINUTES

3 large onions, chopped
3 tablespoons butter
6 tablespoons fresh bread crumbs
1 large clove garlic, finely chopped
Salt and pepper
6 large pork chops, ¾ inch thick
5 tablespoons oil of your choice

2 teaspoons dried thyme
3 large Idaho potatoes, peeled and
   cubed
¼ cup dry white wine
½ cup chicken broth of your choice
2 tablespoons chopped fresh parsley

Sauté the onions in 2 tablespoons of the butter until soft and translucent. Add the crumbs, the chopped garlic, salt, and pepper and mix very well. Cool. Cut a pocket in each chop and stuff with an equal part of the onion mixture, then close each pocket with a toothpick. Brown the chops on each side in 3 tablespoons of the oil, then salt and pepper them and sprinkle half the thyme over them. Cover the pan and cook the chops for 10 minutes on the first side. Uncover the pan, turn the chops over, and sprinkle with the remainder of the thyme. Add a bit of liquid, if necessary, and cook the meat another 15 minutes.

Meanwhile, sauté the potatoes in a mixture of 2 tablespoons oil and 1 tablespoon butter until golden. When the chops are done, remove them to a shallow platter and surround them with the potatoes. Degrease the juices in the frying pan, add the wine and broth, reduce by half, and spoon the cooking juices over the chops, so that some of it will run and be absorbed by the potatoes. Sprinkle with chopped parsley.

ORDER OF DINNER PREPARATION:

1. Calculate the recipe for lemon soup to serve 6 (see formula page 20).
2. Prepare the fruit for the dessert, put it in a large container and chill.
3. Prepare the filling for the chops; stuff the chops, then put on to brown and cook.
4. While the chops cook, prepare salad ingredients and dressing.
5. Prepare the lemon soup.
6. Peel and cook the potatoes; add them to the chops. Keep warm. Degrease the meat juices and make the gravy. Spoon over the meat.
7. Toss the fruit with the maraschino. Keep chilled.
8. Serve the soup.
9. Toss the salad. Serve the pork and potatoes with the salad.
10. Serve the refreshed fruit.

PAN-FRIED PORK

To pan-fry pork, use very thin chops, labeled "thin for breading" by meat packers. If you are willing to spend a lot of calories for a treat, buy those chops and pan-fry them in their own rendered fat, searing them first, then letting them cook slowly through until they become positively candied-like and brown. Serve them with mustard. It is a treat without peer, but the scales will soar!

Thin pork chops, though, are always tastier and more pleasing to the eye and palate if you bread them. To bread, use the same basic ingredients in the same amount as described in the key recipe for breading veal (page 98).

KEY RECIPE: The general method is to trim all traces of fat from the chops, flour them, brush them with egg wash, and coat them with crumbs. But you can introduce a number of welcome variations for a change of taste and pace using either of the following techniques:

For *plain breading and flavored meat*: Mix with the flour that will coat the meat, individually or in combination: ½ teaspoon of allspice or curry, ground ginger, ground cardamom, ground coriander, ground cinnamon, a large pinch of cloves, grated nutmeg.

For *flavored breading and plain meat*: If you wish the meat to remain only slightly flavored, add an herb to the bread crumbs. The herb can be dried or fresh and you can use the following combinations:

1 tiny clove garlic, minced, and 1 tablespoon chopped fresh parsley
¼ teaspoon finely crumbled dried thyme
¼ teaspoon rubbed sage
¼ teaspoon cumin
¼ teaspoon commercial poultry seasoning
¼ teaspoon crushed caraway seeds
1 tablespoon of the crumbs can be replaced by very dry grated Parmesan or Gruyère cheese.

SUGGESTED COMPANY DINNER MENU

COSTOLETTE DI MAIALE BOLOGNESE
Asparagus stir-fried in olive oil and lemon (page 255)
Tomato and cucumber salad (page 252)
Strawberry ice with kirsch (page 285)

SUGGESTED WINE: Valpolicella

SERVINGS: 6

APPROXIMATE TOTAL PREPARATION TIME: 2 HOURS

A dish from the vicinity of Bologna that tastes best when prepared with true Parmigiano Reggiano, or true Swiss Gruyère cheese.

COSTOLETTE DI MAIALE BOLOGNESE
SERVINGS: 6

PREPARATION TIME: 40 MINUTES

MEAT:	SAUCE:
6 paper-thin pork chops, fat entirely removed	3 tablespoons butter
3 tablespoons flour	3 tablespoons flour
1 egg, beaten	1 cup scalded milk
½ cup fresh bread crumbs	Salt and pepper
2 tablespoons grated Parmesan cheese	⅛ teaspoon grated nutmeg
3 tablespoons olive oil or other oil of your choice	1 egg yolk
6 slices prosciutto	2 tablespoons grated Parmesan cheese
	6 tablespoons grated Swiss Gruyère cheese

Flour the chops. Brush them with beaten egg and bread them with the crumbs mixed with the 2 tablespoons Parmesan cheese. Pan-fry them in the hot olive oil.

To make the sauce, heat the butter well. Add the flour and cook 3 minutes. Add the milk and thicken on medium heat, stirring constantly. Season with salt, pepper, and nutmeg. Add the egg yolk, Parmesan cheese, and 3 tablespoons of the Swiss cheese. Put the chops on a long platter. Top each of them with a slice of prosciutto and spoon an equal amount of sauce on each chop. Sprinkle with the remaining Swiss cheese and broil 2 minutes.

ORDER OF DINNER PREPARATION:

1. Bread the pork chops. Let them stand.
2. Prepare the cream sauce for chops. Keep warm in a hot water bath.
3. Peel and cut the asparagus into 1-inch pieces.
4. Cut the tomatoes (peeled, if desired) and peeled cucumbers in slices; prepare salad dressing. Keep both chilled.
5. Pan-fry the pork chops.
6. Stir-fry the asparagus pieces in olive oil and lemon juice.
7. Remove 2 frozen 24-ounce bags of loose strawberries from the freezer.
8. Finish the chop dish; broil the top 2 minutes. Serve the chops, asparagus.
9. Arrange the tomato and cucumber slices on a plate. Spoon the dressing over them and serve.
10. Make the strawberry ice and serve in sherbet glasses.

BROILED PORK

The broiling of pork in an oven does not result in the best of meats. The pork dries out too much, and a stringy dinner is sure to follow. If you charcoal broil, you will obtain better results. Since a lot of charcoal broiling goes on on apartment house balconies, here are a few ideas:

KEY RECIPE: Use ¾-inch cubes of pork meat (shoulder butt is the best). Marinate the meat first, in a marinade that should consist mostly of oil flavored with some lemon rind and juice or pepper. Since the pork meat is very dry, leave the oil on the meat when broiling. Wipe the meat dry before broiling only if the marinade contains much more liquid than oil (see the rules for marinated beef on page 68). Remove large flecks of pepper—they burn and turn acrid.

After marinating, sear the meat very well on all sides by exposing it very, very close to the coals. Then raise the grill 5 inches above the coals and cook the meat for another 10 minutes, turning it at regular intervals. Salt and pepper the meat only after it is cooked.

SUGGESTED EVERYDAY DINNER MENU I

PORK AND PRUNE SKEWERS
Grated carrot salad (page 252)
Strawberries Samuel (page 291)

SERVINGS: 2

APPROXIMATE TOTAL PREPARATION TIME: 1 HOUR

PORK AND PRUNE SKEWERS
SERVINGS: 2

PREPARATION TIME: 30 MINUTES

¾ pound pork shoulder butt, cut into 12 three-quarter-inch cubes
10 soft prunes, pitted
2 tablespoons corn oil

1 teaspoon lemon juice
½ teaspoon finely grated lemon rind

Mix the pork cubes and prunes. Mix the corn oil, lemon juice, and lemon rind. Roll the pork and prunes in the corn oil mixture and let stand 10 minutes or so. Without drying them, skewer the pork and prunes. Sear close to the coals, then raise 5 inches above the coals to let cook to the center.

ORDER OF DINNER PREPARATION:

1. Start the coals or broiler.
2. Make the custard for strawberries. Chill.
3. Marinate the pork cubes and prunes in the oil, lemon juice, and lemon rind mixture.
4. Grate the carrots and make the salad dressing. Chill separately.
5. Clean the strawberries; pour the custard over them. Keep chilled.
6. Skewer the pork and prunes; broil them.
7. Toss the salad. Serve it with the meat dish.
8. Serve the strawberries and custard.

SUGGESTED EVERYDAY DINNER MENU II

LES BROCHETTES SUR LE BALCON
Stir-fried broccoli (page 255)
Sliced tomatoes and fennel salad (page 252)
Sliced pineapple in rum (page 272)

SERVINGS: 2

APPROXIMATE TOTAL PREPARATION TIME: 1 HOUR

Barbecuing is fashionable on Paris balconies and in suburban gardens. This is the favorite skewered pork dish of one of my friends.

LES BROCHETTES SUR LE BALCON

SERVINGS: 2

PREPARATION TIME: 30 MINUTES

¾ pound pork shoulder butt, cut into 12 three-quarter-inch cubes
2 tablespoons olive oil
Cracked black pepper

6 breakfast sausages
Prepared Dijon or Düsseldorf mustard
1 cup fresh bread crumbs

Marinate the cubes of meat 10 minutes in the oil, mixed with a bit of cracked black pepper. Halve each sausage link to make 12 tiny sausages, 1 inch long.

Skewer the meat cubes alternately with the sausages. Sear on all sides very close to the coals. Brush mustard evenly on all sides of the meat cubes. Spread the crumbs on a sheet of paper and roll the skewers into the crumbs. Finish cooking 5 inches above the coals until cooked through.

ORDER OF DINNER PREPARATION:

1. Start the coals (or broiler)
2. Peel and slice the pineapple; sprinkle it with rum and sugar or honey. Chill.
3. Marinate the pork cubes.
4. Peel and cut the broccoli into ¾-inch pieces.
5. Slice the tomatoes and fennel. Make an olive oil and lemon juice dressing. Keep chilled, separately.
6. Skewer the pork and sausages; sear them.
7. Brush the pork and sausage with mustard, roll them in crumbs. Put on to finish cooking.
8. Stir-fry the broccoli while the pork finishes cooking.
9. Serve the meat, broccoli, and salad.
10. Serve the pineapple.

SUGGESTED COMPANY DINNER MENU

BROCHETTES DE VIERVILLE
Pan-fried butternut squash (page 259)
Boston lettuce, avocado and hard-boiled egg salad (page 251)
Two-pear mousse (page 280)

SUGGESTED BEVERAGE: Hard cider

SERVINGS: 6

APPROXIMATE TOTAL PREPARATION TIME: 2 HOURS

This is a regional recipe from Normandy.

BROCHETTES DE VIERVILLE

SERVINGS: 6

PREPARATION TIME: 50 MINUTES

3 pounds pork shoulder butt, cut into 36 three-quarter-inch cubes
4 apples, each cut into 8 chunks
1 onion, sliced
½ teaspoon dried thyme
1 bay leaf, crushed

2 tablespoons applejack or Calvados
Oil of your choice
Salt
Cracked black pepper
½ cup heavy cream, warmed and lightly salted

Combine the pork cubes, apple chunks, onion, thyme, crushed bay leaf, Calvados, and 2 tablespoons of oil and let sit for 30 minutes. Skewer the meat and apples and charcoal broil, following the key recipe (page 117). Season highly with salt and crushed black pepper. As soon as they are cooked, place the brochettes on a long platter and dribble the warmed heavy cream over them. (The onion and thyme are only seasonings, and can be discarded.)

ORDER OF DINNER PREPARATION:

1. Prepare the two-pear mousse; pour it into sherbet glasses or champagne cups. Chill well.
2. Prepare the meat and apple cubes; marinate them.
3. Start the coals or broiler. Skewer the meat and apples to make brochettes.
4. Peel and slice the butternut squash.
5. Clean the lettuce; hard-boil the eggs; make the salad dressing.
6. Start pan-frying the butternut squash slices.
7. Broil the brochettes.
8. Serve the brochettes and squash, and also, if desired, the salad now (or you may serve it after the main course).
9. Serve the mousse.

CURED PORK

Precooked cured ham steaks, smoked pork chops, and boiled ham can be put to very quick use in your everyday dinner preparations. Cured pork in all its forms has a great drawback—the large amount of salt it contains. The customary garnish for cured pork is fresh or canned fruit, the juiciness and tartness of which help to temper the high salt content.

With all the sugar and cream involved in its preparation, cured pork should be given careful consideration, and if at all possible, should not be served on a more than once-a-week basis to prevent a quick soaring of the scales.

You can give cured fully cooked ham steaks and fully cooked smoked pork chops the very same culinary treatment: they may be broiled or pan fried.

KEY RECIPE: Follow the rules for broiling and pan frying given on pages 115 and 117. Do not overbroil, or you will see the meat turn into a mass of unchewable strings. Since cooked cured meats should only be reheated, just sear the surface on each side for 3 to 4 minutes. A few sprinklings of sugar on the surface of the meat before broiling will do wonders for its appearance.

Boiled ham requires no special preparation; it is best reheated in a cream sauce, which once more is there only to temper the large amount of salt contained in the meat.

SUGGESTED EVERYDAY DINNER MENU I

HAM AND FRUIT SOUP
Romaine, cherry tomatoes, green pepper, marinated olive, and feta
cheese salad (page 252)
Coffee pudding (page 289)

SERVINGS: 2

APPROXIMATE TOTAL PREPARATION TIME: 45 MINUTES

HAM AND FRUIT SOUP

SERVINGS: 2

PREPARATION TIME: 10 MINUTES

1 ham steak
1 tablespoon butter or oil of your
   choice
½ teaspoon sugar

1 small jar mixed canned fruit
¼ teaspoon potato starch
Pinch of ground cloves

Brush the steak with half the butter or oil. Sprinkle with half the
sugar. Broil 3 minutes. Turn the steak over, repeat the brushing with
oil and sprinkling with sugar, using the remainder of those two ingredients, and broil 3 more minutes.

Drain the fruit into a colander, reserving ¼ cup of the canning syrup.
Mix the syrup, potato starch, and cloves. Heat the fruit well in a small
pot. Pour over the mixture of syrup and starch and stir gently until
thickened. Serve the ham with the fruit mixture as a separate garnish.

ORDER OF DINNER PREPARATION:

1. Prepare the coffee pudding. Chill.
2. Prepare the salad greens and garnishes; prepare the dressing. Keep
chilled, separately.

3. Prepare the fruit; put it on to heat. Mix the syrup and starch for the thickening.
4. Broil the ham.
5. Thicken the fruit soup.
6. Serve the ham and fruit.
7. Toss the salad and serve.
8. Serve the coffee pudding.

SUGGESTED EVERYDAY DINNER MENU II

EMMENTHALER SCHINKENSCHNITTEN
Stir-fried chopped fresh spinach (page 260)
Grated carrot salad (page 252)
Fresh fruit

SERVINGS: 2

APPROXIMATE TOTAL PREPARATION TIME: 1 HOUR

A substantial dish from the German-speaking part of Switzerland. Gruyère, Appenzell or Sbrinz Swiss may also be used.

EMMENTHALER SCHINKENSCHITTEN
SERVINGS: 2

PREPARATION TIME: 25 MINUTES

3 tablespoons dry white wine
2 tablespoons butter, or fat or oil of your choice
2 slices (⅓ inch thick) Italian or French bread
2 slices (2½ x 4 inches) boiled ham
2 slices (2½ x 2 inches) Emmenthaler or Swiss cheese
1½ tablespoon flour
⅔ cup scalded milk of your choice
¼ cup grated Emmenthaler or Swiss cheese
Salt and pepper

Sprinkle the white wine on the bottom of a 1-quart baking dish. Spread ½ teaspoon butter or other chosen fat on one side of each slice of bread. Put the bread, unbuttered side down, in the baking dish; it will absorb the wine. Fold each slice of ham over one slice of cheese. Put each ham-cheese sandwich on one of the slices of bread. Heat the remainder of the butter or fat in a small saucepan, add the flour, and cook 3 minutes, stirring occasionally. Whisk in the scalded milk and thicken on medium heat. Remove from the heat and add half the grated cheese. Correct the seasoning and pour over the slices of bread, sprinkle with the remainder of the cheese and reheat for 10 minutes in a 350° F. oven. Broil the top 2 minutes to brown, if necessary.

ORDER OF DINNER PREPARATION:

1. Grate the carrots; make the dressing. Chill separately.
2. Wash and chop the spinach.
3. Prepare the slices of bread and the sandwiches of ham and cheese.
4. Make the cream sauce, and add half the cheese; pour the sauce on the bread and ham slices. Place in oven.
5. Stir-fry the chopped spinach.
6. Serve the *schnitten* and spinach.
7. Serve the salad, then the fresh fruit.

SUGGESTED COMPANY DINNER MENU

Zucchini soup (page 29)
JAMBON À LA CRÈME
White rice pilaf (page 261)
Boston lettuce in plain vinaigrette (page 252)
Refreshed nectarines and kiwis (page 276)

SUGGESTED WINES: French Côte de Nuits Villages or California Pinot Noir

SERVINGS: 6

APPROXIMATE TOTAL PREPARATION TIME: 2 HOURS

This ham in cream dish is a specialty of the French province of Burgundy.

JAMBON À LA CRÈME

SERVINGS: 6

PREPARATION TIME: 20 MINUTES

3 tablespoons butter
6 slices (5 x 3 x ⅓ inch) ham
⅓ cup Madeira

1 small truffle, chopped (optional)
1½ cups heavy cream
White pepper

Heat the butter well in one or two large frying pans. Pan-fry the ham until golden on both sides, then remove to a plate and keep warm. Add the Madeira and chopped truffle, if used, to the frying pan and cook down to 3 tablespoons. Add the heavy cream, a good pinch of pepper, and let the sauce reduce to 1 cup, stirring occasionally on low heat. Spoon the sauce over the ham slices.

ORDER OF DINNER PREPARATION:

1. Prepare the nectarines and refresh them; peel the kiwis and slice them. Chill.
2. Clean the lettuce; prepare the dressing; chill both separately.
3. Make the zucchini soup.
4. Cook the pilaf; it will wait for you if your ham is not ready.
5. Pan-fry the slices of ham; keep warm. Prepare the sauce; it can reduce while you are entertaining your guests and eating the soup.
6. Serve the soup.
7. Serve the ham in cream sauce and the pilaf.
8. Serve the salad.
9. Serve the refreshed fruit.

CHAPTER IX

Lamb for a Quick Dinner

I F Y O U cannot eat "medium rare" lamb cooked to a pink juiciness, do not even bother to read or use anything having to do with roasting, broiling, and pan frying in this chapter and proceed directly to the paragraphs concerned with sautéed lamb. Well-done lamb is spoiled lamb, but unless one becomes personally convinced that it is so by direct experience, no amount of talking or writing on the subject will ever convince anyone.

In quick cookery, use first-quality young lamb—it will cook faster. Look for small racks and small legs, the meat of which is very young and cooks in a minimum amount of time.

ROASTED CHOICE CUTS OF LAMB

The following cuts of lamb can be roasted in a relatively short time using an oven preheated to 400° F. to obtain a fast concentration of the juices inside the meat.

Expensive:

> Rib rack (collar)
> Loin rack (rack or saddle)
> Leg

Moderately expensive:

> Square-cut shoulder
> Boned, rolled shoulder

Do not hesitate to buy a rack or leg of lamb one week ahead of time and let it sit in the refrigerator. Set on a rack and loosely cover with a tent of foil. The flavor will improve with the passing of time.

RACK OF LAMB

KEY RECIPE: Have the butcher saw off the extremity of the ribs, split the rack in half through the backbone, and saw off the spiny part of the backbone on both sides. With a knife held flat, remove all but a thickness of ¼ inch from the fat layer on each side and the long, tough white ligament of the backbone. Put the racks on a lightly oiled rack placed in a roasting pan and roast at 400° F.—50 minutes for the loin rack, 45 minutes for the rib rack. Salt and pepper the meat only when two-thirds done.

To carve the loin rack, remove both loin strips with a sharp knife and slice each with the grain in long slivers ⅛ inch thick. To carve the rib rack, cut between the ribs and twist your blade to snap each chop from the backbone.

One single rack will serve 3 persons; 1 double rack will serve 6.

SUGGESTED COMPANY DINNER MENU

Cream of mushroom soup (page 33)
RACK OF LAMB DIJONNAISE
Broiled tomatoes (page 260)
Boston lettuce salad (page 252)
Cantaloupe in port (page 272)

SUGGESTED WINE: French Côte de Nuits Villages or California Pinot
  Noir

SERVINGS: 6

APPROXIMATE TOTAL PREPARATION TIME: 2 HOURS

RACK OF LAMB DIJONNAISE

SERVINGS: 6

PREPARATION TIME: 1 HOUR

1 double rib rack of lamb
2 tablespoons olive oil
3 tablespoons prepared Dijon mustard

½ cup seasoned fresh bread crumbs from French or Italian bread
¼ cup clarified butter (page 9)

Have the butcher trim the rack as indicated in the key recipe (page 128). Remove the fat covering on both sides of the rib rack down to the bare muscle.

Rub each half with 1 tablespoon of oil. Roast 15 minutes in a preheated 400° F. oven. Remove both racks from the oven and brush with mustard. Sprinkle each rack with ¼ cup bread crumbs. Spoon 2 tablespoons clarified butter on each rack and let roast another 30 minutes. Let rest 5 minutes before carving.

ORDER OF DINNER PREPARATION:

1. Trim the rack of lamb of all fat; let stand at room temperature while you work on soup and vegetables.
2. Prepare the soup ingredients and put on to cook.

3. Prepare the tomatoes for broiling; let them stand.

4. Put the meat in to roast for the first 15 minutes.

5. Cut the cantaloupe in pieces or balls; marinate in port. Chill.

6. Brush the meat with mustard, crumb it, and butter it; return to the oven.

7. Prepare the lettuce and dressing.

8. Serve the soup minutes before meat is done. Remove the meat from oven, and just before you sit down to eat your soup, put the tomatoes to broil.

9. Serve the meat and tomatoes.

10. Toss the salad and serve.

11. Serve the melon.

LEG OF LAMB

Have the butcher prepare the leg this way: ask for the hip bone to be removed and the sirloin meat to be tied closed. When you are ready to cook the leg remember that the whole leg (frenched leg with small sirloin attached) will serve 8 to 10 persons; the frenched (shortened) leg, 6 to 8 persons; the small sirloin cut flush with the thigh bone will give you a dainty little dinner for 2 to 3 persons.

Choose a leg of lamb as small as possible so that the frenched leg weighs barely more than 3½ to 4 pounds.

KEY RECIPE: With a sharp paring knife, remove any traces of fat and fell from the whole surface of the leg of lamb, so the meat is completely exposed. Rub the leg with, preferably, olive oil or with any oil of your choice. Set on a rack resting in a roasting pan and roast at 400° F. for 15 minutes per pound. A completely trimmed leg weighing from 3½ to 4½ pounds will be done to a juicy pink color in 1 hour 15 minutes.

SUGGESTED COMPANY DINNER MENU

Fish soup (page 30)
TIAN D'AGNEAU
Iceberg lettuce salad with mint dressing (page 252)
Narcissa Chamberlain's berry salad (page 273)

SUGGESTED WINE: Châteauneuf du Pape or Zinfandel

SERVINGS: 6

APPROXIMATE TOTAL PREPARATION TIME: 2½ HOURS

In and around the Provençal town of Avignon a baking dish is called
a "Tian"; by extension a "tian" has become the name of a dish prepared in a tian—here it is lamb.

TIAN D'AGNEAU

SERVINGS: 6

PREPARATION TIME: 1½ HOURS

4 large Idaho potatoes
3 large cloves garlic
6 tablespoons butter
Veal stock (page 11)
3 ripe, red tomatoes, sliced

Salt and pepper
1 shortened leg of lamb (about 4
   pounds)
Dried rosemary

Peel, then slice the potatoes with a slicer to obtain paper-thin slices.
Rub a large baking dish with 1 clove of the garlic, then butter it with
2 tablespoons of the butter. Add the potatoes and half cover them with
veal stock. Slice the tomatoes, and with the slices slightly overlapping
one another, make a border of tomato slices placed on the potatoes.
Dot the tomatoes and potatoes with 3 tablespoons of the butter. Sprinkle with salt and pepper.

Remove all the fat from the surface of the meat, down to the bare
muscle. Slice the remaining cloves of garlic in fine slivers; cut small
slits just below the surface of the meat and slide the garlic slivers into

each. Rub the leg of lamb with the remaining tablespoon of butter and sprinkle with a bit of dried rosemary (as much as you like, but not *too* much). Place the leg of lamb in the center of the baking dish, on the potatoes. Bake 1 hour and 15 minutes in a 400° F. oven. Salt and pepper the meat when it is three-quarters done. Allow the meat to rest 10 minutes before slicing.

ORDER OF DINNER PREPARATION:

Spread the work over 2 days:

DAY ONE:
Prepare the fish soup. Keep it well chilled.

DAY TWO:
1. Prepare the lamb dish. First the potatoes and tomatoes and then the leg of lamb. Put it in to bake.
2. Prepare the berry salad and chill it.
3. Prepare the iceberg lettuce and its mint dressing. Chill both separately.
4. Prepare the bread slices for the fish soup.
5. Reheat the soup gently and serve it.
6. Serve the leg of lamb.
7. Toss and serve the salad.
8. Serve the dessert.

SUGGESTED EVERYDAY DINNER MENU

SMALL SIRLOIN OF LAMB ROASTED WITH HERBS
Pan-fried zucchini (page 259)
Romaine salad with Parmesan cheese (page 252)
Caramel pudding (page 289)

SERVINGS: 2

APPROXIMATE TOTAL PREPARATION TIME: 1 HOUR 15 MINUTES

SMALL SIRLOIN OF LAMB ROASTED WITH HERBS

SERVINGS: 2

PREPARATION TIME: 45 MINUTES

1 small loin of lamb, cut from the
    leg, rolled and tied
½ teaspoon Provençal herbs (page
    12)

6 fennel seeds, crushed
Salt and pepper

Untie the small loin. Sprinkle the herbs and the crushed fennel seeds, plus a pinch of salt and pepper, inside the meat, then roll closed again and tie. Roast 35 to 40 minutes in a preheated 400° F. oven. Salt and pepper the outside when the meat is three-quarters done.

ORDER OF DINNER PREPARATION:

1. Season and tie the roast; put in the preheated oven to roast.
2. Make the caramel pudding. Chill in the freezer or refrigerator.
3. Clean and slice the zucchini.
4. Prepare the salad and its dressing.
5. Pan-fry the zucchini.
6. Serve the roast and the zucchini.
7. Serve the salad.
8. Serve the pudding.

SHOULDER OF LAMB

You may roast a shoulder either unboned or boned and rolled. If you want it rolled, have the butcher bone it for you and tie it.

A rolled shoulder will cost you more, but it will slice better if you use it for company. Be prepared to roast a boned shoulder 10 minutes longer than a square-cut shoulder, since the bones acting as rods conduct the heat to the center of the meat.

Roasting time at 400° F.: whole shoulder 1 hour, rolled shoulder 1 hour 10 minutes.

SUGGESTED COMPANY DINNER MENU

SHOULDER OF LAMB BOULANGÈRE
Boston lettuce and sliced fennel salad (page 252)
Strawberry ice (page 285)

SUGGESTED WINE: French Hermitage or California Pinot Noir
SERVINGS: 6

APPROXIMATE TOTAL PREPARATION TIME: 1½ HOURS

SHOULDER OF LAMB BOULANGÈRE
SERVINGS: 6

PREPARATION TIME: 1 HOUR 15 MINUTES TO 1½ HOURS

3 tablespoons butter
1 shoulder of lamb, square-cut or rolled
4 large Idaho potatoes

2 large onions
2 tablespoons oil of your choice
Chicken broth of your choice
Salt and pepper

Using 1 tablespoon of the butter, butter a 2-quart baking dish, put the shoulder right on the bottom, not on a rack, and roast in a 400° F. oven for 20 minutes. Meanwhile slice the potatoes very thin, using a Feemster, if possible. Slice the onions, too. Heat the oil and 2 remaining tablespoons butter in a large frying pan and sauté the onions and potatoes. Salt and pepper the mixture, then add it to the dish in which the lamb is roasting and continue roasting another 30 minutes (40 minutes, if rolled). Baste once in a while with a few tablespoons of chicken stock and the juices and fat escaping from the meat. Serve piping hot, on hot plates.

ORDER OF DINNER PREPARATION:

1. Peel and slice the onions and potatoes
2. Roast the meat for the first 20 minutes.
3. Meanwhile, sauté the onions and potatoes in a large frying pan.

4. Add the sautéed vegetables to the meat baking dish and bake another 30 to 40 minutes.

5. Prepare the lettuce and fennel; make the salad dressing. Chill both separately.

6. Serve the lamb.

7. Put bags of frozen strawberries to partially defrost on the kitchen counter.

8. Serve the salad.

9. Make strawberry ice in blender and serve.

PAN-FRIED LAMB

The best pieces for pan frying are:

Expensive:
> Kidney (loin) chops (1 inch thick), although these are better when broiled)
> Rib chops (1 inch thick)
> Leg or shoulder, cut into small (¾-inch) cubes
> Lamb steaks (½ inch thick), cut across the leg

Moderately expensive:
> Lamb patties from the shoulder

Ground lamb, like beef hamburger or ground veal, is an excellent choice for pan frying. But if you buy already ground lamb in a supermarket, you are almost certain to make a bad investment. There will be too much fat and the flavor will not be what you expect, since lamb patties are made with all the odd cuts that are difficult to sell, the shoulder shank being predominant. Shank is delicious only when braised, and lamb patties are mostly for broiling and pan frying.

If you want a good ground lamb, choose a tray of cubes prepared for shish kebabs, so that you will be able to judge the quantity of fat and the quality of the meat, and have the butcher grind it for you. If you plan a larger party, have a whole shoulder boned, trimmed, and ground—you will obtain the best value and the best taste.

If a good-quality ground lamb seems too expensive for your budget, stretch it with an addition of eggs and bread crumbs of your choice, also add parsley and garlic both finely chopped. They will take away any so-called "lamby" taste.

BASIC PROPORTIONS FOR GROUND-LAMB STRETCHERS

Servings	Meat	Eggs	Bread crumbs of your choice	Wheat Germ	Parsley	Garlic
1	3–4 oz.	none	1 T.	1½ tsp.	½ T.	⅛ clove
2	5 oz.	1	2 T.	3 tsp.	1 T.	¼ clove
3	8 oz.	1	6 T.	4½ tsp.	1½ T.	⅓ clove
4	11 oz.	2	½ cup	2 T.	2 T.	½ clove
5	1 lb.	2	⅓ cup	2½ T.	3 T.	¾ clove
6	1 lb.	3	¾ cup	3 T.	¼ cup	1 clove

KEY RECIPE: *For lamb steaks and chops:* Trim off most of the fat, then cut 2 slashes into the surrounding connective tissues of steaks and chops to prevent curling up while cooking. Heat the cooking fat or oil until nearly smoking and sear one side of the meat. Turn over, salt and pepper the seared side, and watch for bright red droplets of meat juice. The steaks will be done as soon as you sear them; if you continue cooking them, they will be tough.

If you desire medium rare chops turn the meat over a second time and continue cooking 2 to 3 minutes on slower heat.

Follow the same principles for lamb patties.

For lamb cubes: If you pan-fry cubes, toss the meat in the very hot fat until brown on all sides.

You can then remove the meat to a plate, keep it hot and deglaze the pan with the liquid of your choice—water, broth, wine, or even tomato sauce. If you use wine, be certain to boil it down by half at least or the sauce will be sour.

SUGGESTED EVERYDAY DINNER MENU I

LAMB STEAKS AU VERT
Steamed brown rice with saffron and basil (page 263)
Tomato and julienne of green pepper salad (page 252)
Blueberry yogurt (page 276)

SERVINGS: 2

APPROXIMATE TOTAL PREPARATION TIME: 1 HOUR

"Au vert" in French culinary jargon means that the dish contains a healthy addition of one or several chopped green herbs.

LAMB STEAKS AU VERT

SERVINGS: 2

PREPARATION TIME: 10 MINUTES

2 lamb steaks (½ inch thick), cut from the leg
2 tablespoons oil of your choice
1 shallot, finely chopped
¼ cup dry vermouth
Salt and pepper
1 tablespoon chopped fresh parsley
1 tablespoon cold fresh butter

Pan-fry the steaks in the oil, following the key recipe (page 136). Discard five-sixths of the fat and quickly sauté the chopped shallot in the remainder, but be careful not to burn it or the deglazing will be very bitter. Add the vermouth, a pinch of salt and pepper, and reduce quickly to 2 tablespoons; add the parsley, and off the heat, whisk in the butter. Pour over the steaks.

ORDER OF DINNER PREPARATION:

1. Steam the rice with the saffron and basil.
2. Mix blueberries into plain yogurt. Chill.

3. Prepare the tomatoes and peppers for the salad; prepare the dressing. Chill both separately.

4. When the rice is done, pan-fry the lamb steaks; make the sauce.

5. Serve the lamb and brown rice.

6. Toss the salad and serve.

7. Serve the yogurt.

SUGGESTED EVERYDAY DINNER MENU II

Lemon soup (page 28)
PAN-FRIED MOUSSAKA
Tomato, sliced zucchini, and red onion salad (page 252)
Apricot compote (page 274)

SERVINGS: 2

APPROXIMATE TOTAL PREPARATION TIME: 1 HOUR

A quick version of the delicious Greek eggplant and lamb concoction.

PAN-FRIED MOUSSAKA

SERVINGS: 2

PREPARATION TIME: 30 MINUTES

1 small eggplant, cut into slices ⅓ inch thick
Salt and pepper
Flour
Oil of your choice (best for this is olive oil)
Lamb patty mixture for 2 (see page 136

¼ cup dry red wine
½ cup tomato sauce of your choice
1 small clove garlic peeled and crushed
⅛ teaspoon dried oregano flowers
1 tablespoon dried dill
1 tablespoon each feta cheese and grated Parmesan cheese

Early in the morning, place the eggplant slices in a flat baking dish and sprinkle with salt. When you are ready to cook dinner, rinse the eggplant slices, pat them dry, and flour them. Pan-fry them until light golden in ¼ cup oil. Keep them warm in a 200° F. oven or covered over a pan of hot water. Discard most of the cooking oil.

Make 2 patties out of the ground lamb and pan-fry, according to the key recipe (page 136), in the remainder of the oil to the degree of doneness you like best—in this preparation they will be good even well done. Remove the patties to the same plate as the eggplant. Discard all the cooking fat.

Add the wine to the frying pan and reduce to 2 tablespoons. Add the tomato sauce, crushed garlic, oregano, and dill and cook together 5 minutes. Correct the seasoning of the sauce. Place 2 slices of eggplant on each plate; top with a meat patty and half of each type of cheese. Cover each patty with half of the remaining eggplant and pour the sauce over.

ORDER OF DINNER PREPARATION:

Divide the work into 2 parts:

Early in the morning:
Slice and salt the eggplant. Refrigerate.

At dinnertime:
1. Prepare the apricot compote. Chill.
2. Prepare the soup.
3. Prepare the salad ingredients and dressing. Chill separately.
4. Prepare the meat patties.
5. Pan-fry the eggplant. Keep it hot in a low oven.
6. Pan-fry the meat patties.
7. While the patties cook, serve the soup.
8. Finish the meat dish; toss the salad and serve with the meat.
9. Serve the compote.

SUGGESTED COMPANY DINNER MENU

Quick minestrone (page 25)
LAMB AND FENNEL SKILLET
Boston lettuce, avocado, and hard-boiled egg salad (page 251)
Cranberry-orange mousse (page 280)

SUGGESTED WINE: Côtes du Rhône or California Cabernet Sauvignon

SERVINGS: 6

APPROXIMATE TOTAL PREPARATION TIME: 2 HOURS

LAMB AND FENNEL SKILLET

SERVINGS: 6

PREPARATION TIME: 30 MINUTES

3 medium fennel bulbs
2 pounds leg of lamb, cut into ¾-inch cubes
2 to 3 tablespoons olive oil or oil of your choice
1 ounce Pernod or ouzo
Salt and pepper
1 cup heavy cream
1½ teaspoons cornstarch

Cut the fennel bulbs in 1-inch strips across. Bring a large pot of water to a boil, add the fennel, bring back to a boil, let boil 2 minutes, then drain. Spread the fennel over a tea towel to dry.

Separate the cubes of lamb into 2 one-pound portions. Heat 2 tablespoons olive oil in a large frying pan and pan-fry 1 pound of the cubes. Remove to a plate and keep hot. Repeat with the second pound of meat. (You may need an additional tablespoon of oil.) Discard all of the cooking oil, return the already cooked meat to the pan and flambé with the Pernod or ouzo. Salt and pepper the meat.

Meanwhile, place the fennel in another pan and reheat it well. Mix the cream and the starch, pour over the fennel, and shake the pan back and forth until the sauce thickens.

Finally, mix the contents of both pans very well. Correct the seasoning and serve.

ORDER OF DINNER PREPARATION:

1. Recalculate the mousse recipe to serve 6 (see formula on page 20); make the mousse and deep chill in the freezer.
2. Cut the vegetables for minestrone; put it on to cook.
3. Prepare the Boston lettuce, avocado, and salad dressing. Chill separately. Wash the egg carefully; add it to the simmering minestrone to hard-boil it, then cool it under cold water.
4. Prepare the lamb and fennel; boil the fennel.
5. Sauté the lamb, flambé with spirits.
6. Serve the minestrone.
7. Pour the cream over the fennel; heat, shaking the pan until thickened. Blend the meat and fennel.
8. Serve the lamb dish.
9. Toss the salad and serve.
10. Serve the mousse.

SAUTÉED LAMB

The best cut of lamb, moderately expensive, for quick sautéing is shoulder, either as chops (½ to ¾ inch thick), or as cubes (¾ inch).

KEY RECIPE: Trim chops of any excess fat. Brown them on both sides. Salt and pepper them, add a bit of liquid (broth or wine, even water). Cover and let cook until the top of a paring knife goes in and comes out of the meat freely. Turn the meat over once while cooking. Degrease the cooking juices and deglaze with more liquid. Add any vegetable garnish 10 minutes before the meat is due to be finished.

Cubes should be browned on all sides, then covered and treated exactly like chops.

SUGGESTED EVERYDAY DINNER MENU I

Sherry soup (page 27)
CÔTELETTES DE MOUTON POREAUX-PENNETIÈRES
Romaine salad with walnuts and leeks (page 251)
Yogurt ice (page 284)

SERVINGS: 2

APPROXIMATE TOTAL PREPARATION TIME: 1 HOUR

"Poreaux" and "pennetières" are the local names given to leeks and potatoes in the north of France, where they are dearly loved and appear in multiple culinary combinations.

CÔTELETTES DE MOUTON POREAUX-PENNETIÈRES
SERVINGS: 2

PREPARATION TIME: 40 MINUTES

2 shoulder lamb chops (½ to ¾ inch thick)
¼ cup oil of your choice
Salt and pepper
¼ cup dry white wine

2 leeks, white part only, finely sliced
2 Idaho potatoes, peeled and cut into ¾-inch cubes
1 tablespoon chopped fresh parsley

Brown the chops in 2 tablespoons of the oil. Salt and pepper them. Add the wine, cover, and cook 15 minutes. Meanwhile, in a second frying pan, sauté the leeks in 1 tablespoon oil until soft, then remove to a plate. Add the last tablespoon of oil to the pan in which the leeks cooked and sauté the potatoes until golden and crisp. Mix leeks and potatoes and add them to the pan containing the chops; continue cooking, covered, for another 10 minutes. Serve sprinkled with parsley.

ORDER OF DINNER PREPARATION:

1. Blend the yogurt, lemon juice, and honey. Store in the freezer, in a shallow dish.
2. Prepare the salad; prepare the dressing. Chill both separately.

3. Chop the leeks; peel and slice the potatoes.
4. Make the sherry soup.
5. Brown the chops; add wine and let cook while you pan-fry the leeks and potatoes. Add the vegetables to the meat cooking pan.
6. Serve the soup.
7. Serve the chops and garnish.
8. Toss the salad and serve.
9. Serve the ice.

SUGGESTED EVERYDAY DINNER MENU II

ALMA'S LAMB CHOPS
White rice pilaf (page 261)
Cucumbers in sour cream and dill dressing (page 251)
Strawberries in kirsch (page 272)

SERVINGS: 2

APPROXIMATE TOTAL PREPARATION TIME: 1 HOUR

ALMA'S LAMB CHOPS

SERVINGS: 2

PREPARATION TIME: 40 MINUTES

2 shoulder lamb chops (½ to ¾ inch thick)
1 tablespoon oil of your choice
1 tablespoon butter
1 onion, chopped
1 carrot, chopped
1 to 1½ teaspoons curry, according to taste
½ cup tomato sauce of your choice
Salt and pepper
1½ teaspoons currants
1 tablespoon pine nuts or chopped almonds
2 tablespoons cream of your choice or yogurt

Brown the chops on both sides in the oil. Remove the chops to a plate; discard the oil. Add the butter to the pan and slowly sauté the onion and carrot. Add the curry powder and cook 2 minutes, stirring well, then add the tomato sauce. Return the chops to the pan, salt and pepper them, and cook, covered, for 20 to 25 minutes. When the chops are done, add the currants, nuts, and cream or yogurt. Correct the seasoning of the sauce and serve.

ORDER OF DINNER PREPARATION:

1. Clean the berries; steep in kirsch. Chill.
2. Brown the lamb chops; while they brown, chop the onion and carrot; sauté the vegetables, add the curry and the tomato sauce, and let cook, with the chops.
3. Prepare white rice pilaf; let cook.
4. Peel and slice the cucumbers; salt lightly. Let them stand.
5. Finish the chops and serve with the rice.
6. Drain the cucumbers of salt water; add sour cream and dill. Serve.
7. Serve the berries.

SUGGESTED COMPANY DINNER MENU

SAUTÉ D'AGNEAU AUX ARTICHAUTS
Gnocchi with paprika (page 269)
Romaine, cherry tomato, green pepper, marinated olive, and feta
  cheese salad (page 252)
Flambéed peaches (page 277)

SUGGESTED WINE: Hungarian Egri Bikavér
SERVINGS: 6

APPROXIMATE TOTAL PREPARATION TIME: 2 HOURS

SAUTÉ D'AGNEAU AUX ARTICHAUTS

SERVINGS: 6

PREPARATION TIME: 50 MINUTES

2 pounds shoulder of lamb, cut into ¾-inch cubes
2 tablespoons oil of your choice
1 to 1½ cups veal stock (page 11), preferably, or chicken bouillon of your choice
Salt and pepper

1 teaspoon dried tarragon
2 paper thin slices lemon, with the rind
2 ten-ounce packages frozen artichoke hearts, defrosted
2 tablespoons cold butter

Brown the lamb cubes in the oil; you may have to do it in two batches, since the cubes should not touch one another while browning. Discard the browning oil.

Add 1 cup of the broth, salt and pepper, the tarragon (well crumbled), and the lemon slices. Cover and cook on low heat for 10 minutes. Add the artichoke hearts and continue cooking, covered, another 15 minutes. Add more broth, if necessary. Before serving, correct the seasoning, and off the heat stir in the butter.

ORDER OF DINNER PREPARATION:

1. Defrost the artichokes.
2. Peel the peaches by immersing them in boiling water for 2 minutes; sprinkle with lemon juice and keep at room temperature, on a plate.
3. Prepare the gnocchi batter.
4. Prepare the salad and salad dressing. Chill separately.
5. Brown the lamb cubes in oil; add the artichokes and finish cooking.
6. Slice onions, then sauté, with paprika, in butter. Set aside, to use as a garnish for the gnocchi.
7. Boil water; poach the gnocchi. Put them in a flameproof serving dish; top with the onion and paprika.
8. Serve the chops and the gnocchi.

9. Toss the salad and serve.

10. Heat the peaches in butter, with sugar. Flambé with liquor or liqueur (bourbon, cognac, kirsch) and serve.

STEWED LAMB

A quick lamb stew, identical to the veal stew described on page 88, can be made quite fast with very young or spring lamb. You may change the basic taste by using, as a vegetable garnish, either a mixture of 1 cup carrots, ½ cup white turnips, and ½ cup small onions; or 3 large or 6 small fresh fennel heads.

Use the following recipe for the amounts of liquid and thickening agent used; flour will be used here for the thickening agent instead of cornstarch, as on page 88, to apply a different technique for the making of white sauce. The recipe will be usable for polyunsaturated diets if the sauce is made with polyunsaturated margarine or oil, and if the egg and cream enrichment is omitted.

SUGGESTED COMPANY DINNER MENU

BLANQUETTE D'AGNEAU AUX CÂPRES
White rice pilaf (page 261)
Green bean salad (page 252)
Moka cake (page 34)

SUGGESTED WINE: French Tavel or California Grenache Rosé

SERVINGS: 6

APPROXIMATE TOTAL PREPARATION TIME: 2½ HOURS

BLANQUETTE D'AGNEAU AUX CÂPRES

SERVINGS: 6

PREPARATION TIME: 1 HOUR 15 MINUTES

3 pounds lean spring lamb, cut into 1-inch cubes
3 cups chicken bouillon of your choice
1 carrot
1 onion, stuck with 2 cloves
Bouquet garni (page 12)

6 small red Bliss potatoes, peeled
3 tablespoons butter
3 tablespoons flour
1 egg yolk
⅓ cup heavy cream
¼ cup capers
Salt and pepper

Immerse the meat in the bouillon and bring to a boil. Add the carrot, onion, and bouquet garni and simmer 35 minutes. Add the potatoes and simmer another 15 to 20 minutes. Remove the cooked meat and potatoes to a casserole.

Heat the butter in a 1-quart saucepan, then add the flour and cook 2 to 3 minutes, stirring occasionally. Whisk in 1½ cups of the cooking broth and thicken on medium heat. Mix the egg yolk and cream in a measuring cup. Gradually add enough hot sauce to fill up the cup, then whisk the mixture back into the bulk of the sauce. Bring back to a boil and remove immediately from the heat. Add the capers, correct the seasoning, and pour over the meat and potatoes.

ORDER OF DINNER PREPARATION:

Spread the work over 2 days:

DAY ONE:
Make the moka cake. Store in the refrigerator.

DAY TWO:
1. Put the lamb stew on to cook.
2. While the stew cooks, boil the beans, cool them, chill them; make their dressing.

3. Remove the cooked lamb to a serving dish. Measure enough broth to make the sauce.

4. With the remaining broth, and if necessary some additional chicken broth, prepare the rice pilaf.

5. Make the meat sauce while the rice cooks.

6. Serve the stew and the rice.

7. Remove cake to room temperature 15 minutes before serving to allow the flavor to develop.

8. Toss the beans in the dressing and serve.

9. Serve the cake.

BROILED LAMB

The following cuts of lamb can be broiled:

Expensive:

        Kidney (loin) chops

        Rib chops, although these are truly better pan-fried

        Leg, cut into cubes for shish kebab and brochettes

Moderately expensive:

    Shoulder, ground for patties or cut into cubes, for shish kebab and brochettes

KEY RECIPE: Trim off any excessive amount of fat, and remove the fell, if this has not been done by the butcher. Cut 2 slashes through the surrounding connective tissues to prevent the meat from curling while cooking. Brush all sides of the meat with a very thin layer of oil. Broil 3 inches below the heat for the following times (see page 149) for medium-rare meat. Salt and pepper the meat only on a well-seared surface, never on the raw meat.

For rib chops (1 *inch thick*): 5 minutes on the first side, 3 to 4 minutes on the second side.

For kidney chops (1¼ *to* 1½ *inches thick*): 7 minutes on the first side, 5 minutes on the second side.

Keep the broiler at all times on high heat if the chop is not thicker than 1½ inches. If a kidney chop is 2 inches thick, expose it to the direct broiling flame for 5 minutes on the first side, then turn the heat down to 350° F. for 5 minutes. Turn the chop over, raise the broiler heat again and broil the second side for 3 to 4 minutes more.

For cubes (*cut from the leg or better part of the shoulder*): 5 minutes on each side.

For lamb patties (3 × 1 *inches*): 5 minutes on the first side, 3 to 4 minutes on the second side.

For butterflied leg of lamb: If you have the butcher remove the fell from, and bone completely, a 4-pound shortened leg of lamb, you will obtain a butterflied leg of lamb, in which all the muscles of the meat are spread open, presenting a thickness of about 2½ inches. Flatten the meat well, oil it lightly on both sides, and broil for a total of about 25 minutes, distributed as follows: on the first side, under direct, high broiler heat, 4 inches from the meat, for 5 minutes, then under 350° F. heat for 8 to 10 minutes; on the second side, under direct, high broiler heat, 4 inches from the meat, for 5 minutes, then 350° F. heat for 5 to 8 minutes.

If the lamb is marinated before broiling, do not wipe off the marinade if the latter is mostly oil; but if it is mostly a liquid, such as wine, wipe the meat dry or its surface will never seal (see the technical details in the chapter on beef, page 68).

The best garnish is, as for beef, salt, pepper, and a small nugget of fresh, cold, unsalted butter. But you can make a compound butter (page 38). The best compound-butter flavorings for lamb are a combination of tomato paste, anchovy paste, and crumbled dried basil; crushed fennel seeds (just a few); chopped fresh mint or crumbled dried mint; chopped garlic and parsley.

SUGGESTED EVERYDAY DINNER MENU I

COSTOLETTE D'AGNELLO
Steamed wheat berries with garlic and parsley (page 264)
Romaine and cucumber salad with plain vinaigrette (page 252)
Fresh fruit

SERVINGS: 2

APPROXIMATE TOTAL PREPARATION TIME: 50 MINUTES TO 1 HOUR

Kidney chops, Sicilian style. In Sicily, the lamb is served as rare as beef.

COSTOLETTE D'AGNELLO

SERVINGS: 2

PREPARATION TIME: 15 MINUTES

2 kidney (loin) chops (1½ inches thick)
2 very small slices prosciutto
Rosemary

1 teaspoon oil
1 tablespoon butter (optional)
1½ teaspoons grated pecorino cheese

Trim and slash the edges of the chops for broiling. Cut a pocket in each chop and stuff the pockets with one slice of prosciutto each. Sprinkle the prosciutto with a bit of rosemary, fresh or dried, then close the pocket with a toothpick. Brush each chop with a thin film of olive oil and broil according to the key recipe (page 148). Mix the butter, if used, and pecorino cheese and let half of the mixture melt on each chop. If butter is not used, sprinkle half the pecorino on each chop.

ORDER OF DINNER PREPARATION:

Spread the work over 2 days:

DAY ONE:
Soak the wheat berries overnight. (This is a *must!*)

DAY TWO:
1. Start the wheat berries steaming.
2. Prepare the romaine and cucumbers; prepare the dressing.
3. Prepare the loin chops for broiling.
4. Chop garlic and parsley and season the wheat berries with the mixture.
5. Put the lamb chops on to broil.
6. While the lamb chops broil, prepare the pecorino butter.
7. Serve the chops and the wheat.
8. Toss the salad and serve.
9. Serve the fresh fruit.

SUGGESTED EVERYDAY DINNER MENU II

BROCHETTES DE LÉRIN
Buttered, boiled green beans (page 255)
Cauliflower, watercress, and tomato salad (page 252)
Cocoa Spanish cream (page 293)

SERVINGS: 2

APPROXIMATE TOTAL PREPARATION TIME: 1 HOUR

A memory from a barbecue party on the island of Lérin off the Mediterranean coast of Provence.

BROCHETTES DE LÉRIN

SERVINGS: 2

PREPARATION TIME: 20 MINUTES

¾ pound lean leg or shoulder of lamb, cut into 8 one-and-one-half-inch cubes

8 small fresh figs

2 tablespoons olive or oil of your choice

1 large lemon, cut in 16 paper-thin slices

2 fresh mint leaves or ⅛ teaspoon dried mint

1 tablespoon butter (optional)

Salt and pepper

In the morning, before going to work, skewer the meat cubes and un-peeled but washed figs alternately. Brush well with olive oil. Place 8 slices of the lemon in a baking dish and set the skewers on them; place 4 of the remaining lemon slices on top of each skewer. Put the meat into the refrigerator to marinate.

That evening, let the meat come back to room temperature before broiling. Discard the lemon slices, then broil according to the key recipe (page 148). While the meat broils, chop the mint leaves, and using a fork, mash them with the butter until the butter turns green. Rub half the butter on each cooked skewer. (If you do not want to use the butter, powder some dried mint leaves on the meat and figs.) Correct the seasoning.

ORDER OF DINNER PREPARATION:

Divide the work into 2 parts:

EARLY IN THE MORNING:

Skewer the meat and marinate it in oil and lemon slices.

AT DINNERTIME:

1. Make the Spanish cream. Chill.

2. Prepare the cauliflower, watercress and tomato for the salad; prepare the salad dressing. Chill separately.

3. Prepare and put the green beans on to cook.
4. Broil the brochettes.
5. Serve the brochettes and the beans.
6. Toss and serve the salad.
7. Serve the Spanish cream.

SUGGESTED COMPANY DINNER MENU

Fresh tomato soup (page 22)
ANN PALMER'S BUTTERFLIED LEG OF LAMB
Stir-fried asparagus (page 255)
Boston lettuce with orange and grapefruit sections (page 251)
Grand Marnier mousse (page 283)

SUGGESTED WINE: California Zinfandel

SERVINGS: 6

APPROXIMATE TOTAL PREPARATION TIME: 2 HOURS

ANN PALMER'S BUTTERFLIED LEG OF LAMB

SERVINGS: 6

PREPARATION TIME: 40 MINUTES

1 leg of lamb, butterflied (page 149)
Oil of your choice

Salt and pepper
Fresh, unsalted butter to taste

Bring the coals of your barbecue to a beautiful white smolder, then add 2 good handfuls of hickory wood chips. Brush the butterflied leg of lamb with a thin film of oil. As soon as the first black exhaust of hickory smoke abates, start broiling the leg following the steps given in the key recipe (page 149). Salt and pepper the meat only when it is seared. As soon as the meat is done, rub it with fresh butter. Serve, cut in paper-thin slivers against the grain of the meat.

ORDER OF DINNER PREPARATION:

Spread the work over 2 days:

DAY ONE:

1. Make the mousse, using the general proportions given on page 283 and using 3½ tablespoons Grand Marnier and the rind of an orange. Freeze the mousse in 6 two- to three-ounce ramequins.

2. Remove fell and fat from the surface of the leg of lamb; bone the leg to butterfly it.

DAY TWO:

1. Prepare and put the soup on to cook.
2. Prepare the asparagus—that is, peel it and cut it in 1-inch chunks.
3. Start the coals.
4. Prepare the lettuce, the orange and grapefruit slices; prepare the salad dressing. Chill separately.
5. Strain the soup.
6. Put the leg of lamb on to broil.
7. While it broils, serve the soup.
8. Stir-fry the asparagus.
9. Serve the lamb and the asparagus.
10. Toss the salad and serve. Remove the mousse from the freezer.
11. Serve the mousse.

Variety Meats for a Quick Dinner

Do not use the following variety meats in quick cookery—you will spend too much time either preparing them for cooking or cooking them:

Brains (they must be skinned carefully)

Sweetbreads (they must soak at length in cold water, then be blanched, cleaned of their connective tissues, and pressed for even cooking)

Tongue in any of its forms—fresh, pickled, or smoked—and tripes (they all must cook a very long time)

You may, if you desire, use heart, kidneys, liver, and some types of sausages.

HEART

In quick cookery heart should be quickly pan fried.

KEY RECIPE: Cut the heart in very thin (⅛ inch) slivers and sauté them very quickly in the fat or oil of your choice. Use stock, wine, or lemon juice to deglaze the pan, and if your diet can afford it, add a little bit of butter to add mellowness to the resultant sauce. Be careful—overcooked heart is as attractive to the taste buds as shoe leather.

SUGGESTED EVERYDAY DINNER MENU

VEAL HEART MAGALI
Noodles with basil and Parmesan (page 269)
Sliced tomato salad (page 252)
Fresh fruit

SERVINGS: 2

APPROXIMATE TOTAL PREPARATION TIME: 45 MINUTES

VEAL HEART MAGALI

SERVINGS: 2

PREPARATION TIME: 10 MINUTES

2 veal hearts
1½ tablespoons olive oil or oil of your choice
Salt and pepper

1 large pinch Provençal herbs (page 12)
¼ teaspoon fennel seeds
Juice of ½ lemon
1 tablespoon butter (optional)

Cut the hearts in thin slivers, removing all tendons and sinews. Heat the oil until almost smoking, add the heart slivers, and sauté a few minutes, then add salt and pepper. Sprinkle with herbs and fennel seeds; mix well. Remove the cooked meat to a plate. Deglaze the pan with the lemon juice, and off the heat, swirl in the butter, if used. Return the meat to the pan and swirl it in the sauce. Correct the seasoning and serve immediately.

ORDER OF DINNER PREPARATION:

1. Slice the tomato; make the dressing. Chill both separately.
2. Prepare the mixture of butter, basil, and Parmesan to season the noodles.
3. Cut the heart in thin slivers; prepare the seasonings on a small plate.
4. Cook the noodles; season them; keep them warm.
5. Pan-fry the heart slivers (it should take you only one or two minutes).
6. Serve the heart and the noodles.
7. Spoon the dressing over the tomato slices.
8. Serve the fruit.

KIDNEYS

KEY RECIPE: *Lamb kidneys:* These are best broiled. Remove the largest part of the fat, cut the beanlike kidney in half lengthwise, starting at the convex side and leaving both sides attached at the fat pad. Brush the kidneys with oil and skewer them butterfly fashion. Broil them for 4 minutes on each side. Serve the kidneys sprinkled with salt and pepper, fresh butter, or a compound butter of your choice. An especially good compound butter for kidneys is the tomato-basil butter on page 149.

Veal Kidneys. These are best sautéed.

KEY RECIPE: Cut the fat off. Cut the kidneys in very thin slivers and sauté in smoking oil just until they turn gray, then flambé with cognac, whiskey, or bourbon. Drain them into a colander and discard the juice they render. Build a small sauce with some wine that you will let reduce at least by half or some stock, herbs, mustard, or any other garnish of your choice. Thicken the sauce lightly with a beurre manié (page 37) or a starch slurry.

SUGGESTED EVERYDAY DINNER MENU

KIDNEY CRUNCH
Spaetzle with cracked black pepper (page 268)
Romaine lettuce salad (page 252)
Sliced oranges in Grand Marnier (page 272)

SERVINGS: 2

APPROXIMATE TOTAL PREPARATION TIME: 50 MINUTES TO 1 HOUR

KIDNEY CRUNCH
SERVINGS: 2

PREPARATION TIME: 15 MINUTES

1 tablespoon corn oil	1 tablespoon bourbon
2 tablespoons blanched slivered almonds	2 tablespoons broth of your choice
	1/16 teaspoon meat extract
2 veal kidneys, slivered	1/2 cup light cream
Salt and pepper	1/2 teaspoon arrowroot starch

Heat the oil and in it, on medium heat, toast the almonds. Remove the almonds to a plate. Raise the heat very high. Add the kidneys to the hot oil and sauté until just gray. Add salt and pepper, then the bourbon, and flambé, shaking the pan back and forth. Drain into a colander. Add the broth, meat extract, and half the cream to the pan and mix well.

Bring to a simmer. Mix the starch with the remainder of the cream and blend both mixtures until thickened. Return the kidneys to the pan until they are just heated through, but do not let them boil. Correct the seasoning. Mix the almonds with the kidneys and serve piping hot.

ORDER OF DINNER PREPARATION:

1. Slice the oranges; sprinkle them with Grand Marnier. Chill.
2. Prepare the romaine and its dressing. Chill both separately.
3. Prepare the spaetzle batter; let stand a while.
4. Sliver the kidneys; prepare the bourbon, broth, meat extract, and mixture of starch and cream.
5. Put the spaetzle on to cook; season with butter and pepper when cooked.
6. Cook the kidneys; do not forget to drain the juices in a colander before making the sauce.
7. Serve the kidneys and the spaetzle.
8. Toss the salad and serve.
9. Serve the oranges.

LIVER

Use chicken livers, calf's or young steer liver cut in paper-thin slices.

KEY RECIPE: Cut slashes through the edge membrane to prevent curling up, and in all cases pan-fry the livers in the fat or oil of your choice. You may either simply flour the liver, or bread it with plain or flavored crumbs as indicated in the key recipe for breaded veal (page 98).

SUGGESTED EVERYDAY DINNER MENU I

BREADED CHICKEN LIVERS
Boiled artichoke hearts (page 254)
Boston lettuce with tarragon dressing (page 252)
Crème Suchard (page 287)

SERVINGS: 2

APPROXIMATE TOTAL PREPARATION TIME: 45 TO 50 MINUTES

BREADED CHICKEN LIVERS

SERVINGS: 2

PREPARATION TIME: 15 MINUTES

Salt and pepper
6 chicken livers
2 tablespoons flour
1 egg
1 teaspoon water

2½ tablespoons oil of your choice
½ teaspoon finely crumbled dried
 tarragon
⅓ cup bread crumbs of your choice
Lemon juice

Lightly salt and pepper the livers, then flour them. Beat the egg, water, oil, and a pinch each of salt and pepper until well combined. Mix the well-crumbled tarragon and crumbs; put them in a small paper bag. Dip the livers in the egg mixture, then drop each into the bag of crumbs and shake. Heat the remaining oil in a frying pan and pan-fry the livers 3 to 4 minutes on each side until golden. Serve sprinkled with lemon juice.

ORDER OF DINNER PREPARATION:

1. Make the crème Suchard. Cool, then chill it.
2. Prepare the Boston lettuce greens; prepare their dressing. Chill separately.
3. Put the artichokes on to cook.

4. While the artichokes cook, bread the livers.
5. Pan-fry the livers.
6. Serve the livers and the artichokes.
7. Toss the salad and serve.
8. Serve the dessert.

SUGGESTED EVERYDAY DINNER MENU II

FOIE DE VEAU AU VINAIGRE
Green beans with garlic and parsley butter (page 255)
Tomato and avocado salad (page 252)
Raspberry yogurt (page 276)

SERVINGS: 2

APPROXIMATE TOTAL PREPARATION TIME: 45 MINUTES

Here is the favorite French way of preparing calf's liver.

FOIE DE VEAU AU VINAIGRE

SERVINGS: 2

PREPARATION TIME: 10 MINUTES

Flour
4 slices (4 × 2 × ⅓ inch) calf's
   liver
1½ tablespoons oil of your choice
3 tablespoons broth of your choice
   or water

2 teaspoons wine vinegar
Salt and pepper
1 tablespoon butter (optional)
1 tablespoon chopped fresh tarragon, chervil, or parsley

Flour the liver slices after slashing through the outside membrane. Heat the oil in the frying pan. Brown each liver slice on one side, then let the liver cook a few minutes on its second side so it is pink but not rare. Remove to a plate. Add the broth or water, vinegar, and a pinch of salt and pepper to the pan, deglazing well. Reduce to 2 tablespoons, turn the heat off, and if desired, swirl in the butter. Strain over the liver slices and sprinkle with the chosen fresh herb.

ORDER OF DINNER PREPARATION:

1. Prepare the raspberry yogurt and keep chilled.
2. String the green beans; wash and put them on to cook.
3. While the beans cook, prepare the garlic and parsley butter.
4. Peel and slice the tomatoes. Chill.
5. Peel and slice the avocado. Prepare the lime dressing and pour it over the avocado. Chill.
6. Prepare the liver slices for pan frying.
7. While the liver cooks, reheat the green beans in the garlic butter.
8. Serve the liver and beans.
9. Spoon the avocado slices and dressing over the tomato slices.
10. Serve the salad.
11. Serve the raspberry yogurt.

SAUSAGES

Good fresh sausages made exclusively with natural ingredients are offered for sale in many stores nowadays. Read the labels and abstain from buying anything containing preservatives and artificial smoke flavorings.

You may pan-fry sausages of the Italian type to render their fat and concentrate their flavor. They are good combined with potatoes. So are frankfurters, provided they are not made with all kinds of sad ingredients bearing no resemblance to good food. Watch the calories, though, because sausages are fat and retain a lot of fat even if they are properly cooked—that is, first well heated in water to melt the fat, then crisped brown in their own fat and patted dry in paper towels, if need be.

SUGGESTED EVERYDAY DINNER MENU I

ITALIAN SAUSAGE SKILLET
Boston lettuce and sliced fennel salad (page 252)
Honeydew melon in Marsala (page 272)

SERVINGS: 2

APPROXIMATE TOTAL PREPARATION TIME: 1 HOUR

ITALIAN SAUSAGE SKILLET

SERVINGS: 2

PREPARATION TIME: 20 MINUTES

2 tablespoons water
4 Italian sausages, cut in ½-inch chunks
2 large potatoes

3 tablespoons oil of your choice
Salt and pepper
Large pinch of well-crumbled dried oregano flowers

Place the water and the sausage chunks in a skillet on medium heat and let the sausage render its fat. As soon as the water has evaporated, the sausage will start crisping. Let the chunks become golden on both sides.

Meanwhile peel the potatoes and cut them in ¾-inch cubes. Heat the oil in a second pan. Brown the potatoes on all sides, turn the heat down to allow the potatoes to cook through, then raise the heat again to crisp them. Remove to a colander lined with paper towels and keep hot. Season with salt and pepper.

As soon as the sausage is golden, discard all traces of fat in the pan. Deglaze the pan juices with a bit of water, toss potatoes and sausage in these juices, and sprinkle with oregano.

ORDER OF DINNER PREPARATION:

1. Prepare the honeydew melon; add Marsala and let steep in refrigerator.

2. Prepare the lettuce and fennel; prepare their dressing. Chill separately.

3. Render the sausage.
4. Peel, dice, and fry the potatoes.
5. Blend the potatoes and sausage.
6. Toss the salad and serve with the sausage skillet.
7. Serve the melon.

SUGGESTED EVERYDAY DINNER MENU II

FRANKFURTERS COMME À LA MAISON
Iceberg lettuce and romaine salad with lime-mint dressing (page 252)
Fresh pears in Cassis (page 272)

SERVINGS: 2

APPROXIMATE TOTAL PREPARATION TIME: 45 MINUTES

"À la maison" is home-style in French. This is my favorite "hot dog" recipe.

FRANKFURTERS COMME À LA MAISON

SERVINGS: 2

PREPARATION TIME: 20 MINUTES

2 large potatoes, peeled and cut into
   1-inch chunks
Water to cover
Salt and pepper

2 tablespoons butter
2 teaspoons chopped fresh chives
4 frankfurters

Cover the potatoes with water. Bring to a boil and simmer 10 minutes. Discard most of the water, add salt and pepper, the butter, and chives, and finish cooking 5 to 7 minutes, tightly covered. Meanwhile, boil the frankfurters. Serve the frankfurters and potatoes with Dijon or Düsseldorf mustard.

ORDER OF DINNER PREPARATION:

1. Peel the pears; rub with lemon juice; spoon over 1 or 2 tablespoons Cassis (or other liqueur of your choice, such as Grand Marnier, Curaçao, etc.)
2. Prepare the lettuce and dressing.
3. Peel the potatoes; cook them for 20 minutes.
4. Cook the frankfurters.
5. Toss the salad and serve, along with the frankfurters and potatoes.
6. Serve the pears.

CHAPTER XI

Chicken for a Quick Dinner

NEVER exceedingly expensive, chicken can be an even better bargain if you learn all the tricks of cutting it and dismembering it yourself. No very great effort or time is involved. Not only will you save money if you buy whole chicken, but you will have the possibility to inspect the cavity yourself and make sure that it presents no physical abnormality. In spite of all health inspections, tumors are frequent and deserve your attention. Discard any chicken showing this kind of physical defect.

The matter of whether organically raised chicken tastes better than the "speed-meal fed" chicken we buy in any supermarket remains doubtful to this author, who tried several brands of organically raised chickens and could not muster special enthusiasm for any of them.

WHOLE CHICKEN

OVEN-ROASTED WHOLE CHICKEN

Choose a chicken weighing as close as possible to 3½ pounds, 4 pounds being the maximum weight. The oven temperature should be 375° F. to 400° F.

KEY RECIPE: Put salt and pepper into the cavity of the chicken, then truss it, as follows:

Take a piece of string 18 inches long and fold it in half. Tie the middle of it around the tail; tie again around the end of the drumsticks, then bring the strings on each side way down into the fold between breast and thigh. Turn the chicken upside down, thread each piece of string through the wings, folded akimbo, and tie as tight a knot as possible on the upper back of the chicken.

After the chicken is trussed, brush it with oil or melted fat, then set it on a rack in a shallow pan. Roast the chicken, with its neck toward the back of the oven, for 20 minutes on its right side, 20 minutes on its left side, and 15 minutes breast up—a total of 55 minutes (the chicken is cooked when the juices running out of the cavity are transparent). Brush the chicken with oil or fat each time you turn it. When the chicken is done, salt and pepper its crisp skin, degrease the pan juices, and serve them plain or mixed with broth, wine, or cream to make a sauce.

For a change of taste you may add herbs to the cavity before roasting, fill the cavity with a stuffing, or make a compound butter and slide it under the skin of the legs and breast (the butter will melt during the roasting; keep brushing the chicken with it as it melts).

If you use 1 chicken for 2 persons, you will obtain 2 warm fresh portions, 2 portions to eat cold, and a carcass to nibble on or make broth with; or 4 warm portions plus a carcass to nibble on or make broth with.

If you use 2 chickens, you will obtain 8 portions and 2 carcasses to nibble on or make broth with.

Finally, a note on leftovers: Do not reheat leftovers of chicken. The meat will taste stale and unpleasant. Serve leftovers cold with mayonnaise or use them in high-protein salads.

SUGGESTED EVERYDAY DINNER MENU I

POULET RÔTI ASCONA
Boiled cauliflower and chives (page 255)
Julienne of green pepper salad (page 252)
Blueberry yogurt (page 276)

SERVINGS: 2

APPROXIMATE TOTAL PREPARATION TIME: 1 HOUR

POULET RÔTI ASCONA

SERVINGS: 2

PREPARATION TIME: 1 HOUR

1 roasting chicken (3½ to 4 pounds)
Salt and freshly ground pepper
1 teaspoon dried basil

½ tablespoon oil or melted fat of your choice
2 large, fresh tomatoes

Truss the chicken (page 167) after having added salt, pepper, and finely crumbled dried basil to the cavity. Brush it with oil or fat and roast 40 minutes (page 167). Remove the stems from the tomatoes. Put the tomatoes on the rack, brush them with some of the cooking juices, and continue roasting the chicken and tomatoes together for 15 minutes. Serve plain, with the degreased pan juices.

ORDER OF DINNER PREPARATION:

1. Preheat the oven. Mix the yogurt and blueberries. Chill.
2. Truss the chicken, season it, and put it in to roast.
3. Prepare the peppers and the dressing.
4. Clean, pare, and boil the cauliflower.
5. Add the tomatoes to the chicken roasting pan.
6. Season the cauliflower.

7. Serve the chicken and vegetables.
8. Serve the salad.
9. Serve the blueberry yogurt.

SUGGESTED EVERYDAY DINNER MENU II

ROAST CHICKEN ISABEL
Saffron rice pilaf (page 261)
Tomato, sliced zucchini, and red onion salad (page 252)
Fresh fruit

SERVINGS: 2

APPROXIMATE TOTAL PREPARATION TIME: 1 HOUR

ROAST CHICKEN ISABEL

SERVINGS: 2

PREPARATION TIME: 1 HOUR

Salt and pepper
1 roasting chicken (3½ to 4 pounds)
1½ tablespoons olive oil or oil of your choice
2 tablespoons fino or amontillado sherry
½ cup light cream
½ teaspoon potato starch

Salt and pepper the cavity of the chicken. Truss the chicken (page 167), rub it with oil, and roast it according to the key recipe (page 167). When the chicken is done, degrease the cooking juices and mix them with the dry sherry. Bring the mixture to a simmer. Mix the cream and starch and blend, stirring, into the simmering gravy. Correct the seasoning of the sauce and serve poured over the chicken.

ORDER OF DINNER PREPARATION:

1. Truss the chicken. Season it and put it in to roast.
2. Prepare the tomatoes, zucchini, and red onion for the salad; prepare the dressing. Chill separately.

3. Make the rice pilaf.

4. Mix the cream and starch for the chicken gravy. Make gravy as soon as chicken is done.

5. Serve chicken and rice.

6. Spoon the dressing over the salad and serve.

7. Serve fruit.

SUGGESTED COMPANY DINNER MENU

POULET MIREILLE
Gnocchi with Provençal butter (page 270)
Romaine, cherry tomato, green pepper, marinated olives and feta cheese salad (page 252)
Maraschino-refreshed fruit (page 276)

SUGGESTED WINE: Italian Soave

SERVINGS: 6

APPROXIMATE TOTAL PREPARATION TIME: 1½ HOURS

POULET MIREILLE
SERVINGS: 6

PREPARATION TIME: 1 HOUR

2 roasting chickens (3½ to 4 pounds each)
2 tablespoons olive oil or oil of your choice
Salt and pepper
Rind of 2 lemons

1 cup chicken broth of your choice
2 ten-ounce boxes frozen artichoke hearts, defrosted
½ teaspoon dried tarragon
2 egg yolks
Juice of 1 lemon

Brush the chickens with oil. Put salt, pepper, and the rind of 1 lemon cut in long strips in each cavity. Roast the chickens, following the key recipe (page 167). While the chickens finish roasting, place ⅓ cup chicken broth, the defrosted artichoke hearts, and the tarragon in a saucepan with salt and pepper. Cook, covered, for 15 minutes. When the birds are done, degrease the cooking juices and mix with ⅔ cup chicken broth. Mix the egg yolks and the lemon juice. Blend some of the gravy into the mixture to slowly warm it, then pour back the warmed mixture into the bulk of the sauce and reheat very well *without boiling*. Correct the seasoning. Serve the chickens accompanied by the lemon sauce and the artichoke hearts.

ORDER OF DINNER PREPARATION:

1. Peel, slice, and refresh the fruit salad. Chill.
2. Preheat the oven; truss and season the chickens; put them in to roast.
3. Prepare the romaine, tomatoes, and pepper for the salad; pit the olives and cut the feta cheese; mix the dressing. Chill all the salad components separately.
4. Make the gnocchi batter; mix the butter and Provençal herbs. Set aside.
5. Put the artichokes on to cook; boil the water for the gnocchi.
6. Cook the gnocchi; season them.
7. Make the lemon sauce for the chickens.
8. Serve the chickens, the artichokes, and the gnocchi.
9. Toss and serve the salad.
10. Serve the refreshed fruit.

WHOLE CASSEROLE-ROASTED CHICKEN

Choose a chicken weighing 3 to 3½ pounds maximum. Use a pot just big enough to contain the chicken or chickens, thick and preferably made of copper or enameled cast iron. Casserole roasting more than 2 chickens at a time, although not impossible, is cumbersome.

KEY RECIPE: Clean and truss the chicken (page 167). Season the cavity. Heat oil to a depth of ⅙ inch in a casserole. Brown the chicken on all sides on medium heat.

Salt and pepper the outside of the chicken lightly; cover the pot and continue cooking on direct slow heat for 45 minutes, turning the bird once or twice while cooking. When the bird is done, the juices will run clear from the cavity. Degrease all the cooking juices and serve with the chicken.

You may, for a change of taste, add herbs in the pot before covering it; add vegetables to the pot halfway through the cooking time of the chicken; deglaze the cooking juices with the wine of your choice to make a more flavorful sauce.

SUGGESTED EVERYDAY DINNER MENU I

POULET ODETTE
White rice pilaf with roasted pine nuts (page 263)
Grated carrot salad (page 252)
Grapefruit in raspberry sauce (page 273)

SERVINGS: 2

APPROXIMATE TOTAL PREPARATION TIME: 1 HOUR 15 MINUTES

POULET ODETTE
SERVINGS: 2

PREPARATION TIME: 1½ HOURS

2 tablespoons dark raisins
2 tablespoons rum
1 roasting chicken (3 to 3½ pounds), trussed (page 167)

2 tablespoons oil of your choice
Salt and pepper
2 tablespoons heavy cream

Soak the raisins for 30 minutes in the rum—they will absorb some of it. Brown the chicken on all sides in hot oil. Salt and pepper it and cover the pot. Let cook 20 minutes. Add the raisins with what is left of the rum. Finish cooking, still covered, until the bird is tender. Degrease the cooking juices completely. Blend in the cream, correct the seasoning, and serve with the raisin sauce.

ORDER OF DINNER PREPARATION:

1. Soak the raisins in rum; roast the pine nuts for the pilaf.
2. Peel and slice the grapefruit; defrost the raspberries in warm water and strain over the grapefruit.
3. Truss, season, and brown the chicken; add salt and pepper, cover, and cook 20 minutes.
4. Add the raisins to the chicken.
5. Make the carrot salad and its dressing. Chill both, separately.
6. Make the rice pilaf; add the pine nuts just before serving.
7. Serve the chicken and the rice.
8. Serve the salad.
9. Serve the dessert.

SUGGESTED EVERYDAY DINNER MENU II

POULET GRANDMÈRE MARIE
Parsleyed potatoes (page 258)
Sliced tomato salad (page 252)
Fresh fruit

SERVINGS: 2

APPROXIMATE TOTAL PREPARATION TIME: 1 HOUR 10 MINUTES

Grandmother Marie was from Lorraine, where this way of cooking beans is very popular. She added the mushrooms and chicken for good measure.

POULET GRANDMÈRE MARIE

SERVINGS: 2

PREPARATION TIME: 50 MINUTES

1 slice bacon
¼ pound mushrooms, quartered
Salt and pepper
1 tablespoon oil of your choice
1 roasting chicken (3 to 3½
    pounds), trussed (page 167)

1 ten-ounce box frozen frenched
    green beans, defrosted
1 tablespoon fresh, unsalted butter

Render the bacon, crumble it, and set aside. Sauté the mushrooms with a bit of salt and pepper in the bacon fat until they are brown and dry. Remove them to a plate. Add the oil to the pan and brown the chicken in the mixture of bacon fat and oil; brown on all sides, then cover and cook 10 minutes. Pat the defrosted beans dry in a towel. Add the mushrooms, green beans, crumbled bacon and butter and continue cooking until the bird is done. The green beans should be brown and overcooked. Serve piping hot.

ORDER OF DINNER PREPARATION:

1. Render the bacon; truss and season the chicken; sauté the mushrooms.

2. Brown the chicken. Defrost the green beans under running cold water; pat them dry. Cover the chicken pot and cook 10 minutes.

3. Peel the potatoes; chop the parsley.

4. Add the beans, bacon, mushrooms and butter to the chicken pot and finish cooking.

5. Put the potatoes on to cook.

6. Prepare the tomato salad and its dressing.
7. Drain and season the potatoes with parsley and butter.
8. Serve the chicken and the vegetables.
9. Serve the salad.
10. Serve the fruit.

BROILED CHICKEN

Choose broilers weighing 2 to 3 pounds; one half broiler per person is an adequate portion.

KEY RECIPE: *With an electric broiler:* Remove the backbone of the chicken, using a very sharp chef's knife. Flatten the chicken very well, pressing hard on the breastbone. Make a hole in the skin on each side of the tail and slip the end of each drumstick into each hole.

Brush both sides of the chicken with melted butter or oil of your choice. Sear the cavity side first, 5 minutes under the direct heat of the broiler, 4 inches away from the flame. Turn the heat down to 350° F. and continue cooking 5 to 7 minutes. Salt and pepper the cooked side. Turn the chicken over. Repeat the same procedure, searing the skin side for 5 minutes under the direct heat, then turning the heat down and finishing cooking at 350° F. for another 5 to 6 minutes. Salt and pepper the skin side.

Keep the oven door ajar during the whole broiling process.

With an incandescent gas broiler: Proceed exactly as you would with an electric broiler, but *keep the door closed* during the whole broiling process.

With a gas broiler: Brush both sides of the chicken with melted butter or the oil of your choice. Sear the cavity side 2 inches away from the flame for 5 minutes. Lower the broiler tray to the lowest rack of the oven and continue broiling for 6 to 7 minutes. Salt and pepper the seared side. Turn the chicken over and repeat the same operation on the skin side.

Keep the oven door closed during the whole broiling process.

To change the basic taste, you may after searing the chicken sprinkle it with bread crumbs plain or flavored, then sprinkle the crumbs with a bit of butter or oil and continue broiling. You can use grated cheese in the same manner. You can make a compound butter with herbs and slide the butter under the chicken skin, or you can marinate the chicken in an oily marinade before broiling.

SUGGESTED EVERYDAY DINNER MENU I

POULET AU FROMAGE
Spaetzle with chive butter (page 269)
Boston lettuce, sliced red radish, and green peppercorn salad (page 252)
Fresh fruit

SERVINGS: 2

APPROXIMATE TOTAL PREPARATION TIME: 45 TO 50 MINUTES

POULET AU FROMAGE

SERVINGS: 2

PREPARATION TIME: 35 MINUTES

⅓ cup grated Swiss Gruyère or Swiss cheese
2 tablespoons chopped fresh parsley

1 broiler (2 to 3 pounds), flattened
1½ tablespoons oil of your choice
Salt and pepper

Mix the grated cheese and parsley. Brush the broiler with the oil and broil, following the key recipe (page 175). Remove the skin from the cooked chicken, sprinkle the exposed meat with the mixture of cheese and parsley and let the cheese melt in the dying oven. Serve promptly, as soon as the cheese starts running.

ORDER OF DINNER PREPARATION:

1. Prepare the salad ingredients and dressing. Chill separately.
2. Prepare the spaetzle batter; prepare the chive butter. Let stand.
3. Start the broiler; prepare the chicken for broiling; brush with oil.
4. Grate the cheese, chop the parsley, and mix well. Set aside.
5. Put the chicken on to broil.
6. Bring water to a boil to cook spaetzle; cook the spaetzle.
7. As soon as the chicken is done, sprinkle with cheese and let melt.
8. Serve the chicken and the spaetzle.
9. Toss the salad and serve.
10. Serve the fruit.

SUGGESTED EVERYDAY DINNER MENU II

Watercress soup (page 23)
LIME-MARINATED CHICKEN
Tomato and avocado salad (page 252)
Cantaloupe in port (page 272)

SERVINGS: 2

APPROXIMATE TOTAL PREPARATION TIME: 50 MINUTES TO 1 HOUR

LIME-MARINATED CHICKEN

SERVINGS: 2

PREPARATION TIME: 25 MINUTES, PLUS TIME TO MARINATE THE CHICKEN
OVERNIGHT

¼ cup olive oil or oil of your choice
½ teaspoon dried basil, positively powdered

1 lime, cut in paper-thin slices
1 broiler (2 to 3 pounds), flattened
Salt and freshly ground pepper

Mix the olive oil and powdered basil very well. Brush both sides of the chicken with the olive oil and apply half the slices of lime on each side of the chicken. Let stand overnight in the refrigerator. When ready to broil, remove the lime slices and broil, following the key recipe (page **175**).

ORDER OF DINNER PREPARATION:

Spread the work over 2 days:

DAY ONE:
Marinate the chicken overnight in basil, lime, and oil. Refrigerate.

DAY TWO:
1. Remove the chicken from the refrigerator; discard the lime slices.
2. Cut the cantaloupe in dice or balls; steep in port.
3. Make the watercress soup.
4. Slice the tomatoes and avocado; make the dressing. Mix the avocado slices and dressing. Chill.
5. Put the chicken on to broil.
6. While the chicken broils, strain and serve soup.
7. Spoon the dressing and avocado slices over the tomato slices. Serve with the chicken.
8. Serve the melon.

SUGGESTED COMPANY DINNER MENU

Cream of broccoli soup (page 32)
COQUELETS GRILLÉS AUX POINTES D'ASPERGES
Tomato and julienne of green pepper salad (page 252)
Narcissa Chamberlain's berry salad (page 273)

SUGGESTED WINE: Alsace Riesling or California Emerald Riesling

SERVINGS: 6

APPROXIMATE TOTAL PREPARATION TIME: 1½ HOURS

In the village of Worth in Alsace a small old-fashioned inn serves these squab chickens with the local white asparagus crop on Easter Sunday. It is a feast!

COQUELETS GRILLÉS AUX POINTES D'ASPERGES
SERVINGS: 6

PREPARATION TIME: 35 MINUTES, PLUS 20 MINUTES TO START THE
BARBECUE

Hickory wood chips
6 squab chickens (1½ to 2 pounds), split in half
½ cup clarified butter (page 9)
Salt and pepper

18 stalks jumbo asparagus, peeled and cooked for 5 minutes in boiling water
Lemon juice

Build a fire with briquettes, add hickory wood chips, and as soon as the worst of the wood smoke has burned off, start broiling the squab chicken halves, 6 halves at a time. Brush well with clarified butter. Sear the cavity side for 5 minutes, 2 inches away from the heat, then raise the broiler 4 inches away from the heat and continue broiling 5 minutes. Season with salt and pepper; turn the chicken over, sear the skin side 2 inches away from the heat, and cook 4 inches away from the coals for another 5 minutes. Push the chicken halves toward the center of the rack and add half the large asparagus, well brushed with butter, at the edge of the rack for 1 or 2 minutes, or until they are heated through.

Remove to plates. Salt and pepper each portion and sprinkle liberally with lemon juice. Broil the other 6 chicken halves, and heat the remaining asparagus, while you eat the first batch.

ORDER OF DINNER PREPARATION:

1. Establish new measurements for cream of broccoli soup so you can serve 6 (see formula on page 20).
2. Cook the broccoli in the broth.
3. Prepare the squab chickens for broiling; peel and blanch the asparagus.
4. Start the coals.

5. Prepare tomatoes and peppers for salad; prepare the dressing. Chill separately.

6. Prepare the berry salad; add the liquor. Chill.

7. Finish the cream of broccoli soup by adding cream and thickener.

8. Broil the first 6 chicken halves; while they broil, serve the soup.

9. Broil half the asparagus.

10. Serve the first 6 halves of chickens with half the asparagus.

11. Broil the remainder of the chickens, then the asparagus.

12. Serve the remainder of the chickens.

13. Spoon the dressing over the salad and serve it.

14. Serve the berries.

WHOLE POACHED CHICKEN

Choose a chicken weighing 3½ to 4 pound maximum.

To poach the chicken, use the best available veal or chicken broth. A very good stock would be the veal stock given on page 11. But you can make a broth with the giblets. If you decide to make your own broth, do so the day before, so that all you have to do is bring the stock to a boil and cook the bird(s). The fastest, but surely not the best, solution is to use a mixture of ⅓ canned concentrated chicken broth and ⅔ water, or even plain water and part of a bouillon cube (watch the salt) to which you add a few aromatics, soup vegetables, the giblets of the chicken, and if possible, a veal bone at the same time as the bird itself.

To poach 1 chicken use a 4-quart pot and 3 quarts of liquid. To poach 2 chickens use a 6-quart pot and 4½ quarts of liquid.

KEY RECIPE: Bring the liquid to a boil. Add all the vegetables— 1 carrot, 1 large onion, 2 leeks or 6 scallions, and 1 small white turnip—1 bay leaf, a pinch of thyme, a large bunch of parsley, and the chicken, seasoned in the cavity and trussed (page 167), and bring back to a steady simmer. Let simmer 55 minutes. The chicken is done when the juices run clear from the cavity. Pour them into a mixing bowl to be sure. This is best done by lifting the chicken out of the water on a large slotted spoon and maintaining it steady with a wooden spoon.

This chicken tastes delicious just plain, served with mustard and pickles, but you can make variations by changing the taste of the sauce served with the chicken. For thickening the sauce, use, per cup of broth, 1½ tablespoons flour, or 3 teaspoons cornstarch, or 1½ teaspoons potato starch.

There are 4 portions per chicken. Poached chickens reheat very well in their own cooking broth. Reheat whatever is left slowly and without ever boiling. Keep the chicken immersed in cold broth when refrigerated. If you have the space, freeze the stock for reuse another time; if you do not have the space, make soup with it.

SUGGESTED EVERYDAY DINNER MENU

POACHED CHICKEN TARRAGON
Carrots cooked in chicken broth (page 256)
Escarole salad with blue cheese dressing (page 252)
Cranberry-orange clafouti (page 300)

SERVINGS: 2

APPROXIMATE TOTAL PREPARATION TIME: 1½ HOURS

POACHED CHICKEN TARRAGON

SERVINGS: 2

PREPARATION TIME: 1 HOUR

1 whole chicken, (3½ to 4 pounds), including giblets, trussed (page 167)
Soup vegetables and aromatics as per key recipe (page 180)
3 quarts water
Salt and pepper

1½ tablespoons dried tarragon
1 tablespoon butter or other fat of your choice
1 tablespoon flour
2 tablespoons heavy cream (optional)

Follow the key recipe (page 180), adding 1 teaspoon dried tarragon, salt and pepper in the chicken cavity and 1 tablespoon dried tarragon to the cooking broth. Revive the remaining ½ teaspoon tarragon in a tablespoon of boiling water or stock. Ten minutes before the chicken is done, remove ¾ cup of broth from the cooking pot. Heat the butter, cook the flour in it for a few minutes, and moisten with the ¾ cup of broth. Add the revived tarragon, bring to a boil, stirring, and simmer 5 minutes. Add the cream, if used. Correct the seasoning and serve the tarragon sauce on the poached chicken.

ORDER OF DINNER PREPARATION:

1. Peel the vegetables for broth, using enough carrots to use half as a vegetable. Bring the water to a boil, add the vegetables, including half of the carrots, and the chicken giblets, and let simmer 10 minutes.

2. Truss and season the chicken; put it on to cook.

3. Prepare the cranberry-orange clafouti. Put it in to bake.

4. Prepare the escarole salad and dressing. Chill separately.

5. When the chicken has only 15 minutes left to cook, add the carrots you will use as a vegetable to the pot. Bring back to a boil.

6. Make the sauce for the chicken; meanwhile, keep the carrots and the chicken hot in their cooking broth by covering the pot with the heat turned off.

7. Serve the chicken and the carrots.

8. Toss the salad and serve.

9. Serve the clafouti.

SUGGESTED COMPANY DINNER MENU

POULARDE POCHÉE AU VINAIGRE
Polenta with fontina cheese (page 266)
Romaine salad with plain vinaigrette (page 251)
Tartelettes aux raisins (page 304)

SUGGESTED WINE: French Graves Blanc or California Sémillon

SERVINGS: 6

APPROXIMATE TOTAL PREPARATION TIME: 2 HOURS

Chicken poached or sautéed with a vinegar sauce is an old French favorite that has been revived in recent years.

POULARDE POCHÉE AU VINAIGRE

SERVINGS: 6

PREPARATION TIME: 1 HOUR

2 whole chickens (3½ to 4 pounds), including giblets, trussed (page 167)
1 double recipe veal stock (page 11)
Soup vegetables and aromatics as per key recipe (page 180)
¼ cup butter
¼ cup flour
½ cup dry vermouth

2 shallots, finely chopped
2 tablespoons excellent wine or cider vinegar
1 teaspoon dried basil
1½ teaspoons tomato paste
Salt and pepper
¼ cup heavy cream
2 tablespoons chopped parsley

Poach the chickens in the veal stock, following the key recipe (page 180). When the chickens are three-quarters done, make a white sauce with the butter, flour, and 2 cups of the cooking broth. Let simmer 10 minutes, skimming it a bit. While the sauce simmers, make a reduction by boiling the vermouth—mixed with the shallots, vinegar, basil, tomato paste, and a good pinch of salt and pepper—down to 2 tablespoons. Mix this reduction with the white sauce and cook together another 5 minutes. Strain the sauce into a clean bowl, add the cream and parsley, and correct the seasoning. Serve the sauce on the poached chicken.

ORDER OF DINNER PREPARATION:

Spread the work over 2 days:

DAY ONE:

1. Make the broth to poach the chicken.
2. Make the pastry for the tartlet shells.

3. Bake the tartlet shells; store them in a cannister.

4. Calculate the measurements of the filling for the tartlet recipe (see page 302).

DAY TWO:

1. Truss, season, and poach the chickens; make the vermouth and herb infusion.

2. Prepare the salad greens and the dressing. Chill both separately.

3. Whip the cream for filling the tartlets. Chill.

4. Prepare the glazing jelly in a small pan.

5. Make the polenta.

6. Make the sauce for the chicken. Add the cheese to the polenta.

7. Serve the chicken and the polenta.

8. Toss the salad and serve.

9. Glaze the tartlets and serve.

CHICKEN PARTS

There is a wide difference of quality between the white meat and the brown meat of chicken. The white meat is delicate and rather bland, and requires careful cooking; it is better not to cook it a long time, to make sure that its long fibers do not turn into unchewable strings. The brown meat is more flavorful, and easier to cook.

FRIED CHICKEN DRUMSTICKS, THIGHS, AND BREASTS

Rather than deep-frying chicken, try frying it in a layer of 1 to 1½ inches of hot oil in a frying pan. The cleaning up is easier.

Serve fried chicken plain, well sprinkled with salt—it is a treat—but be sure to cook only small pieces. Separate the drumstick from the thigh. Split double breasts in half lengthwise, then cut each piece again crosswise to obtain small 2 × 2-inch pieces, which will cook fast.

KEY RECIPE: Allow 1 drumstick and 1 thigh, or 1 drumstick or thigh and ½ breast, per person. Mix 1 tablespoon corn flour for each portion with a pinch each of salt and pepper. Coat the chicken with this mixture, patting to discard any excess flour. Heat oil to the depth of 1½ inches in a skillet until it starts shivering. Add the chicken pieces, not more than four to six at a time, so that they float freely in the oil bath without touching one another. Let the chicken crisp and brown on all sides, then turn the heat down to allow the meat to cook through. Drain the chicken on paper towels.

Just before serving, bring the oil back to a shiver and add the chicken again, to let it crisp. Drain on crumpled paper towels and serve, generously sprinkled with salt. The total cooking time varies between 9 and 12 minutes, depending on the size of the pieces.

CHICKEN CUTLETS (boned chicken breasts)

Chicken cutlets are low in calories and excellent for low-cholesterol diets when prepared with a polyunsaturated oil.

It is important to cook chicken cutlets properly. Since they are made of long fibers kept together by meat juices, the more you cook them the drier they become. Cook them a very short time; if you are pan-frying them, use medium heat; if you are poaching them in butter, use very high heat. In both cases, you want to just coagulate the meat proteins. The cutlets are done as soon as they are resilient under the pressure of your finger.

BONING CHICKEN BREASTS   Slip two fingers under the skin of a double chicken breast and pull it back and off. Put the breast, on its side, on a board. Apply pressure toward the left with your left hand and cut 1½ inches deep along the breastbone, with your knife blade scraping along the bone itself. You now have a gaping pocket. Turn the breast at a 90-degree angle, with the cut close to you. Slide your thumb between meat and bone and hold the meat very firmly. Slide the tip of your blade between the bone and your thumb. Cut to the right, then to the left. You are now holding a boneless cutlet. Cut off the tendon you can see attached to the small fillet.

This boning will take about 5 minutes of your time at first, then 2 minutes will be sufficient once you have mastered the procedure. If you do not want to bone cutlets, buy them boned in the supermarket; be prepared to spend some money for them and to remove the tendons, which butchers always seem to leave.

After you bone the breasts, you should flatten the cutlets—but only slightly. Do not flatten the poor things until they are transparent; you will lose time and true chicken flavor. Simply tap the upper side of each cutlet with the outer right side of your right hand so that the large fillet flattens slightly while the small fillet slides against it. Ready for cooking, the cutlet is ⅓ inch thick and as wide as a woman's hand. Use 1 large cutlet per person; it is usually adequate. If the cutlets come from small chickens, use 2, especially for large appetites.

PAN-FRIED CHICKEN CUTLETS

KEY RECIPE: For cutlets to be pan-fried without breading, simply flour the cutlets. Heat some butter or oil of your choice in a frying pan on medium heat. Sear the large fillet first, turn over, and salt, then sear the small fillet. (Searing the small fillet will cook it through.) To finish cooking the large fillet, turn it over a second time; turn the heat down and let cook another 3 to 4 minutes. A total cooking time of 8 to 10 minutes altogether is amply sufficient. If you want a vegetable garnish, cook it first, then put it to reheat gently around the cutlets during their last 3 to 4 minutes of cooking.

For breading and for instructions on pan-frying cutlets, see the key recipe for breaded veal (page 98).

SUGGESTED EVERYDAY DINNER MENU I

Cream of dill soup (page 33)
CHICKEN CUTLETS PAPRIKA
Tomato slices, zucchini and red onion salad (page 252)
Peach yogurt (page 276)

SERVINGS: 2

APPROXIMATE TOTAL PREPARATION TIME: 1 HOUR

CHICKEN CUTLETS PAPRIKA

SERVINGS: 2

PREPARATION TIME: 20 MINUTES

2 large onions, thinly sliced
2 tablespoons butter or oil of your choice
2 tablespoons dry white wine
Salt and pepper

1 tablespoon mild imported Hungarian paprika
1 tablespoon flour
2 large chicken cutlets
1 tablespoon chopped fresh parsley

Gently sauté the sliced onions in 1 tablespoon of the butter or oil. Add the wine, salt, and pepper; cover and cook until the onion is tender but not mushy. Uncover the saucepan and add the paprika. Let any excess liquid reduce on slow heat and evaporate. Remove from the heat and keep warm.

Heat the second tablespoon of butter or oil in a frying pan. Flour the cutlets and fry them until just cooked, following the key recipe (page 186). Serve the cutlets topped with the onions and well sprinkled with parsley.

ORDER OF DINNER PREPARATION:

1. Prepare the dill soup; cook the dill in the broth.
2. Prepare the tomatoes, zucchini, and onion for the salad; prepare the dressing. Chill separately.

3. Peel the peaches; slice or dice them; blend them with plain yogurt. Chill.

4. Bone the chicken breast or breasts.

5. Slice the onions for the seasoning of the chicken and slowly cook them until tender. Add the paprika.

6. Finish the cream soup by adding the cream and lemon juice.

7. Serve the soup. Cook the chicken cutlets while the soup is being eaten.

8. Spoon the dressing over the salad.

9. Serve the chicken cutlets and the salad.

10. Serve the yogurt and peaches.

SUGGESTED EVERYDAY DINNER MENU II

Julienne of carrot soup (page 25)
CHICKEN CUTLETS NANCY
Boston lettuce and sliced fennel salad (page 252)
Caramel pudding (page 289)

SERVINGS: 2

APPROXIMATE TOTAL PREPARATION TIME: 1 HOUR

CHICKEN CUTLETS NANCY

SERVINGS: 2

PREPARATION TIME: 45 MINUTES

12 asparagus
2 tablespoons slivered almonds
2 large chicken cutlets

2 to 3 tablespoons butter or 2 tablespoons oil of your choice (but
not olive oil)
Salt and pepper

Peel the asparagus and cut them into 1-inch chunks, then parboil in boiling water for 3 to 4 minutes. Drain very well.

Heat 1 tablespoon butter or oil and gently sauté the slivered almonds in it until they turn golden. Remove the almonds to a plate. Pan-fry the cutlets, following the key recipe (page 186), in 1 tablespoon butter or oil; salt and pepper them. As soon as they are three-quarters done, add the asparagus to the pan. Let cook another 2 minutes. Serve the asparagus and cutlets sprinkled with the toasted almonds—and if your diet allows it, heat a third tablespoon of butter until it turns nut brown and pour half of it onto each portion.

ORDER OF DINNER PREPARATION:

1. Prepare the caramel pudding. Chill.
2. Prepare the julienne of carrot soup; put it on to cook.
3. Prepare the Boston lettuce and fennel; prepare their dressing. Chill both, separately.
4. Peel the asparagus for the chicken; parboil them.
5. Sauté the almonds. Set aside.
6. Bone the chicken breasts; flour the cutlets.
7. Serve the soup. While the soup is being eaten, pan-fry the chicken cutlets.
8. Just before serving the chicken, add the asparagus and almonds to the pan.
9. Toss the salad and serve with the chicken.
10. Serve the caramel pudding.

SUGGESTED EVERYDAY DINNER MENU III

CHICKEN CUTLETS ORIENTALE
Buttered, boiled broccoli (page 255)
Tomato salad (page 252)
Cranberry-orange clafouti (page 300)

SERVINGS: 2

APPROXIMATE TOTAL PREPARATION TIME: 1 HOUR 15 MINUTES

CHICKEN CUTLETS ORIENTALE

SERVINGS: 2

PREPARATION TIME: 25 MINUTES

2 large chicken cutlets, flattened
1 teaspoon dark soy sauce
1 tablespoon flour
1 egg
1 teaspoon each water and oil

Salt and pepper
1 tablespoon sesame seeds
3 tablespoons fresh bread crumbs
2 tablespoons butter or oil of your
    choice

Brush the cutlets very lightly with the soy sauce. Let them stand a few minutes to dry, then flour them. Beat the egg, water, and oil with a bit of salt and pepper. Mix the sesame seeds and crumbs. Brush the egg mixture on both sides of the cutlets and coat with the mixture of sesame seeds and crumbs. Heat the butter or oil in a frying pan and brown the cutlets on each side; the total cooking time should not exceed 8 to 10 minutes.

ORDER OF DINNER PREPARATION:

1. Prepare and bake the cranberry-orange clafouti.
2. Slice the tomatoes; prepare the dressing. Chill.
3. Peel and pare the broccoli.
4. Bone the chicken breast; bread the cutlets.
5. Boil the broccoli at the same time you pan-fry the chicken.
6. Butter the broccoli.
7. Serve the chicken cutlets and the broccoli.
8. Spoon the dressing over the tomatoes and serve the salad.
9. Serve the clafouti.

SUGGESTED COMPANY DINNER MENU

Lemon soup (page 28)
SOUTHERN-STYLE CHICKEN CUTLETS
Parsleyed carrots (page 256)
Boston lettuce with orange and grapefruit sections (page 251)
Rum-raisin soufflé (page 297)

SUGGESTED WINE: California Blanc Fumé or Grey Riesling

SERVINGS: 6

APPROXIMATE TOTAL PREPARATION TIME: 2 HOURS

SOUTHERN-STYLE CHICKEN CUTLETS

SERVINGS: 6

PREPARATION TIME: 25 MINUTES

6 large chicken cutlets
1½ tablespoons chopped pecans
1½ tablespoons chopped Smithfield ham
2 tablespoons fresh bread crumbs
1 to 2 tablespoons heavy cream
3 tablespoons flour

1 egg
1 teaspoon each oil and water
Salt and pepper
¼ cup finely ground pecans
¼ cup dry bread crumbs
½ cup clarified butter (page 9)

Cut a pocket in each cutlet. Mix the chopped pecans, ham, fresh bread crumbs, and just enough cream to bind the mixture. Stuff an equal amount of mixture into each pocket and seal by pressing between the fingers. Flour the cutlets, then brush with the egg beaten with the oil, water, and a pinch each of salt and pepper. Coat the cutlets with the ground pecans mixed with the dry bread crumbs and brown on each side in the hot clarified butter; the total cooking time should not exceed 8 to 10 minutes.

ORDER OF DINNER PREPARATION:

Spread the work over 2 days:

DAY ONE:

1. Make the soufflé, using the proportions given on page 297 and replacing the ladyfingers by raisins soaked in rum. Freeze the soufflé, in its baking dish, well covered with plastic wrap.
2. Clarify the butter in which you will cook the chicken breasts.

DAY TWO:

1. Make the lemon soup.
2. Prepare the salad greens, the citrus fruit slices and the salad dressing. Chill separately.
3. Bone the chicken breasts; fill them and bread them.
4. Peel and cook the carrots; season them.
5. Serve the soup.
6. Cook the chicken cutlets while the soup is being eaten.
7. Serve the chicken and the carrots.
8. Put the soufflé to bake in a 400° F. oven for 25 minutes.
9. Toss the salad and serve.
10. Serve the soufflé.

STIR-FRIED CHICKEN CUTLETS The general method is Chinese. Stir-frying means tossing quickly a food, cut in bite-sized pieces, in hot oil over high heat to cook it in a matter of seconds.

KEY RECIPE: Mix well dark soy sauce, cornstarch, and sherry. Toss the chicken cutlets cut into ½-inch cubes in the mixture. Heat some vegetable oil in a wok or a large frying pan and quickly stir-fry the vegetable garnish to keep it crunchy. Push the vegetable to the side of the pan or remove it to a plate, then quickly stir-fry the chicken meat.

With the chicken cubes you may use carrot and

zucchini strips, broccoli and sesame seeds, walnuts and Chinese cabbage, and almonds toasted in oil and snowpeas. You may use any green leafy vegetable you like and any nut you enjoy as a garnish. And you may, if you desire, for this type of Oriental cooking use an infinitely small amount of monosodium glutamate with the regular salt, but do not *ever* use more than a grain.

SUGGESTED EVERYDAY DINNER MENU

STIR-FRIED CHICKEN WITH ROMAINE
White rice pilaf (page 261)
Sliced oranges in Curaçao (page 272)

SERVINGS: 2

APPROXIMATE TOTAL PREPARATION TIME: 40 TO 45 MINUTES

STIR-FRIED CHICKEN WITH ROMAINE
SERVINGS: 2

PREPARATION TIME: 15 MINUTES

2 chicken cutlets
1 teaspoon each dark soy sauce, dry sherry, and cornstarch
1½ tablespoons corn oil
¼ cup natural raw cashew nuts

1½ cups shredded large, deep-green romaine leaves
Salt
MSG (optional)

Cube the meat and marinate it in the mixture of soy sauce, sherry, and starch. Heat ½ tablespoon of the oil in the pan and brown the cashews. Remove them to a plate. Heat another ½ tablespoon oil and quickly stir-fry the romaine; keep it crunchy. Remove it to the same plate as the cashews. Heat the last ½ tablespoon of oil and stir-fry the chicken cubes for 1 minute. Return the greens and nuts to the center of the pan and season with salt and a grain of MSG, if you desire. Serve promptly.

ORDER OF DINNER PREPARATION:

1. Slice the oranges; sprinkle the slices with Curaçao. Chill.
2. Bone and cube the chicken cutlets; marinate in the soy, sherry, and cornstarch mixture; shred the romaine.
3. Put the rice pilaf on to cook.
4. While the pilaf cooks, brown the cashews in hot oil.
5. As soon as the pilaf is done, stir-fry the romaine, then the chicken; then blend the nuts into the mixture.
6. Serve the chicken and the rice.
7. Serve the orange slices.

OVEN-POACHED CHICKEN CUTLETS

KEY RECIPE: Preheat the oven to 475° F. or 500° F. Butter or oil a baking dish. Put the cutlets in the dish, salt and pepper them, and sprinkle them with a few drops of lemon juice. Cover them with a buttered or oiled baking paper or foil, and bake them 7 to 12 minutes, depending on their size. The cutlets are done when they are resilient under the light pressure of your finger.

Reduce the cooking juices and add them to a garnish of your choice—fresh herbs, a compound butter, nuts, ham, and so on. Let your imagination go and scan through your refrigerator for unused bits of this or that.

SUGGESTED EVERYDAY DINNER MENU

CHICKEN ROBERTINA
Romaine, walnut and leek salad (page 251)
Strawberry ice (page 285)

SERVINGS: 2

APPROXIMATE TOTAL PREPARATION TIME: 45 MINUTES

CHICKEN ROBERTINA

SERVINGS: 2

PREPARATION TIME: 30 MINUTES

4 ounces commercial noodles
2 large chicken cutlets
Salt
Lemon juice
2 tablespoons butter, or more if desired

2 tablespoons finely grated Parmesan cheese
2 tablespoons chopped prosciutto
½ teaspoon coarsely cracked black pepper

Boil the noodles, keeping them al dente. Poach the cutlets in a baking dish, following the key recipe (page 194). Cut the cutlets in stripe ½ inch wide crosswise and mix them into the noodles. To the chicken cooking juices add butter, to your taste, and boil hard to reduce to 1 tablespoon. Stir into the noodle-chicken mixture. Just before serving, toss the Parmesan cheese and prosciutto into the mixture and sprinkle with the cracked black pepper.

ORDER OF DINNER PREPARATION:

1. Prepare the salad greens; chop the walnuts; make the salad dressing and chill separately.
2. Bone the chicken; chop the prosciutto.
3. Boil the noodles.
4. Poach the chicken cutlets, cut them in strips.
5. Blend the noodles and chicken; season with prosciutto, cheese, and butter and cooking juices.
6. Remove the frozen berries from the freezer.
7. Serve the noodles and chicken.
8. Toss the salad and serve.
9. Make the strawberry ice in blender and serve.

SUGGESTED COMPANY DINNER MENU

CHICKEN CUTLETS AU POIVRE VERT
White rice pilaf (page 261)
Grated carrot salad (page 252)
Haupia (page 294)

SUGGESTED WINE: Côtes du Rhône or California Zinfandel

SERVINGS: 6

APPROXIMATE TOTAL PREPARATION TIME: 2½ HOURS

"Poivre vert" or green peppercorns from Madagascar have become "the" seasoning in France. The very best are canned in their own juices; those canned in vinegar are not as good—in fact, they are even slightly unpleasant.

CHICKEN CUTLETS AU POIVRE VERT
SERVINGS: 6

PREPARATION TIME: 1½ HOURS

6 large chicken cutlets
3 tablespoons coarsely chopped, blanched pistachios
Salt and pepper
1½ tablespoons butter
Lemon juice
2 slices (6 x 3 inches) boiled ham

2 tablespoons green peppercorns, canned in their own juices
1/16 teaspoon meat extract
¾ teaspoon potato starch
¾ cup heavy cream
2 tablespoons sour cream
Watercress

Cut a pocket in each cutlet. Mix the chopped pistachios with a pinch of salt and stuff each cutlet with 1½ teaspoons of the nuts. Press the edges of the cutlets well to seal them. Put the cutlets in a baking dish that has been well rubbed with 1 tablespoon butter. Salt and pepper them, then sprinkle with lemon juice, cover with baking paper or foil, and cook according to the key recipe (page 194). While the cutlets cook, cut the ham in fine julienne and place the peppercorns in a strainer. Rinse the peppercorns under running warm water to discard the outer skin, and keep only the pale green core of each. Mix the ham and peppercorns and heat gently in 1½ teaspoons butter. Remove the cooked cutlets to a plate and keep warm. Mix the cooking juices with the meat extract and reduce them to 1 tablespoon. Mix the starch and heavy cream, blend in the reduced cooking juices, and thicken on a medium flame. Add the ham and peppercorns, then blend in the sour cream and correct the seasoning. Spoon the sauce on the cutlets and serve, surrounded with bouquets of watercress.

ORDER OF DINNER PREPARATION:

Spread the work over 2 days:

DAY ONE:
1. Blanch and chop the pistachios.
2. Bone the chicken breasts. Wrap them in oiled waxed paper and keep them chilled.

DAY TWO:
1. Slice the pineapple; steep in rum in a deep crystal dish.
2. Make the coconut custard for the Spanish cream; cool it.
3. Stuff the chicken cutlets with chopped blanched pistachios. Prepare the ham and peppercorns; place on a tray or plate with the meat extract and mixture of starch and cream.
4. Whip the egg white and fold into the coconut cream. Pour over the pineapple and chill.
5. Grate the carrots; make the salad dressing. Chill both, separately.
6. Put the rice pilaf on to cook.
7. Poach the chicken cutlets; make the pepper sauce.
8. Serve the chicken and the rice.
9. Toss the carrot salad with its dressing and serve.
10. Serve the Haupia.

CHICKEN LEGS, DRUMSTICKS AND THIGHS

ROASTED CHICKEN LEGS

KEY RECIPE: Brush the chicken with butter or oil. Place it on a rack fitted in a jelly roll or other shallow baking pan.

Concentration roasting for moist chicken and little or no gravy: Preheat the oven to 400° F. Roast 30 minutes, meat side up. Salt and pepper the meat side, then turn the chicken over, salt and pepper the second side, and continue roasting another 25 to 30 minutes (total roasting time 55 minutes).

Slow roasting for tender chicken and a good gravy: Preheat the oven to 325° F.; salt and pepper the meat on both sides and roast 30 minutes meat side up and 1 hour skin side up (total roasting time 1½ hours). To obtain a good gravy, discard the cooking fat in the roasting pan and deglaze the caramelized meat juice with water, broth, wine, or cream.

You may vary the taste of the chicken by sprinkling any herb of your choice on the chicken before roasting it.

The recipes and menus given in the section on whole roasted chicken (pages 168–174) may be applied to roasted chicken legs.

BROILED CHICKEN LEGS Proceed as described under whole broiled chicken (pages 176–178). Observe carefully the techniques of sealing under direct flame first, then turning the heat down to allow the meat to cook through. Note that whole legs will be broiled in 20 to 22 minutes, drumsticks in 15 minutes, and thighs in 15 minutes.

You may also use all the recipes and menus given under whole broiled chicken (pages 176–178).

SAUTÉED CHICKEN LEGS

The choice of the pan is important. The best kind to use is a thick skillet with a lid, or a copper or aluminum sautéing pan 2 to 3 inches deep with straight sides and a flat lid. You may also use an electric frying pan, but slide a piece of aluminum foil between the meat and the dome lid of the pan to reduce the possibility of all-too-quick evaporation of the cooking juices into the large space between chicken and lid if the steam vents of the pan are open; or to prevent an excessive rebasting of the chicken with condensation falling from the lid if the vents are closed.

KEY RECIPE: Brown the chicken on both sides in the fat or oil of your choice, then salt and pepper it. Discard the browning fat or oil and add 1½ to 2 tablespoons of liquid (water, broth, wine) per whole chicken leg. Cover the chicken and cook for 15 minutes. Uncover the pot, turn the meat over, add the vegetable garnish, cover again, and continue cooking until meat and vegetables are tender. The total cooking time is around 40 minutes, and can generally be broken down as follows: 10 to 15 minutes for browning, 10 to 15 minutes for cooking without vegetables, 10 to 15 minutes for cooking with vegetables.

SUGGESTED EVERYDAY DINNER MENU I

POULET SAUTÉ NORTH-SOUTH
Crisp green bean salad (page 252)
Blender blueberry mousse (page 281)

SERVINGS: 2
APPROXIMATE TOTAL PREPARATION TIME: 1 HOUR 15 MINUTES

POULET SAUTÉ NORTH-SOUTH

SERVINGS: 2

PREPARATION TIME: 45 MINUTES

1 onion, sliced
2 tablespoons oil of your choice
2 chicken legs
Salt and pepper
2 to 3 tablespoons water or broth of your choice
2 sun-ripened tomatoes, peeled, seeded, and cut in thick slices (or 3 whole, peeled, canned tomatoes)

2 tablespoons chopped fresh dill or 1 tablespoon dried
2 to 3 tablespoons sour cream

Brown the sliced onion lightly in the oil. Remove it to a plate. Brown the chicken on both sides in the same oil, then salt and pepper it. Discard the browning oil, add some liquid, cover the pan, and cook 15 minutes. Return the onion to the pan, add the tomatoes, a bit more salt and pepper, and the dill. Cover and cook until the chicken is tender. When the chicken is done, remove the meat to the serving plates. Add the sour cream to the vegetables in the pan and scrape well. Do not boil. Spoon the sauce over the chicken.

ORDER OF DINNER PREPARATION:

1. Make the blueberry mousse in the blender. Flavor with a bit of lemon or lime rind and a drop or so of bourbon. Chill in the freezer.
2. Boil the green beans, chill them; prepare the salad dressing.
3. Prepare the onions, tomatoes, and dill for the chicken.
4. Sauté the chicken and serve.
5. Toss the bean salad and serve.
6. Serve the blueberry mousse.

SUGGESTED EVERYDAY DINNER MENU II

POULET PARMENTIER
Boston lettuce salad (page 251)
Fresh pears in Cassis liqueur (page 272)

SERVINGS: 2

APPROXIMATE TOTAL PREPARATION TIME: 1 HOUR

This is a classic French preparation named after Monsieur Parmentier, who introduced the potato to France.

POULET PARMENTIER

SERVINGS: 2

PREPARATION TIME: 50 MINUTES

2 onions, sliced
¼ cup oil of your choice
2 chicken legs
⅓ cup water, white wine, or chicken broth of your choice

Salt and pepper
2 potatoes, peeled and cut in 1-inch chunks
1 tablespoon chopped fresh parsley

Brown the onions lightly in 2 tablespoons of the oil. Remove them to a plate.

Brown the chicken legs in the same oil. Discard the browning oil, return the onions to the pan, and add the broth or water or wine. Salt and pepper the meat, cover, and cook 10 minutes. Meanwhile, sauté the cubed potatoes in the remaining 2 tablespoons of oil until they are golden on all sides. Add them to the pan containing the chicken and continue cooking for another 10 to 15 minutes. Serve sprinkled with parsley.

ORDER OF DINNER PREPARATION:

1. Peel the pears; sprinkle them with lemon juice; spoon some Cassis liqueur over them and chill them well.

2. Prepare the salad greens and the salad dressing. Chill separately.

3. Prepare the onion and potato garnish for the chicken; brown the onions and chicken legs.

4. While the chicken legs are cooking, pan-fry the potatoes in oil in another frying pan.

5. Blend the potatoes and chicken and finish cooking together.

6. Toss the salad and serve with the chicken.

7. Serve the pears.

SUGGESTED COMPANY DINNER MENU

POULET SAUTÉ AU PORTO
White rice pilaf (page 261)
Romaine, leek, and walnut salad (page 251)
Maraschino-refreshed fruit (page 276)

SUGGESTED WINE: Médoc, Mercurey, or Santenay

SERVINGS: 6

APPROXIMATE TOTAL PREPARATION TIME: 1½ HOURS

POULET SAUTÉ AU PORTO
SERVINGS: 6

PREPARATION TIME: 45 MINUTES

6 chicken legs
3 tablespoons oil of your choice
Salt and pepper
2 tablespoons cognac brandy or whiskey
½ pound button mushrooms or larger mushrooms, quartered

3 tablespoons white or tawny port
6 croutons
2 tablespoons butter
1 teaspoon potato starch
1 cup heavy cream

Brown the chicken in the oil, then salt and pepper it. Discard the cooking oil, add the chosen spirits, and flambé. Cover the pan and cook 15 minutes. Add the mushrooms and port and cook another 10 minutes.

Meanwhile, brown the croutons in the butter. When the chicken is done, remove chicken to a plate. Raise the heat, and if necessary reduce the cooking liquids in the pan to 1½ tablespoons. Mix the starch and cream and add the mixture to the pan; stir over medium heat until lightly thickened. Correct the seasoning, then spoon the sauce over the chicken and decorate each plate with a butter-fried crouton.

ORDER OF DINNER PREPARATION:

1. Refresh the fruit with maraschino. Chill well.
2. Prepare the salad; prepare the dressing. Chill separately.
3. Prepare the mushrooms for the chicken dish.
4. Brown the chicken; flambé it. Cook it for 15 minutes.
5. Prepare the rice pilaf; put it in to cook.
6. Add the mushrooms and port to the chicken pot. Finish cooking the chicken.
7. Make the sauce for the chicken.
8. Serve the chicken and the rice.
9. Toss the salad and serve.
10. Serve the fruit salad.

CHAPTER XII

*Fish and Shellfish
for a Quick Dinner*

FISH

Fish is quick cooking and excellent for your health. It used to be quite accessible to all budgets, but it has for many reasons become quite expensive. The fish supplies of the oceans are dwindling: some species have completely disappeared, and many are on their way to extinction as a result of overfishing and pollution.

For the best quality, go to a specialized fish store and have the fish merchant cut or prepare fish steaks or fillets under your very eyes. Make sure that the fish eyes are clear and transparent. Be wary of supermarket bargains; buy frozen fish only if there is nothing else available and do not—under any circumstances—buy those prepackaged trays of fish tightly sealed in plastic wrap. Even the shortest time under a plastic wrap will be long enough to start unpleasant, if not dangerous, anaerobic fermentations.

Whenever you can rationalize the time—probably on a weekend—and it does not require more than 35 to 40 minutes, make a fish stock:

TRUE FISH STOCK

3 pounds fish heads and bones (no skins, please)
2 large onions, sliced thick
1 large bouquet garni (page 12)
⅓ carrot, thickly sliced

4 cups water
1 cup dry white wine
½ teaspoon salt
5 peppercorns

Place all the ingredients except the salt and pepper in a 4-quart pot. Bring slowly to a boil, then simmer 30 minutes, adding salt and pepper in the last 10 minutes of cooking. Strain the stock and store it. Freeze it in ½-cup baby-food jars if you have the space; or reduce it to a glaze by cooking it down by three-quarters of its volume if you do not have storage space in your freezer. These keep well, even if only refrigerated —but fish glaze and stock should be reboiled twice a week if not frozen.

To remake fish stock from fish glaze, mix by volume ¼ fish glaze and ¾ water.

If you do not want to make fish stock, use a mixture by volume of ½ clam juice, ¼ white wine, and ¼ water. Any unused amount of clam juice can be used in a soup or frozen for later use.

And when you use a wine in cooking fish, be sure to use a good-quality dry white wine from California or France, not from New York State. If you use dry vermouth, be prepared for a pleasant but definitely different taste in your fish sauce.

BASIC PROPORTIONS FOR FISH SAUCES

1–2 servings	*3–4 servings*	*5–6 servings*
¼ cup each stock and wine	½ cup each stock and wine	¾ cup each stock and wine
or	or	or
¼ cup clam juice plus 2 T. each water and wine	½ cup clam juice plus ¼ cup each water and wine	¾ cup clam juice plus 6 T. each water and wine
1 T. butter or margarine plus 2 tsp. flour	2 T. butter or margarine plus 1⅓ T. flour	5 tsp. butter or margarine plus 2 T. flour
or	or	or
½ tsp. potato starch	1 tsp. potato starch	1½ tsp. potato starch

Oven-Poached Fish Steaks, Fillets, and Small Fish

KEY RECIPE: Place the fish fillets, steaks, or small fish in a buttered or oiled baking dish, add the fish stock and dry white wine, chopped onion, and herbs if used. Salt and pepper lightly and cover with a buttered or oiled baking paper. Bake in a 375° F. to 400° F. oven until the fish is easily pierced by the tip of a knife.

Strain the cooking juice into a 1-quart saucepan and boil hard for a few minutes. Thicken the sauce with a beurre manié of butter or margarine and flour (page 37), or a slurry made of a bit of cold milk and potato starch to obtain a light sauce. Correct the seasoning and spoon over the fish.

Any herb or seasoning of your choice may be added to the cooking broth to vary the taste of the sauce.

SUGGESTED EVERYDAY DINNER MENU I

PERCH FILLETS, TURKISH STYLE
Parsleyed rice pilaf (page 263)
Boston lettuce, avocado and hard-boiled egg salad (page 251)
Fresh fruit

SERVINGS: 2

APPROXIMATE TOTAL PREPARATION TIME: 40 TO 45 MINUTES

PERCH FILLETS, TURKISH STYLE
SERVINGS: 2

PREPARATION TIME: 30 MINUTES

1 tablespoon oil of your choice
6 perch fillets
6 canned Italian plum tomatoes, plus 2 tablespoons canning liquid
2 scallions, white part only, coarsely chopped

1 green pepper, finely chopped
1 teaspoon ground coriander
Salt and pepper
4 slices (¼ inch thick) of lemon
1 tablespoon chopped fresh parsley
1 tablespoon butter (optional)

Use the 1 tablespoon oil to oil a baking dish. Put the fillets in the dish and surround them with the tomatoes, chopped coarsely and mixed with the scallions, green pepper, and the coriander. Salt and pepper the fish and top with the lemon slices and a buttered or oiled baking paper. Bake 7 to 9 minutes in a 400° F. oven, then remove to serving plates. Pour the vegetables and cooking juices into a pot and boil them very hard for about 5 minutes. Add the chopped parsley; correct the seasoning. Swirl in the butter, if desired, and pour over the fish.

ORDER OF DINNER PREPARATION:

1. Prepare the salad greens; slice the avocado, sprinkle it with lemon juice; prepare the dressing. Chill separately. Boil the egg and chill.

2. Put the rice pilaf on to cook; chop the parsley to garnish both it and the fish.

3. Prepare the baking dish for the fish; chop the tomatoes, pepper, scallions; slice the lemon. Arrange the fish and vegetables in the baking dish and bake.

4. Keep the fish warm on a plate and finish the fish sauce.

5. Add the parsley to the pilaf; serve the pilaf and fish.

6. Toss the salad and serve.

7. Serve the fruit.

SUGGESTED EVERYDAY MENU II

POACHED TROUT WITH HERB SAUCE
Boiled potatoes (page 258)
Tomato, sliced zucchini, and red onion salad (page 252)
Sliced peaches in Curaçao (page 272)

SERVINGS: 2

APPROXIMATE TOTAL PREPARATION TIME: 40 MINUTES

POACHED TROUT WITH HERB SAUCE
SERVINGS: 2

PREPARATION TIME: 25 MINUTES

1 tablespoon oil of your choice
2 trout (brook or rainbow), fresh or frozen and thawed
⅓ cup each fish stock (page 205) and dry vermouth or ⅓ cup clam juice plus 2 tablespoons each water and dry vermouth
1 shallot, finely chopped

½ teaspoon each dried tarragon, chives, and chervil
2 tablespoons chopped fresh parsley
1 teaspoon wine vinegar
Salt and pepper
⅓ teaspoon potato starch
1 tablespoon butter (optional)

Oil a baking dish with the 1 tablespoon oil and put the trout in it. Put 1½ tablespoon fish stock or clam juice aside and mix the remaining liquid ingredients with the shallots, the herbs, 1 tablespoon of the parsley, the vinegar, and a bit of salt and pepper, and pour over the fish. Cover with a buttered or oiled baking paper and bake for 15 minutes in a preheated 400° F. oven. Strain the cooking juice into a small saucepan, boil it hard for a few minutes, and thicken with a slurry of potato starch and the reserved clam juice or stock. Swirl in the butter, if desired, correct the seasoning and pour into a small bowl; add the remaining tablespoon of parsley. Remove the top skin of the trout and spoon a few tablespoons of the sauce on each of them.

ORDER OF DINNER PREPARATION:

1. Slice the peaches; sprinkle with Curaçao. Chill.
2. Prepare the tomatoes, zucchini, and onion slices for the salad; prepare the dressing. Chill separately.
3. Peel the potatoes; cut them in chunks; put them on to cook.
4. Prepare the trout for poaching; put them in to poach. Prepare the starch slurry in a cup.
5. Finish the fish sauce.
6. Serve the fish and the potatoes.
7. Spoon the dressing over the salad and serve.
8. Serve the peaches.

SUGGESTED COMPANY DINNER MENU

FILETS DE SOLE AU SAFRAN
Basil-flavored rice pilaf (page 263)
Raw spinach with anchovy dressing (page 251)
Bûche Ardéchoise (page 312)

SUGGESTED WINE: Beaujolais Blanc or California Pinot Chardonnay

SERVINGS: 6

APPROXIMATE TOTAL PREPARATION TIME: 2 HOURS 15 MINUTES

FILETS DE SOLE AU SAFRAN

SERVINGS: 6

PREPARATION TIME: 35 MINUTES

6 tablespoons butter
Salt and pepper
6 double fillets of grey sole or winter
   flounder
1 onion, chopped
¾ cup each fish stock (page 205)
   and white wine or ¾ cup clam
   juice plus 6 tablespoons each
   water and wine

⅟₁₆ teaspoon powdered saffron
1 teaspoon finely crumbled dried
   basil
1 dime-sized piece orange rind
½ pound fresh mushrooms
1½ tablespoons flour
Juice of ½ lemon
2 tablespoons chopped fresh parsley

Butter a baking dish with 1 tablespoon of the butter. Salt and pepper
the double fillets of sole and roll them, skin side in, cigar fashion. Mix
the chopped onion, the liquid, the saffron, dried basil and orange rind
and pour around the fish. Cover with a buttered baking paper and
bake for 15 minutes in a preheated 400° F. oven. While the fish cooks,
sauté the mushrooms in 1 tablespoon butter; salt and pepper them and
cover them so they render all their juices. Set aside.

As soon as the sole fillets are cooked, remove them to a plate to keep
warm. Boil the cooking juices very hard for about 5 minutes, then
strain them into the pan containing the mushrooms. Bring the mixture
to a boil and thicken with a beurre manié (page 37) made of 2
tablespoons butter and 1½ tablespoons flour. Add fresh lemon juice to
the sauce and swirl in the remainder of the butter. Correct the seasoning and pour over the fillets of sole. Sprinkle with the chopped parsley.

ORDER OF DINNER PREPARATION:

Spread the work over 2 days:

DAY ONE:

Bake the cake. It will keep very well in the refrigerator loosely covered
with plastic wrap.

DAY TWO:

1. Clean the spinach carefully; roll in a terry towel and refrigerate; make salad dressing. Chill both separately.

2. Prepare the sole dish for baking; chop the onion; prepare the mixture of liquids, saffron powder, basil, and orange rind. Set aside.

3. Sauté the mushrooms so that they render all their juices. Set aside.

4. Put the rice pilaf on to cook.

5. Poach the fillets of sole.

6. Remove the poached fillets to a warm platter; make the fish sauce.

7. Serve the fillets and the rice.

8. Bring the cake to room temperature for better flavor.

9. Toss the spinach salad and serve.

10. Serve the cake.

COURT-BOUILLON POACHED FISH FILLETS, FISH STEAKS, OR SMALL FISH

You can also poach fish in a hot water bath or court bouillon bath. If you use water, use at least 2 quarts salted with 2 tablespoons of salt, or make a quick court bouillon as follows:

QUICK COURT BOUILLON

YIELD: 1½ QUARTS

PREPARATION TIME: 30 MINUTES

1 quart clam juice	1 carrot, coarsely chopped
2 cups white wine	1 very large bouquet garni (page
2 cups water	12)
⅓ cup vinegar	1 tablespoon salt
2 large onions, coarsely chopped	6 peppercorns

Put all the ingredients in a pot, bring to a boil, and boil hard for 15 minutes before immersing the fish. Do not discard the court bouillon after using it. If you have the space, freeze it to be able to reuse it. If you do not have enough space, use salted water, which you can discard every time.

You can, if you want, also poach your fish in a mixture of half milk and half water, well seasoned with a bit of salt and a lot of pepper.

KEY RECIPE: Please observe the following method very accurately for best results:

Use steaks not thicker than 1 inch or small fish, such as trout or small red snappers. Bring the court bouillon or water to a rolling boil; immerse the fish in the liquid and bring back to a rolling boil. Cover the pan, remove from the heat, and let stand, covered, for 8 minutes for steaks, 10 minutes for small snappers, and 12 minutes for trout.

Serve the fish with salt, pepper, and fresh butter or a compound butter.

This operation is best done in a fish poacher because the fish can be put on the rack, but you can do it in any pot the fish will fit in if you do not own a poacher. Be sure that at least 4 inches of water cover the fish.

SUGGESTED EVERYDAY DINNER MENU I

Fresh tomato soup (page 22)
FRINTON SALMON STEAKS
Creamed peas (page 257)
Refreshed nectarines (page 276)

SERVINGS: 2

APPROXIMATE TOTAL PREPARATION TIME: 45 MINUTES

FRINTON SALMON STEAKS

SERVINGS: 2

PREPARATION TIME: 15 MINUTES

Salted water
2 large salmon steaks (1 inch thick)

2 tablespoons butter or margarine
1½ teaspoons anchovy paste

Bring the court bouillon or water to a violent boil. Immerse the fish into the boiling liquid. Bring back to a violent boil and remove from the heat. Let stand eight minutes. Cream the butter or margarine with the anchovy paste and serve on the salmon.

ORDER OF DINNER PREPARATION:

1. Prepare the tomato soup; put it on to cook.
2. Refresh the nectarines, peel and slice the kiwis; sprinkle with liqueur and chill.
3. Prepare the court bouillon or water for the salmon; prepare the anchovy butter.
4. Strain the soup.
5. Cook the peas; make the cream sauce.
6. Serve the soup. While the soup is being eaten, cook the salmon.
7. Serve the salmon and the peas.
8. Serve the nectarines.

SUGGESTED EVERYDAY DINNER MENU II

COD STEAK IN FENNEL BUTTER
Pan-fried zucchini (page 259)
Tomato and julienne of pepper salad (page 252)
Strawberry shortcake (page 309)

SERVINGS: 2

APPROXIMATE TOTAL PREPARATION TIME: 1 HOUR

COD STEAKS IN FENNEL BUTTER

SERVINGS: 2

PREPARATION TIME: 15 MINUTES

2 cod steaks (1 inch thick)
Salted water
2 tablespoons butter or oil of your choice

½ teaspoon fennel seeds
Lemon juice to taste
Salt and pepper

Cook the cod steaks in the hot salted water, following the key recipe (page 212). While the fish sits in the water bath, heat the butter or oil in a small pan and add the fennel seeds. Let stand, off the heat, until the fish is ready, then squeeze as much lemon juice as you like into the fennel butter, add salt and pepper, and mix well. Strain over the fish steaks.

ORDER OF DINNER PREPARATION:

1. Bake the cake for the shortcake.
2. Prepare the tomatoes, pepper, and dressing for the salad. Chill separately.
3. Slice the zucchini; bring the water to cook the fish to a boil.
4. Clean the strawberries; whip cream, if you use it; cut the cake into 8 portions (freeze any unused) and prepare 2 shortcake portions.
5. Pan-fry the zucchini; in a small saucepan, prepare the fennel butter.
6. Poach the cod steaks.
7. Serve the cod steaks with the fennel butter and the zucchini.
8. Spoon the dressing on the salad and serve.
9. Serve the shortcake.

SUGGESTED COMPANY DINNER MENU

TROUT WITH AVGOLEMONO SAUCE

White rice pilaf (page 261)
Romaine, cherry tomato, green pepper, marinated olive, and feta
cheese salad (page 252)
Rote Grütze (page 290)

SUGGESTED WINE: Well-chilled Greek retsina (Kokineli)

SERVINGS: 6

APPROXIMATE TOTAL PREPARATION TIME: 1½ HOURS

TROUT WITH AVGOLEMONO SAUCE

SERVINGS: 6

PREPARATION TIME: 30 MINUTES

Court bouillon (page 211)
6 trout, fresh or frozen and defrosted
2 tablespoons chopped fresh dill

3 egg yolks
Lemon juice to taste
Salt and pepper

Bring the court bouillon to a violent boil, and in it cook the trout
following the key recipe (page 212).

To make the sauce, put ¾ cup of the court bouillon in a small saucepan and add the dill. Mix the egg yolks and as much lemon juice as
you like. Add half of the hot court bouillon to the eggs bit by bit, then
pour the mixture back into the small saucepan. Reheat very well, *without boiling*, correct the seasoning, and spoon over the trout after removing the top skin of each of them.

ORDER OF DINNER PREPARATION:

Spread the work over 2 days.

DAY ONE:

1. Make the fruit pudding; pour it into custard cups; cover the cups with clear plastic wrap. Keep refrigerated.
2. Make the court bouillon for the trout; let cool and refrigerate.

DAY TWO:

1. Prepare the salad ingredients and dressing. Chill separately.
2. Chop the dill for the trout sauce.
3. Whip the cream for the dessert. Chill well.
4. Bring the court bouillon to a boil.
5. Put the rice pilaf on to cook.
6. Poach the trout; make the lemon-dill sauce.
7. Serve the trout and the rice.
8. Toss and serve the salad.
9. Serve the pudding, after topping it with the cream.

PAN-FRIED FISH STEAKS OR SMALL FISH
Small fish, such as trout, sardines, tinker mackerel, and baby whiting, and fish steaks of all kinds can be pan-fried in a matter of minutes and add variety to your dinner table.

KEY RECIPE: As a frying medium use either butter or the oil of your choice. The best choice for the taste and the appearance of the fish is, of course, clarified butter (page 9)

Flour the fish, or bread it, exactly as described in the key recipe for pan-fried breaded veal (page 98). If you want a more solid and better-colored crust around the fish when you only flour it, dip the fish in milk first; the layer of flour gathered by the milk will be thicker than it would if the fish had only its natural juices to attract the flour. If you flour only, mix some seasoning into the flour, and let the fish stand for a few minutes to allow the flour to absorb all traces of moisture very well.

As so as you are ready to pan-fry, heat the fat or oil very well and brown the fish on one side; make sure that you build a good, solid crust. Then turn the fish over and brown the other side, making sure that there is plenty of fat or oil so that the fish always slides freely on the bottom of the pan. As soon as the crust is solid and golden on both sides, turn the heat down to finish cooking it through. (This will be necessary only if the piece of fish is between ¾ and 1 inch thick.)

SUGGESTED EVERYDAY DINNER MENU I

Cream of spinach soup (page 32)
SAUMON À LA LYONNAISE
Pan-fried mushrooms (page 257)
Strawberries in kirsch (page 272)

SERVINGS: 2

APPROXIMATE TOTAL PREPARATION TIME: 45 MINUTES

SAUMON À LA LYONNAISE

SERVINGS: 2

PREPARATION TIME: 15 MINUTES

2 salmon steaks (¾ inch thick)
Flour
Salt and pepper
¼ cup clarified butter (page 9)
   or oil of your choice

1 onion, thinly sliced
1 tablespoon chopped fresh parsley
2 teaspoons vinegar
1 tablespoon fresh, unsalted butter
   (optional)

Flour the salmon steaks with flour seasoned with a bit of salt and pepper. Pan-fry the steaks in 3 tablespoons of the butter or oil, according to the directions given in the key recipe (page 216).

While the salmon is cooking, sauté the onion in the remaining butter or oil. Add salt and pepper, then cover the pan and let cook until soft and translucent. When the onion is done, add the parsley and the vinegar, and correct the seasoning. Remove the pan from the heat, and if you desire, swirl the fresh butter into the soft onion and parsley mixture. Spoon half of the mixture on top of each salmon steak.

ORDER OF DINNER PREPARATION:

1. Clean the strawberries; steep them in kirsch. Chill.
2. Clean and slice the mushrooms. Set aside.
3. Slice the onion for the salmon; chop the parsley.
4. Put the cream of spinach soup on to cook; prepare the mixture of starch/milk or cream to thicken the soup. Set aside.
5. Pan-fry the mushrooms; keep them warm; in the same pan sauté the onion for the salmon.
6. Pan-fry the salmon steaks.
7. While they cook, thicken the cream of spinach soup.
8. Serve the soup.
9. Serve the salmon and the mushrooms.
10. Serve the strawberries.

SUGGESTED EVERYDAY DINNER MENU II

SARDINES OF SMELTS À LA PERSILLADE
Parsleyed potatoes (page 258)
Grated carrot salad (page 252)
Coffee pudding (page 289)

SERVINGS: 2

APPROXIMATE TOTAL PREPARATION TIME: 45 MINUTES

"Persillade" is the glorious parsley and garlic mixture of Provence. It should always be crisp and golden for true flavor.

SARDINES OR SMELTS À LA PERSILLADE

SERVINGS: 2

PREPARATION TIME: 15 MINUTES

12 sardines or smelts, heads left on
Flour
Salt and pepper

3 tablespoons butter or oil of your choice
2 tablespoons chopped fresh parsley
1 small clove garlic, minced

Flour the sardines with flour seasoned with salt and pepper, and pan-fry them in 2 tablespoons of the butter or oil, about 3 minutes on each side. When the fish are done, remove them to a plate; discard the cooking fat or oil. In the same frying pan, heat well the last tablespoon of butter or oil, and in it sauté the mixture of parsley and garlic until crisp and golden. Pour it over the sardines and serve.

ORDER OF DINNER PREPARATION:

1. Prepare the coffee pudding. Chill.
2. Prepare the carrot salad and its dressing. Chill both, separately.
3. Peel potatoes; cut them in cubes; put them on to cook.
4. Chop the parsley and garlic for the persillade and the parsley for the potatoes.
5. Flour the fish; pan-fry them.
6. While the fish cook, toss the salad.
7. Pan-fry the persillade; pour it over the fish.
8. Serve the fish and potatoes.
9. Toss the salad and serve.
10. Serve the pudding.

BROILED FISH STEAKS, FILLETS, OR SMALL FISH FOR DINNER

KEY RECIPE: *For broiled fish steaks and large fillets, ¾ to 1 inch thick.* Brush the steaks or fillets with melted butter or oil and coat their top sides with 1 tablespoon fresh bread crumbs. Sprinkle the crumb coating with some melted butter or oil. Place the fish on a buttered or oiled cake rack placed over a jelly roll pan and broil 3 minutes, 4 inches away from the flame.

Turn the steaks or fillets over, brush the second side with more butter or oil, sprinkle with another tablespoon of fresh crumbs, and sprinkle the crumbs with more melted butter or oil. Broil another 4 minutes, 4 inches away from the flame. Serve plain, with lemon juice, or with a compound butter (page 38).

For whole small broiled fish: Use small whole fish such as trout, tinker mackerel, small red snappers, small red mullets, sardines, small bluefish or butterfish.

Clean the fish cavity and salt and pepper it. Do not remove the head of the fish. Brush the fish with oil. If it is a bit large, cut 2 or 3 slashes ⅛ inch deep into each side of the fish for better penetration of the heat. Squeeze the fish between two cake racks placed over a jelly roll pan. Broil about 4 minutes on the first side, then turn over by grasping both cake racks at once and turning both the racks and the fish upside down. Broil 4 to 5 minutes on the second side.

You may, before broiling, sprinkle the fish with any herb of your choice to perk up its basic taste.

SUGGESTED EVERYDAY DINNER MENU I

BROILED SHAD FILLET
Pan-fried potatoes with parsley (page 259)
Boston lettuce salad (page 252)
Sliced oranges in Grand Marnier (page 272)

SERVINGS: 2

APPROXIMATE TOTAL PREPARATION TIME: 45 MINUTES

BROILED SHAD FILLET

1 large shad fillet (the whole side of a medium fish)
1 slice bacon

3 tablespoons fresh bread crumbs
2 tablespoons melted butter or oil
Salt and pepper

Shad is so tender that it need not be turned over. It will broil in 6 to 8 minutes exposed to the flame on the meat side only.

Place the shad, skin side down, on the lightly buttered or oiled broiler rack. Set aside. Render the bacon slowly in a small pan, then crumble it and mix it with the bread crumbs. Brush a bit of bacon fat on the surface of the fillets, sprinkle with the mixture of crumbs and bacon, and sprinkle the crumbs with melted butter or oil. Broil 7 to 8 minutes, 4 inches away from the flame.

ORDER OF DINNER PREPARATION:

1. Peel and slice the oranges; sprinkle them with Grand Marnier. Chill well.

2. Render the bacon for the shad.

3. Prepare the lettuce and its dressing; chill both, separately.

4. Peel and cube the potatoes; start cooking them. While they cook, chop the parsley.

5. Prepare the mixture of bacon and crumbs for the shad.

6. Prepare the shad for broiling; broil it.
7. Serve the shad and the potatoes.
8. Toss the salad and serve.
9. Serve the oranges.

SUGGESTED EVERYDAY DINNER MENU II

Julienne of carrot soup (page 25)
BROILED BABY BLUEFISH OR BUTTERFISH
Buttered, boiled potatoes (page 258)
Pineapple slices in rum (page 272)

SERVINGS: 2

APPROXIMATE TOTAL PREPARATION TIME: 45 TO 50 MINUTES

BROILED BABY BLUEFISH OR BUTTERFISH

SERVINGS: 2

PREPARATION TIME: 15 MINUTES

4 small bluefish or butterfish
Olive oil or oil of your choice
Salt and pepper
2 tablespoons butter or margarine

1½ teaspoons prepared Dijon mustard
1 tablespoon capers

Clean the fish. Salt and pepper them in the cavities and broil, following the key recipe (page 220). When the fish are done, cream the butter or margarine with the mustard and add the capers. Spread this butter over the fish.

ORDER OF DINNER PREPARATION:

1. Peel and slice the fresh pineapple; sprinkle lightly with sugar or honey and rum. Chill.
2. Prepare and put the carrot soup on to cook.

3. Peel and cube the potatoes; put them on to cook.
4. Prepare the bluefish for broiling.
5. Prepare the mustard and caper butter.
6. Serve the soup while you broil the fish.
7. Serve the fish and the potatoes.
8. Serve the pineapple.

SUGGESTED COMPANY DINNER MENU

Cream of mushroom soup (page 33)
BROILED SALMON STEAKS GREAT CYRUS
Cucumbers in dill butter (page 256)
Sliced tomato salad (page 252)
Two-pear mousse (page 280)

SUGGESTED WINE: Pouilly-Fuissé or California Blanc Fumé

SERVINGS: 6

APPROXIMATE TOTAL PREPARATION TIME: 1½ HOURS

BROILED SALMON STEAKS GREAT CYRUS

SERVINGS: 6

PREPARATION TIME: 15 MINUTES

¼ cup melted butter
¾ cup fresh bread crumbs
6 salmon steaks
Salt and pepper
½ cup water
Juice of ½ lemon

1 tablespoon prepared Dijon mustard
½ cup fresh, unsalted butter
2 tablespoons heavy cream, whipped
1 tablespoon chopped parsley

Using the melted butter and fresh bread crumbs to coat them, broil the salmon steaks, following the key recipe (page 220). When they are done, serve them with the mustard butter, made as follows:

Put the water, lemon juice, ¼ teaspoon salt and a good pinch of pepper in a small saucepan and let cook down to 3 tablespoons. Mix in the Dijon mustard, and over very low heat whisk in the fresh, unsalted butter, tablespoon by tablespoon. Add the heavy cream and parsley and spoon over the salmon steaks.

ORDER OF DINNER PREPARATION:

Spread the work over 2 days:

DAY ONE:

Make the two-pear mousse. Spoon it into sherbet glasses; cover each glass with plastic wrap. Keep refrigerated.

DAY TWO:

1. Slice the tomatoes; prepare their dressing. Chill both separately.
2. Clean and slice the mushrooms; cook them in broth.
3. Peel, seed, and cut the cucumbers in triangular chunks; cook in boiling water. Chop the dill, mix it with the butter that will season the cucumbers.
4. Mix the water, the lemon juice, salt, and pepper for the fish sauce. Reduce it, add the mustard. Keep warm. Whip the cream for the sauce.
5. Prepare the salmon steaks for broiling.
6. Finish the soup with its cream enrichment.
7. Finish the fish sauce. Keep it barely lukewarm.
8. Broil the salmon. Serve the soup while it broils.
9. Roll the cucumbers in the warmed dill butter.
10. Serve the salmon with the sauce and the cucumbers.
11. Spoon the dressing over the salad and serve.
12. Serve the dessert.

BAKED FISH STEAKS AND SMALL FISH

KEY RECIPE: *Baking fish in an open dish:* Brush steaks or fillets with oil or melted butter, sprinkle with bread crumbs, if desired, and bake in a 375° F. to 400° F.

oven. The fish is done when the tip of a knife inserted at its center comes out hot.

For small fish, cut slashes, at 1-inch intervals, ⅓ inch deep through the top fillet of the fish to make the penetration of the heat easier. Brush with oil or melted butter and bake in a 350° F. to 375° F. oven for 10 minutes per pound.

The best sauce is lemon juice mixed with melted butter and parsley.

Baking fish in aluminum foil: This method is especially recommended for persons who have to limit their intake of fats, for the foil can be brushed with a minimal amount of butter, margarine, or oil. Put the fish steaks or fillets or any small fish on a piece of foil, brushed with as little fat or oil as you desire. (If you intend the vegetable garnish to be enjoyed with the fish, presauté it before you put it to bake with the fish.) Salt and pepper the fish, close the foil on top of the fish with a drugstore wrap, and tuck the ends under. Bake in a 400° F. oven for 12 to 15 minutes. (Fish baked in foil cooks fast because of the high heat conduction of the aluminum foil.) To serve, cut the foil open and add 1 tablespoon of cream or butter, if you desire.

SUGGESTED EVERYDAY DINNER MENU I

ROUGETS AUX COURGETTES
Steamed brown rice with Provençal herbs (page 262)
Romaine, walnut and leek salad (page 251)
Raw apple mousse (page 279)

SERVINGS: 2

APPROXIMATE TOTAL PREPARATION TIME: 1 HOUR 15 MINUTES

In Provence, this combination of fish and zucchini is an everyday lunch or dinner dish.

ROUGETS AUX COURGETTES

SERVINGS: 2

PREPARATION TIME: 20 TO 30 MINUTES

4 small zucchini
2 tablespoons or more olive oil or oil of your choice
Provençal herbs (page 12)

4 small red snappers or 1 large ocean perch
Lemon juice
Salt and pepper

Wash the zucchini, remove the stems and the rounded ends, and slice in ¼-inch-thick slices. Brush the dish with 1 tablespoon olive oil. Line the dish with the zucchini slices and sprinkle well with Provençal herbs. Put the fish on the zucchini, brush with the second tablespoon or more of oil, and bake in a 375° F. oven, 20 minutes for the small red snappers or 30 minutes for the large ocean perch. Serve with plain lemon juice, salt, and pepper.

ORDER OF DINNER PREPARATION:

1. Peel the apple; make the raw apple mousse. Chill.
2. Prepare the romaine and chop the walnuts; make the dressing. Chill both, separately.
3. Prepare the zucchini and fish dish.
4. Prepare the rice for steaming; put the rice on to steam.
6. Ten minutes later, bake the fish.
7. Serve the fish dish and the rice.
8. Toss the salad and serve.
9. Serve the apple mousse.

SUGGESTED EVERYDAY DINNER MENU II

TINKER MACKERELS, CALABRIA STYLE
Pan-fried eggplants (page 256)
Romaine and iceberg lettuce with mint dressing (page 252)
Natillas y Naranjas (page 292)

SERVINGS: 2

APPROXIMATE TOTAL PREPARATION TIME: 1 HOUR

TINKER MACKERELS, CALABRIA STYLE
SERVINGS: 2

PREPARATION TIME: 30 MINUTES

4 tinker mackerels
Salt and pepper
2 tablespoons olive oil or oil of your
choice

1 sweet red onion, sliced
1 tomato, sliced
Large pinch of crumbled dried oregano

Clean the tinker mackerels. Salt and pepper their cavities. Rub ½ tablespoon of the olive oil on each of 2 sheets (12 x 10 inches) of aluminum foil. Set 2 tinkers on each sheet. Sauté the onion slices and the tomatoes in the other tablespoon of olive oil for 2 to 3 minutes. Add the oregano and mix well. Let cool slightly, then top the tinkers with the vegetables and more salt and pepper. Close the foil and bake in a preheated 400° F. oven for 15 to 18 minutes. Open the foil before serving.

ORDER OF DINNER PREPARATION:

Divide the work into 2 parts:

EARLY IN THE MORNING:
Salt the eggplant slices.

AT DINNERTIME:

1. Slice the oranges; make the custard. Chill both, separately, very well.
2. Prepare the salad greens and dressing. Chill both, separately.
3. Sauté the onion and tomatoes for the fish. Cool slightly.
4. Prepare the tinker mackerels for baking.
5. Bake the fish.
6. While they are baking, pan-fry the eggplant slices.
7. Serve the fish and eggplant.
8. Toss the salad and serve.
9. Pour the custard over the oranges and serve.

SUGGESTED EVERYDAY DINNER MENU III

SALMON SIMPLEX
Sliced cucumber and romaine salad (page 252)
Crème Suchard (page 287)

SERVINGS: 2

APPROXIMATE TOTAL PREPARATION TIME: 1 HOUR

SALMON SIMPLEX

SERVINGS: 2

PREPARATION TIME: 30 MINUTES

2 tablespoons butter or oil of your choice
2 salmon steaks
Salt and pepper
¼ pound fresh mushrooms, sliced
¼ cup sour cream
1½ teaspoons chopped chives, fresh or frozen

Cut 2 pieces (12 x 10 inches) of foil. Rub each of them with ½ tablespoon of the butter or oil. Set the salmon steaks on the foil and salt and pepper them. Heat the remaining tablespoon of butter or oil and sauté the mushrooms until they render their moisture. Salt and pepper them, cool them slightly, then put half of them on each salmon steak. Close the foil tightly and bake in a preheated 400° F. oven for 15 to 18 minutes. In a small saucepan, heat, *but do not boil,* the sour cream, a pinch of salt and pepper, and the chives. Open the foil and spoon half of the cream on each salmon steak.

ORDER OF DINNER PREPARATION:

1. Make the dessert. Chill.
2. Slice the cucumbers; clean the romaine; make the dressing. Chill all the salad elements separately.
3. Cook the mushrooms for the salmon; let them cool slightly.
4. Prepare the salmon for baking; bake the salmon.
5. Prepare the cream and chives mixture.
6. Open the foil wrappers and pour the cream over the salmon steaks.
7. Serve the salmon.
8. Toss the salad and serve.
9. Serve the dessert.

DEEP-FRIED FISH

There is no doubt that fish can be deep fried very fast, and that some fish with a dry, tightly woven texture can gain from being deep fried. But a dubious pleasure remains for the quick cook to face—the cleaning of the oil bath after use.

KEY RECIPE: If you care to deep-fry fish, all you have to do is bring oil for deep frying to 370° F. in a deep-fryer. Flour the fish or bread it as indicated in the key recipe for breaded veal (page 98) and immerse it in the hot oil until it is golden.

When fried in an oil bath at the correct temperature, fish will be crisp and dry outside and very moist inside. Serve with lemon juice and parsley.

SHELLFISH

Be careful—all shellfish is high in cholesterol, as well as expensive, so limit its use. Why not keep it for quick cookery entertaining?

SHRIMP

For the sake of saving time, use flash-frozen peeled and deveined shrimp. You may use any of the following techniques to cook them. The methods are multiple, but those described here are the fastest and give good, tender results.

Before you use shrimp, defrost them in the refrigerator for 12 hours. All it takes is letting the bag stand overnight on the lowest shelf of your refrigerator.

BOILED SHRIMP   Boiled shrimp can be used best in high-protein salads (pages 245–251).

KEY RECIPE: Bring about 4 quarts of water to a boil. Add 3 to 4 tablespoons salt. Put about 10 frozen or defrosted shrimp in a colander or a large strainer with a long handle. Immerse the shrimp in the wildly boiling water. Watch the shrimp carefully; as soon as they curl up into semicircles, remove from the water and put to drain in a terry towel. Repeat with the remainder of the shrimp. Be careful—it takes no more than 2 minutes to cook large defrosted shrimp; any shrimp that is curled up into an almost complete circle will be overcooked.

PAN-FRIED SHRIMP

KEY RECIPE: Pat the defrosted shrimp very dry in paper towels. Heat the butter or oil of your choice in a skillet until very hot. Add the shrimp and toss on high heat until the shrimp curl up in semicircles; this will require no more than 2 to 3 minutes. (Any shrimp that is curled up into a complete circle will be overcooked.) Remove from the heat and add seasonings and any herb of your choice. You may, if you want, add plain cream or cream mixed with other spices to make a sauce.

SUGGESTED COMPANY DINNER MENU

SHRIMP CRÈME-MOUTARDE
Stir-fried asparagus (page 255)
Boston lettuce, avocado, and hard-boiled egg salad (page 251)
Raspberry tart (page 303)

SUGGESTED WINE: French Muscadet or California Folle Blanche

SERVINGS: 6

APPROXIMATE TOTAL PREPARATION TIME: 1½ HOURS

SHRIMP CRÈME-MOUTARDE

SERVINGS: 6

PREPARATION TIME: 15 MINUTES

1½ pounds frozen medium shrimp, defrosted
3 tablespoons butter
Salt and pepper
1½ cups heavy cream
1 tablespoon cornstarch
2 tablespoons prepared Dijon mustard
2 tablespoons finely chopped fresh parsley

Pat the shrimp dry with paper towels. Heat the butter and toss the shrimp in it until they curl up in a semicircle. Salt and pepper them, then remove to a plate, leaving any shrimp juice in the pan. Reduce the shrimp juice to 1 tablespoon. Mix 1¼ cups of the heavy cream with the starch, pour into the pan, and stir with a whisk until the mixture boils and thickens. Mix the mustard and the remaining heavy cream, and off the heat and whisking, add it to the cream sauce. Add the shrimp and reheat *without boiling*. Add the parsley; correct the seasoning and serve immediately.

ORDER OF DINNER PREPARATION:

Spread the work over 2 days:

DAY ONE:

1. Make the pastry for the tart; let it rest for 15 minutes.
2. Shape the tart shell. Let the shaped shell rest 30 minutes before baking it. Bake it; as soon as it is done, cool it on a rack and store in a cannister.

DAY TWO:

1. Wash the raspberries; prepare the jelly for melting in a small pan.
2. Prepare salad greens and avocado; hard-boil 2 eggs; make salad dressing. Chill all the ingredients, separately.
3. Prepare the asparagus for stir frying.
4. Prepare the mixture of cream and starch for the shrimp sauce; have the mustard at hand. Chop the parsley.
5. Stir-fry the asparagus.
6. Stir-fry the shrimp; remove them to a dish.
7. Make the cream sauce; add the mustard. Blend with the shrimp and parsley.
8. Serve the shrimp and the asparagus.
9. Toss the salad and serve. Melt the currant jelly on low heat.
10. Whip cream for pie; fill shell with cream and berries. Brush with melted currant jelly and serve.

BROILED SHRIMP

KEY RECIPE: Skewer large shrimp, making sure that the tail of each shrimp is tucked under the upper part of the next shrimp tail. Roll them in melted butter or oil, then in seasoned fresh bread crumbs. Use 3 table-spoons crumbs for each skewer of 6 to 8 large shrimp. Broil 4 inches from the flame for 5 minutes, turning once or twice while broiling.

You may vary the basic taste by adding herbs or grated cheese to the crumbs. Serve with melted butter and—only when there is no cheese in the crumbs—lemon juice.

BAKED SHRIMP   Baking shrimp is also possible—and a rather fast operation it is—but it is unfortunately not the very best for the shrimp, which, if one does not pay great attention to the baking time, turn to rubber with awesome facility.

KEY RECIPE: The method consists in piling the defrosted shrimp in an ovenproof dish, basting them liberally with lemon juice and butter and baking them in a 400° F. oven for 15 minutes; considering a longer baking time means courting disaster. To protect the top layer of shrimp from the intense heat of the oven, sprinkle it with a heavy blanket of seasoned fresh bread crumbs liberally basted with melted butter.

This dish is made very caloric by all that butter, but it is delicious. If the butter does not frighten you, try it and use, per person, 8 large shrimp, ⅓ cup fresh bread crumbs, and 4 tablespoons butter.

SCALLOPS

In quick cookery use only the least expensive deep-sea scallops, and avoid preparing them with a roux-based sauce, which to be good must be skimmed and very well reduced, an operation that takes time. There is nothing worse than an overcooked scallop floating in a badly reduced sauce made with wine and milk or cream without any fish stock or shell-fish juice. The following ways of cooking scallops are fast:

PAN-FRIED SCALLOPS

KEY RECIPE: Cut the scallops across in thin slices (⅛ inch). Heat some butter or oil in a frying pan and toss the scallops on high heat in the hot fat or oil until they turn white. Stop the cooking, then add salt and pepper—and any spices or fresh herbs you may like.

SUGGESTED EVERYDAY DINNER MENU

SCALLOPS KARABASENN
Pan-fried tomatoes with garlic and parsley (page 260)
Cauliflower and watercress salad (page 252)
Blender strawberry mousse (page 282)

SERVINGS: 2

APPROXIMATE TOTAL PREPARATION TIME: 45 MINUTES

This scallop dish is an adaptation of one from Brittany.

SCALLOPS KARABASENN
SERVINGS: 2

PREPARATION TIME: 20 MINUTES

½ cup dry white wine
2 chopped shallots
1 clove garlic, minced
3 tablespoons chopped fresh parsley
¼ cup clam juice

½ pound sea scallops, cut in ⅛-inch slices
¼ cup butter or margarine
Salt and pepper
½ cup fresh bread crumbs

Mix the wine, shallots, garlic, and 1 tablespoon of the parsley; cook down by half and add the clam juice. Sauté the scallop slices for 2 or 3 minutes in 1½ tablespoons butter or margarine with a pinch of salt and pepper. Combine the cooked scallops with the reduction of wine and clam juice and ¼ cup of the bread crumbs. Mix well, then turn into 2 small au gratin dishes. Cover each with half the remaining crumbs and parsley mixed together. Melt the remaining butter and spoon half of it on each dish; pass under the broiler for 1 minute.

ORDER OF DINNER PREPARATION:

1. Make the blender mousse. Store it in the freezer.
2. Clean and slice the cauliflower; clean the watercress; prepare their dressing. Chill all the salad ingredients separately.
3. Chop the shallots, garlic, parsley; make bread crumbs in the blender if you do not have any ready in a jar in the freezer.
4. Mix the wine, chopped shallots, and garlic in a small pot and reduce by half. Add clam juice.
5. Sauté the scallops; mix them with the wine-reduction mixture and bread crumbs; broil.
6. Pan-fry the tomatoes.
7. Serve the scallops and the tomatoes.
8. Toss the salad and serve.
9. Serve the mousse.

BROILED SCALLOPS

KEY RECIPE: Use sea scallops of medium size. Brush them with melted butter or oil and skewer 6 to 8 per person. Broil, 4 inches away from the flame, for 5 to 6 minutes, turning once while cooking. Serve with plain lemon juice or a compound butter (page 38).

SUGGESTED EVERYDAY DINNER MENU

BROILED SCALLOPS WITH HERB BUTTER
Tarragon rice pilaf (page 263)
Boston lettuce salad (page 252)
Yogurt ice (page 284)

SERVINGS: 2

APPROXIMATE TOTAL PREPARATION TIME: 45 MINUTES

BROILED SCALLOPS WITH HERB BUTTER
SERVINGS: 2

PREPARATION TIME: 10 MINUTES

12 to 16 scallops, depending on size
1 tablespoon olive oil or oil of your choice
Salt and pepper
2 tablespoons butter

1 teaspoon lemon juice
1 teaspoon each finely crumbled dried tarragon and chervil
½ teaspoon each fresh chopped parsley and chives

After brushing the scallops with the oil, broil them, following the key recipe (page 235). As soon as they are done, sprinkle the scallops with salt and pepper and serve them with a compound butter made by creaming together with a small whisk the butter, lemon juice, and crumbled and chopped herbs.

ORDER OF DINNER PREPARATION:

1. Blend the yogurt, lemon juice, and honey or sugar. Store in the freezer.
2. Clean and prepare the lettuce; make the dressing. Chill both, separately.
3. Make the herb butter for the scallops.
4. Make the rice pilaf.

5. Skewer the scallops.
6. Broil the scallops.
7. Serve the scallops with their herb butter; serve the rice pilaf.
8. Toss the salad and serve.
9. Serve the yogurt ice.

DEEP-FRIED SCALLOPS Although these should reasonably be kept for an occasional treat at an "eat-in-the-rough" restaurant at the seashore, they can be done at home very easily.

KEY RECIPE: Preheat oil for deep-frying to 370° F. Flour the scallops, or bread them as indicated in the key recipe for breaded veal (page 98), and deep-fry them until golden. Serve with salt, pepper, and lemon juice.

LOBSTER

The main drawbacks of lobster are its price and the tremendous amount of butter it is usually eaten with, so keep it for quick-cookery entertaining.

The best way to cook lobster is to boil or bake it. In only these two ways is the whole flavor of the shellfish completely respected; no sauce is allowed to interfere with its sweetness.

It is, however, not easy to bake a large number of lobsters in a small kitchen. Boiled lobster is easier and less messy than baked lobster when you have more than 4 persons at your dinner table.

But, whether you boil or bake the lobster, use this butter with it. This amount will serve 6 persons; use one 1½-pound lobster per person.

CLINGING, FOAMING BUTTER FOR LOBSTER

¼ cup water
Juice of 1 lemon
¼ teaspoon salt

⅛ teaspoon white pepper
¾ cup soft unsalted butter

Boil the water, lemon juice, salt, and pepper, down to 3 tablespoons. Turn the heat down, let the contents of the pan cool a bit, then beat in the soft butter, tablespoon by tablespoon. Keep the heat very low to prevent melting the butter and breaking the emulsion of the reduced liquid and butter.

BOILED LOBSTER

KEY RECIPE: To boil 1½-pound lobsters use:
3 quarts of water and 3 tablespoons salt for 1 lobster
5 quarts of water and 5 tablespoons salt for 2 to 3 lobsters
6 quarts of water and 6 tablespoons salt for 3 to 4 lobsters
8 quarts of water and ½ cup salt for 5 to 6 lobsters

Bring the water to a violent boil. Add the lobsters, pushing them deep down into the water, bring back to a boil, and barely simmer for 15 minutes, *never more.*

BAKED LOBSTER

KEY RECIPE: Put the lobster on a board. Rub the top of the head with your thumb for 1 minute to immobilize the lobster, then cut in half lengthwise. Remove the gravel bag between the eyes and the center vein. Sear the meat side of each lobster half in hot butter or oil, then sprinkle with salt and pepper. Finish cooking by putting it in to bake for 12 minutes in a 375° F. oven.

CRABMEAT

For the sake of economy of time, use commercially picked-over crabmeat, but be prepared to spend a great deal of money for it. There is no doubt that the king of crabs is the Maryland blue, closely followed by the Dungeness, but the Alaskan king is also very good if fresh instead of frozen. Reserve all of them for quick-cookery entertaining. Below is an attractive recipe for expensive entertaining.

SUGGESTED COMPANY DINNER MENU

Fresh tomato soup (page 22)
CRABE AU POIVRE VERT
Buttered green beans (page 255)
Romaine salad with mint dressing (page 252)
Orange compote (page 274)

SUGGESTED WINE: French Chassagne-Montrachet or California Pinot
Chardonnay

SERVINGS: 6

APPROXIMATE TOTAL PREPARATION TIME: 1 HOUR 15 MINUTES

CRABE AU POIVRE VERT

SERVINGS: 6

PREPARATION TIME: 30 MINUTES

3 tablespons green peppercorns,
   packed in their own juices
   (page 196)
1½ cups heavy cream
Salt

1 pound picked-over crabmeat, preferably back fin meat
3 tablespoons butter
1 tablespoon Cognac
6 toast points

Place the peppercorns in a strainer and rinse them very well under
running cold water to discard all traces of the outer membranes; keep
only the pale green core. Cook the cream down by half, stirring well
with a whisk at regular intervals. Add salt to suit your taste, and the
peppercorns. Heat the crabmeat gently in the butter. Heat the Cognac
in a small saucepan; light it with a match and pour it, flaming, over
the crabmeat. Mix the cream into the crab and serve immediately on
toast points.

ORDER OF DINNER PREPARATION:

1. Prepare the orange compote. Chill in refrigerator.
2. Prepare the salad greens; prepare the dressing. Chill separately.
3. Make the tomato soup; put it on to cook.
4. Reduce the cream for the crabmeat sauce.
5. Peel and cook the green beans; prepare their seasoning butter.
6. Prepare the toast points for the crab.
7. Rinse the peppercorns and add them to the cream sauce.
8. Strain the soup. Serve it.
9. Heat and flambé the crabmeat and mix in cream.
10. Serve the crabmeat and the beans.
11. Toss the salad and serve.
12. Serve the orange compote.

MUSSELS AND CLAMS

To be fast with mussels and clams is a problem, considering the large amount of scrubbing to be done—and *well* done if one does not want a gritty dinner plate. If you are inexperienced, remember that scrubbing the shells of clams or mussels requires about ½ hour per quart, although clams are easier than mussels. Scrub with a tough plastic scrubber with a very rough mesh. Then let the clams or mussels soak about 20 minutes in highly salted water (1 tablespoon per quart), to release the sand they contain.

While they soak, prepare whatever herbs and liquids you need to steam the shellfish open. The steaming is a matter of 5 minutes.

KEY RECIPE: Use New England steamers, soft-shelled clams, razor clams and mussels. (Beware of the months of May through October—the shells are invaded by micro-organisms that render the shellfish very dangerous for human consumption.)

Put the shellfish in a large pot, add the chopped garnish of aromatic vegetables and coarsely ground pepper. The liquid used to produce the steam, which will force the shells open, may be water, white wine, cider (as sour as possible), or vermouth, alone or in combination. (The best combination is half water, half wine.) Toss well to mix; this is best done by covering the pot and holding it closed with your thumbs on the lid while you hold the pot handles with the other four fingers of each hand.

To steam the shellfish, keep the lid on the pot, put on rather high heat, and continue tossing every minute for 4 to 5 minutes. Any shellfish that does not open while steaming must be discarded.

SUGGESTED EVERYDAY DINNER MENU

MOULES SAINT MALO
French bread and unsalted butter
Boston lettuce salad (page 252)
Flambéed apples (page 277)

SERVINGS: 2

APPROXIMATE TOTAL PREPARATION TIME: 1 HOUR TO 1 HOUR 15 MINUTES

MOULES SAINT MALO

SERVINGS: 2

PREPARATION TIME: 1 HOUR

1 quart mussels, scrubbed
1 large shallot, chopped
1 onion, chopped
¼ cup each water and very dry, acid cider
Small bouquet garni (page 12)

Pepper
¼ cup each heavy cream and sour cream
Salt, only if necessary
2 tablespoons chopped fresh parsley

Steam the mussels, following the key recipe (page 240), with the chopped shallot and onion, the water, cider, bouquet garni, and pepper. Mix both creams and the parsley very well with a bit of salt, if necessary.

Remove the steamed mussels to deep soup plates. Pour the cream mixture into the cooking juices and heat well, *without boiling*. Strain half of the sauce onto each portion of mussels. Eat the remainder of the strained cooking juices as you would a soup.

ORDER OF DINNER PREPARATION:

1. Scrub the mussels; let them stand 20 minutes in salted water.
2. Chop the shallot and onion for the mussel garnish.
3. Prepare the Boston lettuce salad and its dressing; chill both, separately.
4. Peel the apples; slice them and sauté them in butter, preferably in a stainless-steel pan. Keep them in the pan.
5. Steam the mussels open; make their sauce.
6. Serve the mussels with bread and butter.
7. Toss the salad and serve.
8. Sweeten the apples with as much sugar as you like; reheat them well to melt the sugar and flambé them with applejack or Calvados—or even whiskey.

SUGGESTED EVERYDAY DINNER MENU II

VONGOLE DEL MARINAIO
Cappellini with basil and Parmesan (page 269)
Romaine salad with mint dressing (page 252)
Fresh fruit

SERVINGS: 2

APPROXIMATE TOTAL PREPARATION TIME: 1 HOUR TO 1 HOUR 15 MINUTES

This dish is featured at the small Ristorante del Marinaio in San Remo. The clams and pesto there are worth the airplane fare to Italy.

VONGOLE DEL MARINAIO

SERVINGS: 2

PREPARATION TIME: 30 MINUTES

1½ quarts soft-shelled clams (use a mixture of different types of clams if possible)
Juice of 1 lemon
2 cloves garlic, finely chopped

⅓ cup finely scissored fresh basil leaves
¼ cup each water and wine
Pinch of salt
Coarsely cracked black pepper

Place the clams in a pot with all the aromatics and liquids. Toss well together and steam, following the key recipe (page 241). Eat the clams and drink the juices—it is food for the gods.

ORDER OF DINNER PREPARATION:

1. Prepare the salad greens; prepare the dressing. Chill separately.
2. Prepare a mixture of butter, basil, and Parmesan cheese to season the cappellini.
3. Scrub the clams.
4. Prepare the aromatics to steam the clams.
5. Bring the water for the cappellini to a boil.
6. Steam the clams.
7. Serve the clams.
8. Cook and season the cappellini and serve it.
9. Toss the salad and serve it.
10. Serve the fruit.

OYSTERS

Pollution has made our enjoyment of raw oysters a very dangerous proposition. If you eat raw oysters, you are taking a chance with hepatitis. Cooking would destroy the bacteria or viruses the shellfish may contain, but oysters should never be boiled, fried or baked, only poached.

There is, however, a way out of this dilemma. If you can locate oysters that you know for sure are free of any hepatitis or mercury pollution, be certain to buy and eat them only in the R months. During the warmer months oysters carry the same microorganisms as mussels and clams, organisms that are not destroyed by cooking or poaching. So do enjoy oysters on the half shell only if you are absolutely certain that their geographic origin is an *unpolluted deep-sea area*, not a bay.

Oysters are best eaten as Mother Nature made them, served with a slice of light rye bread very lightly buttered and washed down with a glass of steely-dry white wine.

CHAPTER XIII

Salads, Vegetables, Grains, and Starches in Quicker Cookery

SALADS

HIGH-PROTEIN SALADS FOR DINNER

Consider a high-protein salad for a quick summer dinner; all you will have to do is put it together—provided you plan ahead. If you consider making a shrimp salad, there is no problem, for you can always buy cooked shrimp; but if you use meat, you have to plan on having it already on hand. So plan a high-protein salad the day after you have roasted a chicken or you have cooked a ham or turkey, of which there will be plenty left over.

The dressing can be either mayonnaise or, if you prefer, the classic mixture of oil and acid (vinegar or lemon juice) called "vinaigrette."

(The most delicious salad dressings are made with olive oil, walnut oil, or sunflower oil. Lemon juice blends better with olive oil than vinegar.) If you feel that you must restrict your intake of dressing because of its calorie content, do not toss the salad with the dressing before serving but present it in a small bowl for each guest to help himself/herself to any amount felt to be suitable for his/her own use. Any leftover dressing can be used for another green salad. Vinaigrette can be flavored with any chopped aromatic or herb you like.

BASIC VINAIGRETTE WITH LEMON AND OLIVE OIL
YIELD: 1 CUP

3½ tablespoons lemon juice
1 teaspoon salt

½ teaspoon cracked black pepper
¾ cup olive oil

BASIC VINAIGRETTE WITH VINEGAR AND OIL

¼ cup cider or red or white wine
    vinegar
1 teaspoon salt

½ teaspoon cracked black pepper
¾ cup oil of your choice

This salad, with its combination of ham, salami, eggs, tomatoes, olives, and caviar, is a summer dinner favorite with many German families.

RUSSISCHE EIER
SERVINGS: 2

PREPARATION TIME: 20 MINUTES

2 eggs
1 slice boiled ham, finely chopped
Mayonnaise (page 42)
6 leaves lettuce

4 slices Genoa salami
2 tomatoes, quartered
6 black olives
1 teaspoon caviar (optional)

Hard-boil the eggs. Shell them, cut them in half; remove the yolk of each half egg, mash it with the boiled ham and 2 tablespoons of mayonnaise. Spoon the mixture back into the egg whites.

Present the salad as follows: Place 3 lettuce leaves on each plate and fill them with 2 half eggs each, 2 slices of salami rolled into cones and filled with the black olives, and tomato quarters. If you desire, sprinkle the caviar over the eggs and offer the mayonnaise in a small bowl.

For dessert, serve fresh fruit or a fruit ice.

This is one of the multiple versions of the famous salad from Nice.

SALADE NIÇOISE

SERVINGS: 2

PREPARATION TIME: 30 MINUTES

2 potatoes
2 quarts cold water
1 cup fresh green beans
1 sweet green pepper
1 sweet red pepper
2 large sun-ripened tomatoes
½ small sweet red onion
4 large leaves lettuce

1 can (6½ ounces) waterpack tuna
4 anchovy fillets
6 oil-cured black olives
1½ tablespoons lemon juice
Salt and pepper
1 tablespoon finely chopped fresh basil or 1 teaspoon dried
4½ tablespoons olive oil

Scrub the potatoes. Immerse them in 2 quarts of cold water and bring quickly to a boil. Boil 10 minutes, add the green beans, and boil another 10 minutes. Drain the vegetables. Peel and slice the potatoes, then cool them and the beans. Slice both peppers in fine julienne after discarding all the seeds. Slice the tomatoes and the sweet onion. Mix together all the vegetables except the tomatoes, tossing well.

Make a border with the tomato slices and the lettuce leaves. Pile the vegetable mixture at the center of the plate. Add the tuna, the anchovies, and the olives. Make a dressing with the lemon juice, salt, pepper, basil, and olive oil; whip well and pour onto the salad, or serve in a small bowl.

For dessert, serve fresh fruit or a fruit ice.

The salad below is the specialty of a Swiss friend, who called it a "health" plate.

SCHWEIZER SALATPLATTE

SERVINGS: 2

PREPARATION TIME: 30 MINUTES

4 beautiful leeks, white part only
6 jumbo asparagus
½ cup boiled ham
4 medium canned sardines
4 slices of salami, rolled into cones
2 medium tomatoes

4 leaves lettuce
Chopped fresh parsley
½ cup mayonnaise (pages 42–43)
1½ tablespoons ketchup
1 tablespoon chopped chives
Salt and pepper

Cook the leeks in boiling salted water for 7 to 8 minutes. Trim and peel the asparagus and cook them in salted water for 8 minutes.

Arrange the vegetables and meats attractively on the platter and sprinkle with chopped parsley. Serve with a dressing made of the mayonnaise mixed with the ketchup and the chives. Correct the seasoning of the dressing with salt and pepper, if necessary.

For dessert, serve fresh fruit or a fruit ice.

This unusual combination of fruit, rice, and meats evolved in the kitchen of a Danish farmer's wife.

KRISTINE'S SALAT

SERVINGS: 2

PREPARATION TIME: 30 MINUTES

¼ cup raw rice of your choice
1 banana, thinly sliced
1 pear, diced
1 apple, diced
¼ cup each cooked ham and cooked
    chicken, diced in ⅓-inch cubes
12 pineapple chunks
4 leaves lettuce

2 oranges, sliced
¼ cup heavy cream, whipped
⅓ cup mayonnaise (pages 42–43)
1 tablespoon lemon juice
Salt and pepper
1½ tablespoons dried currants
1 tablespoon chopped walnuts

Boil the rice until tender but not mushy; drain it and pat it dry. Mix it with the banana slices, the pear, apple, ham, and chicken cubes, and the pineapple chunks. Toss all these ingredients well. Arrange the lettuce leaves and the orange slices around a platter, and in its center put the fruit mixture. Fold the whipped cream into the mayonnaise; add a dash of lemon juice and a pinch each of salt and pepper, if desired. Pour over the fruit and sprinkle with the combined currants and walnuts.

As dessert, serve a piece of plain cake or cookies.

The author of this recipe lives in Algiers. She neither reads nor writes —and she has memorized hundreds of recipes.

SHRIMP SALAD FATMA

SERVINGS: 6

PREPARATION TIME: 1 HOUR 15 MINUTES

3 tablespoons red wine vinegar
2 tablespoons prepared Dijon mustard
1 small red onion, very finely chopped
2 tablespoons green peppercorns, packed in their own juice or in vinegar
¾ cup olive oil

2 tablespoons chopped flat-leafed parsley
2 pounds medium boiled shrimp (page 230)
6 sweet red peppers
6 sweet green peppers
12 fresh plum tomatoes, sliced
3 tablespoons chopped fresh coriander

Combine the vinegar, mustard, onion, green peppercorns, and oil into a dressing. (It is a good idea to rinse the peppercorns under running water to discard their outer membrane before adding them to it.) Toss the shrimp with ⅔ of the dressing. Cut each pepper, red and green, into quarters, discarding all the ribs and seeds. Flatten the quarters on a cookie sheet, skin side up. Broil them slowly, 4 inches away from the flame, until they blister, then wrap them in several layers of paper towels. Unrolling the paper towels only as you go along, peel the skin off each pepper wedge. Peel the tomatoes by immersing them in boiling water for 2 minutes, then pulling the skin off. Slice the tomatoes lengthwise.

Arrange the platter as follows: Make an outer border by overlapping the tomato slices; sprinkle the tomatoes with the chopped coriander. Then make a second border by overlapping the pepper wedges, alternating the colors. In the center of the platter, pile the shrimp salad and sprinkle it with a ribbon of chopped parsley. Dribble the remainder of the dressing on the tomatoes and peppers.

As dessert, serve fresh fruit.

PLAIN SALADS SERVED WITH DINNER

To prepare a head of lettuce, escarole, romaine, or chicory: wash it first under running cold water, then separate the leaves and tear bite-sized pieces from the center rib. Wash the edible pieces of greens at least twice under running water, then blot them dry in a terry towel.

Peel tomatoes and peppers, if you desire, as indicated in shrimp salad Fatma (page 250).

Prepared greens and vegetables for salad and salad dressings should be chilled separately if they have to wait in the refrigerator; a green salad should be tossed only at serving time to prevent wilting. Salads of sliced vegetables such as tomatoes, zucchini, and onions should be arranged tastefully on a serving platter and then chilled. Only avocado slices must be tossed with their dressing early to prevent oxidation; the dressings of all other sliced vegetables should be spooned over them just before serving.

For dressing, use one of the plain vinaigrettes (page 246). Or, if you prefer, for acid use yogurt or sour cream (as much as you enjoy when tasting). The choice of the oil is yours, the best taste coming from olive, walnut, and sunflower oil.

COMBINATIONS:

In the following list the ingredients listed on the left agree particularly well with the dressing components appearing opposite them on the right:

Sliced cucumbers and romaine	Vinaigrette made with sour cream and dill
Boston lettuce, avocado, and hard-boiled egg	Vinaigrette made with lime (juice and rind) and olive oil
Romaine, white part of 1 leek, and 2 tablespoons chopped walnuts	Vinaigrette made with lemon juice, half heavy cream and half walnut oil
Raw mushrooms and fresh spinach leaves	Vinaigrette, plus anchovy paste
Boston lettuce with orange and grapefruit sections	Vinaigrette made with lemon juice and heavy cream

Boston lettuce, sliced red radishes, and green peppercorns preserved in vinegar	Plain vinaigrette
Boston lettuce and finely sliced fennel	Plain lemon juice and olive oil dressing
Finely sliced cauliflower, watercress, and tomatoes	Plain vinaigrette, plus a bit of Dijon mustard
Romaine and cucumbers	Lemon juice and olive oil, plus 1 teaspoon chopped fresh mint
Sliced tomatoes, peeled or unpeeled	Vinaigrette, plus 1 chopped shallot and chopped basil leaves
Sliced tomatoes and fennel	Olive oil and lemon juice
Belgian endive and orange slices	Vinaigrette, plus prepared Dijon mustard
Romaine, cherry tomatoes, green pepper, marinated olives, and feta cheese	Lime juice and rind, olive oil, and an abundant sprinkling of fresh dill
Grated carrots	Sour cream or yogurt, plus olive oil, a tiny clove of mashed garlic and a healthy addition of chopped parsley
Escarole, garlic croutons and crumbled bacon	Vinaigrette, plus blue cheese and sour cream
Tomatoes and cucumbers	Vinaigrette, plus chopped dill
Tomatoes and julienne of peppers	Olive oil and lemon juice, plus 1 chopped shallot
Cooked small green beans, kept slightly crunchy	Vinaigrette, plus finely chopped shallot and prepared Dijon mustard
Tomatoes, sliced zucchini, and sliced red onion	Olive oil and lemon juice, plus prepared Dijon mustard
Tomatoes and avocado	Olive oil and lime (juice and rind), plus chopped fresh coriander leaves
Iceberg lettuce and Romaine	Lime (juice and rind) and olive oil, plus a pinch of fresh mint

FRESH VEGETABLES

The world of vegetable cookery is such a jungle of variety that in this chapter I have restricted my listing of recipes to those that are definitely the fastest.

Avoid long baking and braising; cook the vegetables in the shortest possible time to preserve the vitamins. The controversy remains over whether to boil vegetables covered, in a very small amount of salted water, or uncovered, in a large amount of salted water kept at a rolling boil; there is still much discussion on which method is nutritionally better. The fact is that you will lose vitamins either way, so from the two methods choose the one that, for your personal taste, gives the best results for taste, texture, and color.

To cream boiled vegetables, roll them in white (cream) sauce, well seasoned, and flavored with a pinch of nutmeg (page 35). Plain boiled vegetables are best seasoned with salt, pepper, and a bit of fresh butter or a compound butter (page 38). If butter is off your list, use unsalted margarine.

You can also pan-fry some vegetables—preferably in oil, in a frying pan—or even stir-fry them (the Chinese way of pan-frying), which is done over a blasting flame, usually in a wok, but it can also be done in a very large frying pan. The great advantage of stir frying over the other methods is that it keeps a larger amount of vitamins; but its great disadvantage is the cutting of the vegetables into bite-sized pieces, which can be time consuming for inexperienced hands.

The deep-frying process can also be used, but with the usual reservations for fried food in the everyday diet.

If it is no sin when one works long hours to use frozen vegetables, it definitely remains a sacrilege to use those vegetables sold frozen in all types of horrible gooey cream sauces, sweet and sour sauces, or so-called gourmet European sauces. Please use your own butter, your own cream sauce—the taste of your vegetable dishes will be better and their calorie producing capacities lower.

BASIC PROPORTIONS FOR VEGETABLE SERVINGS

	1–2	3–4	5–6
Fresh vegetable, to be peeled and trimmed	¾ lb.	1 lb.	1½ lbs.
Frozen vegetable, already peeled and trimmed	5 oz.	10 oz.	20 oz.
If creamed you will need	½ cup light white sauce	1 cup light white sauce	1¼ cups light white sauce

APPLES

As a vegetable:

PAN-FRY: Peel (because of wax coating) and slice apples. Pan-fry in butter or tasteless oil (sunflower, corn, etc., *not* olive). Season with a pinch of cinnamon or lemon rind.

USES: Preferably with pork and poultry.

ARTICHOKES

Small frozen hearts:

PAN-FRY: Defrost small frozen artichoke hearts, cut in quarters, and pan-fry in butter or olive oil. Sprinkle with tarragon.

BOIL: Immerse small frozen artichoke hearts, still frozen, in boiling salted water. Serve with fresh butter or margarine plus lemon juice.

USES: Preferably with veal, poultry, ham.

ARTICHOKES

Large fresh:

BOIL: In a large amount of salted water, cook large fresh artichokes until the bottoms are easily pierced by a skewer. Serve with vinaigrette (page 246) or mayonnaise (pages 42–43).

USES: Preferably with veal, poultry, ham.

ASPARAGUS

When fresh asparagus are bent from head to root, they break naturally at the place where the stem stops being edible. Peel asparagus from the top down with a potato peeler. Frozen asparagus is easily peeled while still solidly frozen. (Peeling prevents uneven cooking of tip and stalk.) Tie asparagus in bundles of even-sized stalks.

BOIL: In a large amount of salted water cook medium asparagus 6 minutes; large asparagus, 9 minutes; jumbo asparagus, 10 to 11 minutes. Serve with lemon butter or hollandaise (page 39). It is delicious, too, plain with just salt and pepper.

CHINESE-STEAM: Use tiny asparagus, cut in 1-inch pieces; do not peel. Place on flat Chinese steaming basket in one single layer. Place over boiling water, cover, and steam 3 to 4 minutes. The asparagus will be crunchy.

STIR-FRY: Stir-fry in oil, cut in 1-inch pieces. The asparagus will be crunchy.

USES: With all egg dishes; preferably with white meats, but also with red meats.

BEANS
Green and wax:

BOIL: For *fresh beans,* 7 to 8 minutes for small beans; 10 to 12 minutes for large beans. Season with fresh butter, lemon juice, and parsley; garlic and parsley; or cream with a good pinch of nutmeg. For *frozen beans,* boil 5 minutes.

STIR-FRY: Use frozen frenched beans, defrosted and dried well in a terry towel. Stir-fry in oil.

USES: With all meats.

BROCCOLI AND CAULIFLOWER

BOIL: For fresh, cut in flowerets, 8 minutes in a large amount of water. For *frozen,* 4 to 5 minutes. Serve with butter or margarine and chives.

STIR-FRY: In oil of your choice, sprinkled with sesame seeds.

USES: With all meats.

CABBAGE

For all methods, cut in thin strips with knife or vegetable cutter.

STIR-FRY: For fresh flavor, crunchiness and maximum vitamins. Use oil, just sprinkle with salt and pepper.

BOIL: Very fast in boiling salted water. Drain, pat dry, and season with fresh butter or unsalted margarine and caraway seeds.

USES: Best with pork.

CARROTS

Fresh only, please; the frozen ones are *dead*.

BOIL: 7 to 8 minutes, peeled and cut in chunks. Season with butter and nutmeg, or butter, parsley, and lemon juice.

STIR-FRY: Peel and cut in julienne with a vegetable cutter. Stir-fry in oil and season with salt, pepper, lemon juice, and fresh chopped parsley.

USES: Best with veal and poultry.

CORN

BOIL: On the cob; use only fresh. Immerse in violently boiling salted water, bring water back to a boil, remove the pot from the heat, and serve with plain butter, salt, and pepper.

    Off the cob; use fresh or frozen corn, preferably the pale yellow niblets. Immerse in boiling water, turn the heat off, and let stand a few minutes. Drain and season with salt and pepper, a pinch of sugar, and fresh butter.

USES: Best with broiled meats, red or white.

CUCUMBERS

Peel and cut in quarters lengthwise, cut out the seeds, and cut in small triangular pieces.

BOIL: 3 to 4 minutes in salted water. Season with butter and herb of your choice (tarragon, mint, basil, or dill).

USES: Preferably with all white meats.

EGGPLANT

PAN-FRY: Use only small eggplants. Slice them ⅓ inch thick, sprinkle with salt, and let stand about 20 minutes. Rinse, pat dry, and flour.

Pan-fry in olive oil or oil of your choice. Serve with chopped garlic and parsley.

USES: All meats; best with pan-fried lamb or beef.

MUSHROOMS

PAN-FRY: Slice the mushrooms and pan-fry in butter or oil on high heat until the moisture has evaporated. Add salt, pepper, chopped garlic, and parsley.

STIR-FRY: Slice the mushrooms and stir-fry 2 to 3 minutes in oil. Add salt and pepper and serve plain; or blend Dijon mustard and freshly chopped parsley into the mushroom juices.

USES: All meats, red or white.

ONIONS

PAN-FRY: *Sliced:* On rather high heat at first, to color, in oil or butter; turn heat down to cook through. Just before serving, sprinkle with a pinch of salt and sugar and a bit of pepper.

BRAISE: This is an exception. Put small frozen silverskin onions in a small covered saucepan with 1 tablespoon butter, 1 tablespoon water, salt, and pepper. Cook 30 minutes on low heat. Add chopped parsley.

USES: For pan-fried, all roasted or pan-fried red meats; for braised, all white meats, especially veal.

PEAS

BOIL: *Medium peas:* boil 5 minutes with a sprig of mint. Serve with butter and just a touch of orange rind.

BRAISE: *Small early peas:* this is an exception. Braise with chopped Boston lettuce leaves and 1 or 2 white onions, salt, pepper, and a pinch of sugar. Cooking time will be about 15 minutes.

SWEET PEPPERS

Red and green bell peppers, long Italian peppers.

PAN-FRY: Cut in slivers or julienne. Pan-fry on medium heat in olive oil or other oil of your choice until the juices run out of the vegetable and it starts to discolor. Add Provençal herbs (page 12), oregano, or a good pinch of cumin.

STIR-FRY: Cut in slivers or julienne. Stir-fry on high heat in oil of your choice to keep brightly colored and crunchy.

USES: All dishes of meat and poultry.

POTATOES

Use only fresh potatoes; canned or frozen potatoes are spoiled potatoes. As portions use 1 small potato per person. As a matter of interest, one potato weighing 4 ounces will produce the following amount of calories, depending on how it is cooked:

> Boiled: 87 calories
> Baked: 106 calories
> Pan-fried in oil: 250 to 325 calories

The offender to your weight is not the potato itself but whatever you put on it:

> Butter (1 T.): 100 calories
> Margarine (1 T.): 100 calories
> Sour cream (1 T.): 29 calories

BOIL: In jackets (new potatoes, red potatoes). Boil 20 minutes, starting the cooking in cold water. Serve plain, rolled in meat juice, or with minimum amount of butter or sour cream, salt, and pepper.

Peeled and cut in 1½-inch cubes (Russet or Maine potatoes). Boil in water or stock for 20 minutes. Add either butter or sour cream, and any of the following herbs or seasonings: mint, chives, tarragon, basil, parsley, dill, cumin, or Swiss or any other cheese.

Peeled, cut, and mashed. Boil in water 20 minutes. Strain through a conical strainer, using the bottom of a highball glass as a pestle. Add, for each 2 persons, a bit of butter and/or 1 slice crumbled bacon or chives, a solid pinch of nutmeg, or 1 tablespoon crumbled blue cheese of your choice.

BAKE: If you do not mind the time and heat in the kitchen, wash, prick, and bake Idaho or Maine potatoes 1 hour at 400° F.

PAN-FRY: In ½-inch layer of oil and/or butter or mixture of both. Seal on high heat to build a golden crust outside, turn the heat down to cook through, then raise the heat again to finish coloring. Drain on several layers of crumpled paper towels.

Sliced potatoes will crisp in 10 minutes; ½-inch cubes of raw potato will crisp and cook in 15 to 20 minutes.

Salt the potatoes when they are done only. You may add any chopped herb you like; best are parsley, dill, and caraway seeds mixed. Or you can mix the fried potatoes with 2 shallots or 2 scallions, or the white of 1 leek or 1 onion or 1 red or green pepper, slivered and fried golden in a matter of minutes in the same oil as the potatoes.

USES: For boiled, in skin or cubed plain, with fish; cubed or mashed and seasoned with any meat, adapting the seasoning to the meat. For baked, with all red meats and roasted poultry. For pan-fried, with all red pan-fried meats.

Sweet Potatoes

BOIL: Peel and cut in 1-inch cubes. Boil 15 minutes. Serve with plain butter, salt, and pepper.

USES: Preferably with white meats.

Squash

PAN-FRY: Summer squash and young zucchini on medium heat with salt and pepper until juices start running out of vegetables. Add chopped parsley, dill or basil.

Large zucchini should be cut in large slices slantwise, floured, and pan-fried in olive oil on high heat until golden on both sides. Serve with garlic and parsley, finely chopped.

As for winter squash, specifically butternut squash, peel and cut in slices ⅓ inch thick. Pan-fry in butter or plain vegetable oil on initial high heat, then turn the heat down to cook through. Recrisp just before serving with salt and pepper.

USES: Summer squash—all meats and poultry, winter squash—poultry.

Spinach and Other Greens (Mustard, Chard, Beet Greens)

BOIL: Use frozen whole-leaf spinach and other greens; the chopped ones contain second-choice leaves that were bruised or even stained before freezing.

> For 2 minutes after coming to a second boil. Drain and squeeze excess water out with a high-ball glass. Season with a bit of butter and/or nutmeg. You may also use grated Parmesan cheese; 1 slice cooked, crumbled bacon for each 2 persons; 1 hard-boiled egg chopped for each 2 persons.

STIR-FRY: Wash fresh greens well and pat dry in a towel. Chop coarsely and stir-fry on blasting heat for 1 or 2 minutes.

USES: With all meats and poultry.

Tomatoes

Only fresh, sun-ripened tomatoes must be used in cooking; the winter hothouse tomatoes are lifeless and tasteless—good only for the decoration of salads.

Some high-quality, expensive, vine-ripened winter tomatoes from California can successfully be ripened in the warmth of a winter kitchen and acquire some flavor: buy those tomatoes in fancy greengrocers' stores; they are not to be found in supermarkets. To prepare summer and high-quality winter tomatoes (beefsteak tomatoes):

PAN-FRY: Cut the tomatoes in ⅓-inch slices. Flour and pan-fry on high heat in olive oil or oil of your choice for 2 minutes on each side. Serve with salt and pepper and finely-scissored basil leaves, or with garlic and parsley.

QUICK STEW: Use exclusively Italian plum tomatoes. Cut in quarters. Sauté on medium heat until tomatoes lose their natural juices. Add either garlic and parsley, chopped parsley or chopped dill.

BROIL: Cut large tomatoes in half; push out the seeds with the fingertips. Sprinkle with olive oil and Provençal herbs (page 12) and broil 4 inches from the source of heat for 3 to 4 minutes.

USES: With all meats and poultry.

To prepare canned tomatoes (for winter use): use well-drained Italian, Greek, or California plum tomatoes: can be used for pan-frying in the winter when high-quality tomatoes are not available. Drain them very well.

PAN-FRY: On very high heat in olive oil or other oil of your choice; season with chopped parsley and garlic, Provençal herbs (page 12), oregano, basil, or dill.

USES: With all meats and poultry.

GRAINS

The grains are the classic white rice, bulghur, cornmeal, the newly popular wheat berries (wheat kernels), barley, millet, and brown rice. All whole grains are a welcome addition to the modern diet. If you have never eaten anything rougher than bland, tasteless white rice, make sure that you start with half portions of whole grains so that your internal equilibrium does not find itself jolted by all the bran whole-grain cereals contain.

In the following recipes, each grain has been treated and cooked the fastest possible way; grain leftovers may be used in soups.

RICE

WHITE RICE PILAF

BASIC PROPORTIONS FOR WHITE RICE PILAF

2 servings	*3–4 servings*	*5–6 servings*
1 chopped onion	2 small chopped onions	2 large chopped onions
1½ T. butter or oil of your choice	2 T. butter or oil of your choice	¼ cup butter or oil of your choice
½ cup long-grain rice	1 cup long-grain rice	1½ cup long-grain rice
1 cup hot stock of your choice *	2 cups hot stock of your choice *	3 cups hot stock of your choice *
Salt and pepper	Salt and pepper	Salt and pepper
Seasonings of your choice (pages 263–264), if desired	Seasonings of your choice (pages 263–264), if desired	Seasonings of your choice (pages 263–264), if desired

* Note that the volume of liquid is always twice that of rice.

KEY RECIPE: Use this method of cooking rice in preference to any one given on the commercial rice box. Sauté the onion in butter until golden. Add the rice and toss in the butter until the grains burn the top of your hand. Add the hot stock; if you have no stock, water will do. Bring to a boil, add salt and pepper and seasonings of your choice, if desired. Stretch a paper towel over the opening of the pot to catch the steam and cover with the pot lid. Let cook 20 minutes on slow heat. Stir with the fluff the rice.

STEAMED BROWN RICE

BASIC PROPORTIONS

2 servings	*3–4 servings*	*5–6 servings*
1 cup stock of your choice or water *	2 cups stock of your choice or water *	3 cups stock of your choice or water *
½ cup brown rice	1 cup brown rice	1½ cups brown rice
1 T. butter or oil of your choice	1½ T. butter or oil of your choice	2 T. butter or oil of your choice
Salt and pepper	Salt and pepper	Salt and pepper
Seasonings of your choice (pages 263–264), if desired	Seasonings of your choice (pages 263–264), if desired	Seasonings of your choice (pages 263–264), if desired

* Note that the volume of liquid is twice that of the rice.

KEY RECIPE: Use a double boiler. Bring the stock to a boil in the top part of the double boiler over high, direct heat. Add the rice and butter or oil. Add salt and pepper and the seasonings. Bring back to a boil. Meanwhile, bring 2 cups of water to a boil in the bottom container of the double boiler. Place the container of rice over the boiling water, stretch a paper towel over it, and cover it with the pot lid. Cook 30 to 35 minutes, or until the rice has absorbed all the liquid. Fluff with a fork.

SEASONINGS FOR RICE   The taste of the basic pilaf or steamed brown rice can be modified by adding any of the following seasonings:

FOR EVERY DAY (2 *servings*)

CURRY: Use ⅓ teaspoon for each serving. Cook the curry in the butter or oil used in the cooking of the rice.

ONIONS AND SHALLOTS: Sauté 1 small chopped onion or 1 small finely minced shallot in the butter or oil used in the cooking of the rice.

ANCHOVY PASTE: Dissolve anchovy paste in the water before cooking the rice. Add as much as you personally like, but watch the salt level of your dish.

TOMATOES OR TOMATO PASTE: Add 1 sautéed tomato per person, plus chopped garlic and parsley, or dissolve 2 teaspoons tomato paste in the stock before cooking the rice.

SAFFRON: Add saffron to the stock according to your taste and budget before adding it to the pan.

SAFFRON AND BASIL: Add saffron and crumbled basil to the stock.

HERBS: Add any chopped fresh herb of your choice to the cooked rice.

CHEESE: Add the quantity of cheese you desire to the cooked rice. The very best melting cheese for rice is the Italian Fontina.

NUTS AND RAISINS: Add the quantity of nuts and dark raisins you desire to the cooked rice. Use the nuts you like; but walnuts, pecans, pine nuts, and cashews will be better if you pan-fry them a bit in butter before adding them to the rice.

FOR COMPANY DINNERS (6 *servings*)

BLACK TRUFFLES: Add 1 small diced black truffle to the white rice pilaf only, after the rice has finished cooking.

WHITE TRUFFLES: Add 1 small diced white truffle to the white rice pilaf only, after the rice has finished cooking.

WHITE TRUFFLES, FONTINA, AND PROSCIUTTO: Add 1 small sliced white truffle, ½ cup finely diced fontina, and 3 tablespoons finely chopped prosciutto to the white rice pilaf only, after the rice has finished cooking.

MUSHROOMS: Add ¼ pound coarsely chopped mushrooms, presautéed in butter or oil and flavored with chopped garlic and parsley.

OTHER GRAINS

STEAMED WHOLE-WHEAT BERRIES

BASIC PROPORTIONS FOR
STEAMED WHOLE-WHEAT BERRIES

2 servings	*3–4 servings*	*5–6 servings*
½ cup wheat berries	1 cup wheat berries	1½ cups wheat berries
1 cup stock or broth of your choice *	2 cups stock or broth of your choice *	3 cups stock or broth of your choice *
1 T. butter or oil of your choice	1½ T. butter or oil of your choice	2 T. butter or oil of your choice
Salt and pepper	Salt and pepper	Salt and pepper

* Note that the amount of liquid is twice that of the berries.

KEY RECIPE: Soak the berries overnight at room temperature, in just enough water to cover them. To cook them, immerse them in the cold stock and bring to a boil. Add butter, salt, and pepper and simmer until the berries have tripled their volume and start breaking open, or about 40 minutes.

STEAMED BULGHUR

BASIC PROPORTIONS FOR BULGHUR

2 servings	*3–4 servings*	*5–6 servings*
½ cup bulghur	1 cup bulghur	1½ cups bulghur
1 T. butter or oil of your choice	1½ T. butter or oil of your choice	2 T. butter or oil of your choice
1 cup hot stock of your choice *	2 cups hot stock of your choice *	3 cups hot stock of your choice *
Salt and pepper	Salt and pepper	Salt and pepper
Seasonings of your choice (page 266), if desired	Seasonings of your choice (page 266), if desired	Seasonings of your choice (page 266), if desired

* Note that the volume of liquid is twice that of grain.

KEY RECIPE: Sauté the bulghur in the hot butter until it is well coated with fat and the cereal burns the top of your hand. Add the hot stock, salt, pepper, and seasoning of your choice, if desired. Cover with a paper towel to catch the steam, then with the pot lid, and cook on slow heat for 20 minutes.

STEAMED MILLET

BASIC PROPORTIONS FOR STEAMED MILLET

2 servings	*3–4 servings*	*5–6 servings*
1⅓ cups stock of your choice *	2⅔ cups stock of your choice *	4 cups stock of your choice *
⅓ cup millet	⅔ cup millet	1 cup millet
1 T. butter or oil of your choice	1½ T. butter or oil of your choice	2 T. butter or oil of your choice
Seasonings of your choice (page 266), if desired	Seasonings of your choice (page 266), if desired	Seasonings of your choice (page 266), if desired

* Note that the volume of liquid is 4 times that of the millet.

KEY RECIPE: Proceed exactly as for whole-wheat berries (page 264), but without presoaking. The cooking time is around 35 minutes.

CORNMEAL POLENTA

BASIC PROPORTIONS FOR CORNMEAL POLENTA

2 servings	*3–4 servings*	*5–6 servings*
1½ cups stock of your choice or water	3 cups stock of your choice or water	6 cups stock of your choice or water
6 T. yellow cornmeal	¾ cup yellow cornmeal	1½ cups yellow cornmeal
Salt and pepper	Salt and pepper	Salt and pepper
1 T. butter	1½ T. butter	2 T. butter
Seasoning of your choice (see below), if desired	Seasoning of your choice (see below), if desired	Seasoning of your choice (see below), if desired

* Note that the volume of liquid is 4 times that of the cornmeal.

KEY RECIPE: Bring the stock to a violent boil, add the cornmeal in one continuous stream, stirring, until the mixture reboils. Cook, stirring occasionally, for about 25 minutes or until the spoon can stand in the mixture. Stir in the butter and seasoning.

If you wish to add extra seasoning, you could add 1 slice cooked, crumbled bacon for each 2 persons or you could sprinkle each portion with 1 tablespoon grated Parmesan, Sardo, Romano, Gruyère, or Fontina cheese.

SEASONINGS FOR OTHER GRAINS Although these grains have a lovely, rich, unusual flavor, you can add to them (with the exception of the cornmeal polenta, seasonings for which are given with the recipe) any of the following herbs to make a variation from the basic recipe:

Chopped fresh scallions; parsley; marjoram; garlic; parsley and garlic, mixed together; dill; French thyme or lemon thyme; rosemary; green and red peppers; celery.

STARCHES

NOODLES

The fastest available noodle dishes can be made by using commercial enriched egg noodles or whole-wheat egg noodles bought in an honest organic food store.

Cook the noodles as indicated on the package and keep them slightly chewy, or as the consecrated Italian expression goes, al dente. As portions use 2 to 3 ounces of noodles per person, which is equivalent to 1 pound for 6.

Seasonings for noodles can be found on page 269.

SPAETZLE

If you like fresh noodles but have no time to make them, try making spaetzle, the little batter dumplings of Switzerland and Germany. They are finished in a matter of minutes, taste delicious, and are seasoned exactly like noodles. You might even like to try them on company; although spaetzle are no deluxe item, they are delicious and novel enough to please palates that have never encountered them.

The white-flour spaetzle are better for taste, the whole-wheat for nutrition. The bran in whole-wheat spaetzle gives them a lightly crunchy texture which can be quite pleasing or quite unpleasant, according to your taste. Try both and see which you prefer. They are prepared exactly the same way.

WHITE-FLOUR SPAETZLE

BASIC PROPORTIONS FOR WHITE-FLOUR SPAETZLE

2 *servings*	3–4 *servings*	5–6 *servings*
⅔ cup flour	1 cup flour	1½ cups flour
2 small eggs	3 eggs	4 large or 5 small eggs
2–3 T. milk	¼–⅓ cup milk	½ cup milk
¼ tsp. salt	½ tsp. salt	¾ tsp. salt
⅛ tsp. grated nutmeg	¼ tsp. grated nutmeg	¾ tsp. grated nutmeg

WHOLE-WHEAT FLOUR SPAETZLE

BASIC PROPORTIONS FOR WHOLE-WHEAT FLOUR SPAETZLE

2 *servings*	3–4 *servings*	5–6 *servings*
⅔ cup whole-wheat flour	1¼ cups whole-wheat flour	2 cups whole-wheat flour
2 small eggs	3 eggs	5 eggs
2 T. milk	¼ cup milk	7 T. milk
¼ tsp. salt	½ tsp. salt	¾ tsp. salt

KEY RECIPE: Bring a large pot of water to a boil. Add 1½ teaspoons salt per quart of water and turn down to a simmer.

Put the flour, eggs, milk, salt, and nutmeg, if used, in a mixing bowl and stir with a whisk until you obtain a smooth batter. Pour about ½ cup of the batter on a small chopping board or on the bottom of a clean 9-inch cake pan. With a long spatula, shave ¼-inch ribbons of batter directly into the salted water; the spaetzle are cooked in a matter of minutes, just as soon as they come floating to the surface of the water. Lift them out with a slotted spoon and rinse them under warm water; repeat with the remainder of the batter and season with salt, pepper, and butter, or any other fat or oil of your choice.

SEASONINGS FOR NOODLES AND SPAETZLE As a seasoning choose any of the following for all noodles and spaetzle:

Cracked black pepper

Poppy seeds and a pinch of grated lemon rind

Chopped fresh or crumbled dried basil and grated Parmesan cheese

Grated cheese of your choice (Swiss, fontina, hickory-smoked, Cheddar, and Parmesan are the best)

Brown rather than fresh butter

Imported Hungarian paprika

Chopped fresh scallions and a few drops of soy sauce

Any fresh herb, such as parsley, plain or combined with garlic; dill; tarragon; basil

Chopped Italian parsley, garlic, and chopped Italian salami

GNOCCHI OR NOCKERLN

Gnocchi, or nockerln, are quick, lovely little dumplings, whose principal virtues are that they cook fast and taste delicious. Their principal drawback is that they need loads of butter to taste good. So you may want to keep gnocchi for your quick-cookery entertaining.

BASIC PROPORTIONS FOR GNOCCHI

2 servings	3–4 servings	5–6 servings
½ cup water	1 cup water	1½ cups water
2 T. butter or margarine	¼ cup butter or margarine	6 T. butter or margarine
Large pinch of salt	½ tsp. salt	¾ tsp. salt
Pepper	Pepper	Pepper
½ cup sifted flour	1 cup sifted flour	1½ cups sifted flour
1 jumbo egg	2 jumbo eggs	3 jumbo eggs
Pinch of grated nutmeg	¼ tsp. grated nutmeg	⅓ tsp. nutmeg

KEY RECIPE: Bring a large pot of water to a boil. Add 1½ teaspoons salt per quart of water, turn down to a simmer, and keep ready to cook the gnocchi.

Put the water, butter, salt, and pepper in a large saucepan and bring to a boil. Remove the pot from the heat and add the flour. Mix until a ball forms. Return to the burner and stir well, on high heat, for a few minutes. Remove from the heat and beat in the eggs, one by one.

Although the following method may seem complicated to a novice, it is the easiest for shaping the gnocchi. Fit a pastry bag with a plain ½-inch nozzle and put the batter in the bag. With your left hand squeeze ¾-inch pieces of batter out of the bag and cut each piece off with the back of a knife, letting it fall into the simmering pot of water.

The gnocchi, which cook in a matter of minutes, are done just as soon as they come floating to the surface of the water. Remove them to a colander, using a slotted spoon, and season them immediately with butter or cream.

SEASONINGS FOR GNOCCHI All the seasonings given for noodles and spaetzle (page 269) are usable, but you may want to try these other ideas for quick-cookery entertaining (the proportions given are for 6 persons):

For beef, reduce 1 cup heavy cream by half, then add 1 tablespoon chopped fresh chives

For chicken or veal, 1 finely chopped white or black truffle

For any meat, 1 tablespoon imported Hungarian paprika and 2 small onions, finely chopped and cooked in butter until soft

CHAPTER XIV

Quicker Desserts

FRUIT DESSERTS

All-fruit desserts are best for polyunsaturated diets.

FRESH FRUIT

The quickest and fastest of all desserts—and the healthiest, too—is a piece of delicious fresh fruit. Fresh fruit, alas, unless you have your own fruit trees, is almost a headache for the busy person. Most of the fruit sold is picked green and then refrigerated; if sugar does not form in its pulp, the result is a very disappointing mouthful of hard, grainy tartness, if not acidity. To buy fresh fruit in a supermarket is to play Russian roulette with your taste buds and your pocketbook! Plan ahead, if you can; buy the best quality offered by a better grocery store. Keep the fruit in a paper bag in a not too warm room and open the bag at regular intervals—your nose will tell you when pears, peaches, apricots, or nectarines are ready. Berries will be sold to you almost ready to eat, but a 24-hour stay in a paper bag placed in the vegetable crisper of the refrigerator will bring on a last ripening, which will make the difference between eating vaguely flavored acid water and a true berry.

FRUIT SALADS
Fruit salads are a mixture of cut-up uncooked fruit.

KEY RECIPE: Peel and cut the fruit in small slices or dice; add a flavoring, if desired—a liquor or brandy. Let the fruit marinate in the liquor for as much as two hours. Five minutes before serving, add as much sugar—or better, as much honey—as you desire, and toss well.

The flavorings mentioned below will blend best with the fruits they accompany:

Oranges	Grand Marnier, Curaçao, Cointreau, Triple Sec
Cantaloupe	Tawny port or white port
Honeydew melon	Marsala
Strawberries	Kirsch, Curaçao, Grand Marnier
Raspberries	Framboise (raspberry brandy), kirsch
Fresh red and black currants	Cassis
Blueberries	Lime juice and rind and a bit of bourbon
Apples	Applejack or Calvados, rum
Pineapple	White rum
Peaches	Curaçao, Triple Sec
Pears	Pear brandy or liqueur, almond liqueur, Cassis, Grand Marnier
Grapefruit	White rum or a red berry juice or puree
Italian plums	Dark rum, or quetsche (plum brandy) or slivovitz
Cherries	Maraschino, cherry brandy, kirsch

GRAPEFRUIT IN RASPBERRY SAUCE

SERVINGS: 2

PREPARATION TIME: 10 MINUTES

1 small pink grapefruit
1 small white grapefruit

1 box frozen raspberries, defrosted
Honey to taste

Peel the grapefruit down to the pulp and separate the slices. Place half the slices of each grapefruit into 2 dessert bowls or glasses. Defrost the berries in hot water, then drain the canning syrup completely. Puree the berries in the blender, add honey to suit your taste, and spoon over the grapefruit slices. (If you are quick, finding 2 minutes to strain the puree over the fruit will make all the difference in the world!)

NARCISSA CHAMBERLAIN'S BERRY SALAD

SERVINGS: 6

PREPARATION TIME: 10 MINUTES

1 quart strawberries
1 pint each raspberries and blueberries

Lemon juice
2 to 3 tablespoons raspberry brandy
Sugar to taste

Hull and wash the strawberries. Pick over the raspberries and blueberries. Sprinkle with lemon juice and the raspberry brandy. Toss well and refrigerate. Just before serving, sprinkle with sugar to taste.

FRUIT COMPOTES

Use fresh fruit in later spring, summer and fall and dried fruit soaked overnight in a bit of white wine during the winter months and early spring.

KEY RECIPE: Peel the fruit first, if you want, to remove the preservatives and waxes that are present on most purchased fruit. (To peel a thin-skinned fruit such as an apricot or a peach, immerse it 1 minute in boiling water.) Mix water or wine and sugar (¾ cup sugar for each 2 cups of liquid) in a frying pan and add the fruit, peeled, if you desire, and cut in halves or quarters. Let poach until a large needle goes in and out freely. (That is the only way to test the doneness of fruit, since every single fruit has a different cooking time.)

Use only a small amount of the syrup to serve with the fruit. Keep the remainder refrigerated to cook other fruit.

APRICOT COMPOTE

SERVINGS: 2

PREPARATION TIME: 15 MINUTES

6 large, ripe apricots
1 cup water
⅓ cup sugar

1½ teaspoons apricot jam
2 teaspoons kirsch, Cognac, or Curaçao

Peel and poach the fruit according to the key recipe (page 273). Remove the fruit to a serving dish. Mix ¼ cup syrup with the apricot jam and the liqueur and pour over the fruit.

ORANGE COMPOTE

SERVINGS: 6

PREPARATION TIME: 20 MINUTES

6 large oranges, preferably navels
⅔ cup sugar
1 cup orange juice

1 teaspoon orange flower water (optional)
2 tablespoons Cognac or brandy

Peel the oranges down to the pulp with a knife and slice them in ¼-inch slices. Put them in a serving dish. Bring the sugar and orange juice to a boil and pour it, boiling hot, over the oranges. Let cool to room temperature, then add the orange flower water, if desired, and Cognac or brandy. Spoon the syrup from the bottom of the dish to the top several times to mix well.

DRIED FRUIT COMPOTE FOR THE WINTER

SERVINGS: 6

PREPARATION TIME: 30 MINUTES, PLUS 12 HOURS FOR SOAKING THE
FRUIT

1 pound mixed dried fruit, preserved without sulfur dioxide	½ cup orange or apple juice
1½ cups dry white wine	¼ teaspoon ground cinnamon
	1 whole clove

In the morning, before going to work, wash the dried fruit and put it in a bowl. Add the white wine and let soak until you come home. Then add the juice, cinnamon, and the whole clove and put to cook on slow heat, until the fruit is tender. Transfer to a crystal dish, cool, and refrigerate.

Pass a small jar of honey for your guests to add to the fruit as they desire.

REFRESHED FRUIT

There are two kinds of refreshed fruit, those made with perfect fruit and those made with imperfect, so-called "for quick-sale" fruit.

KEY RECIPE: *With perfect fruit:* Use only perfect fruit of any type, as you would for a fruit salad. Slice it thin, add to it a bit of sugar and ⅓ cup of excellent wine or liqueur, or a mixture of both, and place in a bowl embedded in another bowl filled with ice. Toss the fruit every 5 minutes for 30 minutes.

With imperfect fruit: Pit the fruit if necessary, trim any spot or stain and slice or dice coarsely. Bring a pot of water to a boil and add the fruit. As soon as it comes floating to the top of the water, lift it with a slotted spoon and put it in a bowl. Sprinkle with a bit of sugar and chill.

MARASCHINO-REFRESHED FRUIT

SERVINGS: 6

PREPARATION TIME: 45 MINUTES, INCLUDING TIME FOR CHILLING

¼ cup blueberries
¼ cup raspberries
½ cup strawberries
¼ cup white seedless grapes
2 large, ripe pears, peeled and sliced

3 peaches, peeled and sliced
3 apricots, sliced
½ cup pitted Bing cherries
½ cup maraschino
Sugar to taste

Mix all the berries with the grapes, sliced pears, peaches, apricots, and pitted cherries. Add the maraschino, toss well, and chill on ice. Add sugar 10 minutes before serving, and only if necessary.

REFRESHED NECTARINES AND KIWI

SERVINGS: 2

TOTAL PREPARATION TIME: 10 MINUTES

2 ripe nectarines
1 kiwi fruit

3 tablespoons almond liqueur or 2 tablespoons honey

Immerse the nectarines 1 minute in boiling water and peel them. Halve them, remove the pit. Immerse the nectarine halves in the water again and let them come floating back to the surface. Peel and slice the kiwi fruit. Mix the nectarines, kiwi fruit, and almond liqueur together and chill.

Fruit Yogurt

Buy plain, unsweetened yogurt; the sweetened type is perfectly useless.

KEY RECIPE: Cut fruit to your taste into the bowl of yogurt; add a bit of honey, if you desire, and keep chilled until ready to use. This is healthy, delicious, refreshing, and made in a matter of minutes. The best com-

binations for 2 persons are made with ½ cup
yogurt and ½ cup of the following:

> Sliced strawberries
> Blueberries
> Diced peaches
> Diced pears

FLAMBÉED FRUIT

Butter, liquor, fruit, and a frying pan can help create gorgeous combinations, but watch those calories!

KEY RECIPE: Sauté the fruit in butter, sprinkle it with sugar, and flambé it with 1 ounce (2 tablespoons) of liquor. To make matters even more disastrous for your waistline—and more delicious—how about topping it off with some whipped cream? You need not buy one of those fancy flambéing pans; a good old frying pan will do.

FLAMBÉED BANANAS

SERVINGS: 2

PREPARATION TIME: 7 TO 8 MINUTES

1 tablespoon butter
2 bananas
Juice and rind of 1 orange

1 to 2 tablespoons sugar
2 tablespoons Cognac or white rum

Heat the butter. Cut each peeled banana in two lengthwise and fry in butter on each side. Mix the orange juice and rind and sugar, add to the pan, and cook 2 minutes. Add the Cognac or rum to the pan, and averting your face and head, immediately light to flambé.

FLAMBÉED PINEAPPLE

SERVINGS: 6

PREPARATION TIME: 20 MINUTES

1 large, ripe pineapple
2 tablespoons butter
½ cup unsweetened pineapple juice
¼ cup sugar

¼ cup white rum
2 tablespoons chopped macadamia
nuts

Peel the pineapple. Cut it in slices ⅓ inch thick and remove the core. Heat the butter and sauté the pineapple slices on each side until they brown a bit, then add the pineapple juice mixed with the sugar and cook until the syrup thickens. Heat the rum in a small saucepan, light it, and averting your face and head, pour it flaming over the pineapple. Sprinkle with the macadamia nuts.

QUICK DESSERT MOUSSES

You can very easily have a mousse for dessert. Make it just before dinner and eat it fast, so that it barely has time to separate.

The foam used to make a mousse can be heavy cream, whipped until semistiff—that is, until the cream falls from the beaters in soft blocks; medium cream, whipped until stiff; or egg whites, whipped until they can carry the weight of an uncooked egg in its shell. Use the latter for polyunsaturated diets, although eating raw egg white can be dangerous, for no one is ever sure that commercially sold eggs are not contaminated with salmonella.

The ingredients used to give the mousse its taste are usually either a fruit puree or egg yolk whipped with sugar and a flavoring agent.

FRUIT MOUSSES

CLASSIC FRUIT MOUSSES

In classic cookery, when time is available, a fruit mousse is best made by cooking down a fresh fruit puree and sugar to a very thick consistency, then cooling it. A foaming agent folded into the fruit base will then give it the light and airy consistency of the mousse. In quick cookery, the puree of fruit should be made as follows:

KEY RECIPE: Grate the raw fruit or mash it with a fork. Purees made in the blender will be fine if you do not mind the thin consistency of the finished mousse. Lemon juice added to the base will help make it stiffer and stabilize it. You may add a bit of liqueur to the base of any mousse—use the ideas given on page 272.

Whip the foaming agent (cream or egg whites), then beat one quarter of it into the base and fold in the remainder. Keep in the freezer until ready to use, covered with foil or plastic wrap.

BASIC PROPORTIONS FOR CLASSIC FRUIT MOUSSES

2 servings	*3–4 servings*	*5–6 servings*
⅔ cup fruit puree	1 cup fruit puree	1¼ cups fruit puree
1 tsp. lemon juice	2 tsp. lemon juice	1 T. lemon juice
1–2 T. sugar or honey	2–4 T. sugar or honey	6–8 T. sugar or honey
⅓ cup heavy or medium cream or 2 egg whites	⅔ cup heavy or medium cream or 3 egg whites	1 cup heavy or medium cream or 4 egg whites

RAW APPLE MOUSSE

SERVINGS: 6

PREPARATION TIME: 7 TO 8 MINUTES, PLUS 10 MINUTES TO PRECHILL THE CREAM

2 small apples, grated—and peeled if you desire to eliminate the wax
1 teaspoon lemon juice
1 teaspoon lemon rind, finely grated
1 tablespoon honey
1 tablespoon Calvados or applejack
⅓ cup heavy or medium cream or 2 egg whites

Mix very well the grated apples, lemon juice and rind, honey, and Calvados, then follow the key recipe (above). Keep frozen until ready to use.

BLUEBERRY MOUSSE

SERVINGS: 2

PREPARATION TIME: 7 TO 8 MINUTES, PLUS 10 MINUTES FOR
PRECHILLING THE CREAM

½ cup blueberries, mashed with a fork
1 teaspoon lemon juice
Pinch of grated lemon rind

1 tablespoon honey, or more, to taste
⅓ cup heavy or medium cream or 2 egg whites

Follow the key recipe (page 279). Keep in the freezer until ready to use.

CRANBERRY-ORANGE MOUSSE

SERVINGS: 2

PREPARATION TIME: 5 MINUTES

⅓ cup canned cranberry-orange relish
1 tablespoon Grand Marnier

⅓ cup heavy or medium cream or 2 egg whites

Mix the relish and Grand Marnier. Whip the cream or egg whites and add to the flavored relish as described in the key recipe (page 279). Keep in the freezer until ready to use.

TWO-PEAR MOUSSE

SERVINGS: 6

PREPARATION TIME: 10 MINUTES

1 large, very ripe avocado, peeled
1½ tablespoons lemon juice
Grated rind of 1 lemon
2½ tablespoons honey, or more, to taste

2 tablespoons rum
2 small jars (4½ ounces) baby-food pear puree
1¼ cups heavy cream
¼ cup chopped macadamia nuts

Puree the avocado in the blender or by pushing it through a conical sieve or strainer. Add to it 1 tablespoon of the lemon juice, the lemon rind, the honey, and half the rum. Empty the baby-food pear puree into a dish, add the remaining lemon juice and the remainder of the rum to it and mix well.

Whip the cream until it falls in soft blocks from the beaters. Fold half of it into the avocado puree and half of it into the pear puree. Pour the mousse into dessert dishes in alternate layers and stir once to obtain a marbled effect. Sprinkle each portion with a few chopped macadamia nuts.

SUPER-QUICK BLENDER FRUIT MOUSSES

KEY RECIPE: If you are in the worst of hurries, no need to take out an electric mixer and bowl—blend all ingredients together on medium high speed in the blender container. You will obtain a very quick mousse, which can be served seconds afterwards. However, the finished mousse will taste a lot better if you make it before dinner and let it chill in the freezer while you are enjoying the first part of your meal.

The very best thing to use are, of course, berries— especially strawberries and raspberries. But anything you have in the way of fruit can be prepared this way; it is a very good way to use overripe apricots, plums, nectarines, and peaches. You may, if you wish, add a bit of liqueur or brandy as indicated on page 272.

During the winter months, you can use fruit sold frozen in plastic bags without sugar syrup—or if need be, canned fruit completely drained of its canning syrup.

BLENDER STRAWBERRY MOUSSE

SERVINGS: 2

PREPARATION TIME: 5 MINUTES

⅓ cup strawberries, fresh or frozen
    and defrosted
1½ teaspoons lemon juice
1 tablespoon honey or more to taste

⅓ cup medium cream
1 tablespoon Grand Marnier,
    Curaçao, or kirsch

Follow the key recipe (page 281). Blend the liqueur into the finished mousse and chill, after pouring into 2 custard cups.

BLENDER APRICOT MOUSSE

SERVINGS: 6

PREPARATION TIME: 5 MINUTES

1⅓ cups coarsely chopped apricots,
    fresh or frozen and defrosted
2 tablespoons lemon juice
¼ cup honey, or more, to taste

1⅓ cups heavy cream
2 tablespoons kirsch or Cognac
2 tablespoons chopped pistachios

Make the mousse, following the key recipe (page 281). Blend in the liqueur, then pour the mousse into 6 small custard cups and sprinkle with the pistachios. Chill until serving time.

EGG MOUSSES

The flavoring of an egg mousse is beaten into the yolks at the same time as the sugar. It may be any liquor or spirit you like, a citrus fruit juice and rind, or melted chocolate.

BASIC PROPORTIONS FOR EGG MOUSSES

2 servings	*3–4 servings*	*5–6 servings*
1 whole egg	2 egg yolks 1 whole egg	3 egg yolks 1 whole egg
2 T. sugar	3–4 T. sugar	⅓ cup sugar
Flavoring of your choice *	Flavoring of your choice *	Flavoring of your choice *
⅓ cup heavy or medium cream or 2 egg whites	⅔ cup heavy or medium cream or 3 egg whites	1 cup heavy cream or medium or 4 egg whites

* The quantity of flavoring will vary with the type of flavoring: use 1½ teaspoons liquor or brandy per serving; 1 tablespoon citrus fruit juice and ½ teaspoon citrus fruit rind per serving; 1 ounce of semisweet chocolate per serving and per egg.

KEY RECIPE: Beat the egg yolk, whole eggs, or combination of egg yolks and whole eggs with the sugar until the mixture falls from the beaters forming a flat uninterrupted ribbon. Beat the foaming agent (cream or egg whites).

Beat one quarter of the foaming agent into the base and fold in the remainder. Positively keep in the freezer until ready to use, covered with foil or plastic wrap, or the mousse will separate.

Prepare the mousse as close as possible to dinner-serving time, since mousses made with heavy cream will be mellow even if solidly frozen, but made with egg whites they will be hard as a rock.

SABRA MOUSSE

SERVINGS: 6

PREPARATION TIME: 10 MINUTES

3 egg yolks
1 whole egg
⅓ cup sugar
Finely grated rind of one orange

1 ounce semisweet chocolate, melted
 and cooled
3½ tablespoons sabra liqueur
1 cup heavy cream, whipped

Put the yolks and whole egg, sugar, and orange rind in a large bowl. Beat until very thick and a ribbon forms. Beat in the cooled chocolate and the sabra liqueur. Beat the cream, mix one quarter of it in the yolk base, and fold in the remainder. Keep in the freezer until ready to use.

TANGERINE MOUSSE

SERVINGS: 2

PREPARATION TIME: 7 TO 8 MINUTES

2 tablespoons sugar or honey
Rind of 2 tangerines
1 tablespoon tangerine juice
1 egg

1½ tablespoons orange liqueur
⅓ heavy or medium cream or 2 egg
 whites

Mash the sugar and tangerine rind together to extract the rind taste. Add the tangerine juice to dissolve the sugar. Discard the rinds. Add the egg to the sugar and beat until a ribbon forms, then beat in the orange liqueur. Beat the cream or egg whites; mix one quarter of the egg whites into the tangerine base and fold in the remainder. Store in the freezer until ready to use.

QUICK ICES

YOGURT ICE

You can make a very quick, refreshing and healthy ice using yogurt, honey, and either lemon juice or fresh fruit.

KEY RECIPE: Mix 1 cup yogurt with as much honey as you like and as much lemon juice as you like. Pour into a freezer tray and let become semisolid. If you wish to use fresh fruit instead of the lemon juice, simply mix the honey and fruit and puree in the blender; stir into the yogurt and freeze until semisolid. No exact proportions are needed for this—use as much yogurt, honey, lemon juice, or fruit as you like.

Frozen Fruit Ice

Raspberries, strawberries, nectarines, and apricots are the star fruit for this preparation, but use any frozen fruit you have—and as much as you desire, or as much as your diet requires.

KEY RECIPE: Let the fruit defrost superficially but remain hard at the center. Crush it with a fork. Put honey or sugar at the bottom of the blender container, add the crushed fruit and blend. You will obtain a thickish fruit puree that is absolutely delicious.

QUICK PUDDINGS AND CUSTARDS

Although it is wise in everyday cookery to limit your dessert to fresh fruit or a fruit dessert, there are a few classic puddings and custards that you can make in a jiffy. Watch the calories—all of them contain either flour or other starch or eggs—or even both—as a thickener.

Puddings

FLOUR-BASED PUDDINGS

Start by making a plain pudding using the following proportions. You may then add beaten egg whites and/or cream to lighten the pudding and flavorings to brighten its basic taste.

BASIC PROPORTIONS FOR FLOUR-BASED PUDDINGS

2 servings	*3 servings*	*4 servings*	*5–6 servings*
1 egg yolk	2 egg yolks	3 egg yolks	4 egg yolks
1½ T. sugar	2¾ T. sugar	¼ cup sugar	7 T. sugar
1½ T. sifted flour	2¾ T. sifted flour	¼ cup sifted flour	⅓ cup sifted flour
½ tsp. vanilla extract	¾ tsp. vanilla extract	1 tsp. vanilla extract	1½ tsp. vanilla extract
⅓ cup cold milk	⅔ cup cold milk	1 cup cold milk	1⅓ cups cold milk
Small pinch of salt	Pinch of salt	Pinch of salt	Large pinch of salt
Flavoring of your choice	Flavoring of your choice	Flavoring of your choice	Flavoring of your choice
1 egg white (optional)	2 egg whites (optional)	3 egg whites (optional)	4 egg whites (optional)
2 T. heavy cream (optional)	¼ cup heavy cream (optional)	½ cup heavy cream (optional)	¾ cup heavy cream (optional)

If you use honey instead of sugar as a sweetener, use one fourth less honey than the amount of sugar given in the recipe, but then use 2 tablespoons flour for each egg yolk in the recipe. For example, the recipe for 6 servings made with honey will read:

4 egg yolks	1⅓ cups cold milk
5¼ tablespoons honey	4 egg whites
½ cup sifted flour	¾ cup heavy cream (optional)
1½ teaspoons vanilla extract	

You may use the milk of your choice, whole or skim; whole milk tastes better. The optional egg whites and cream at the end of each list of ingredients can, if you wish, be beaten and folded into the basic pudding. The cream obtained is considerably lighter and smoother.

As for the flavoring, add—besides the vanilla, which is here to temper the strong egg taste—any liqueur of your choice or any pure extract of your choice. The most common liquors and spirits are: rum, Curaçao, Grand Marnier, and kirsch; but you can also use almond extract, almond liqueur, green Chartreuse, sabra liqueur, or raspberry brandy.

KEY RECIPE: Use a thick-bottomed pot. Mix the yolks and sugar and beat 3 minutes until almost white and foamy. Blend in the flour. Mix the vanilla extract and milk. Dilute the other ingredients with the milk; put on medium heat and bring to a boil. Stir constantly (you may use the hand electric mixer on slow speed) until the mixture boils and thickens. Turn into a bowl and let cool 3 minutes Add liqueur or spirit to your taste. Then if you wish to lighten the pudding, beat the egg whites, stir in one quarter of their volume and fold in the remainder. Chill the cream.

If you wish to add whipped cream, whip the cream, not too stiff, and fold it into the chilled pudding.

CRÈME SUCHARD

SERVINGS: 2

PREPARATION TIME: 10 MINUTES

Flour-based pudding for 2, with egg whites (page 286)

1 tablespoon rum
1 ounce bittersweet Swiss chocolate

Make the basic pudding as indicated in the key recipe (page 287 above). Add the rum. Beat the egg white. Chop the chocolate in small pieces, sprinkle it over the egg white, and fold all together into the pudding. Turn into custard cups.

CRÈME AUX FRAMBOISES

SERVINGS: 6

PREPARATION TIME: 40 MINUTES

Flour-based pudding for 6, with egg
   whites and cream (page 286)
3 tablespoons framboise (raspberry
   brandy)

1 pint fresh raspberries or 2 boxes
   frozen raspberries, thawed and
   well drained
2 tablespoons confectioners' sugar
2 tablespoons chopped, blanched
   pistachios or almonds

Make the cream, following the key recipe (page 287), flavoring it with
raspberry brandy. Chill the cream well. Put half of it in an attractive
dish. Sprinkle that first layer with raspberries; top the berries with the
remainder of the cream. Keep chilled. Just before serving, sprinkle the
top of the cream with a mixture of confectioners' sugar and pistachios
or almonds.

STARCH-BASED MILK OR FRUIT-PULP PUDDINGS

Although these puddings can be made with egg yolks, for everyday use
keep them egg free; they taste best made with whole milk or fruit
pulp pureed in a blender, but using skim milk is perfectly acceptable.

BASIC PROPORTIONS FOR STARCH PUDDINGS

2 servings	*3–4 servings*	*4–5 servings*	*5–6 servings*
¾ cup milk or fruit puree	1 cup milk or fruit puree	1¼ cups milk or fruit puree	1½ cups milk or fruit puree
2 tsp. potato starch	3 tsp. potato starch	4 tsp. potato starch	5 tsp. potato starch
3 T. sugar	¼ cup sugar	⅓ cup sugar	½ cup sugar
Pinch of salt	Pinch of salt	Pinch of salt	Pinch of salt
Flavoring of your choice	Flavoring of your choice	Flavoring of your choice	Flavoring of your choice

If you use honey instead of sugar, use one quarter less than the
amount of sugar given in the recipe but use 1¼ teaspoons starch for
each quarter cup of milk. The recipe for 6 servings made with honey
should read:

1½ cups milk or fruit puree   6 tablespoons honey
6¼ teaspoons potato starch   Flavoring of your choice

Use the same flavorings as for the flour-based puddings (page 286).

KEY RECIPE: Mix the cold milk, starch, honey, or sugar and bring to a boil on medium heat, stirring constantly. Pour into small dessert cups and let cool before chilling in the refrigerator, or for faster results, in the freezer. Plastic wrap stretched over the top of each container will prevent the formation of a thick skin while cooling.

COFFEE PUDDING

SERVINGS: 2

PREPARATION TIME: 10 MINUTES

¾ cup milk of your choice   3 tablespoons sugar
1 tablespoon instant coffee powder   Pinch of salt
   or Sanka powder   1 tablespoon brandy or Cognac
2 teaspoons potato starch

Make the pudding, following the key recipe (above) and dissolving the coffee well into the milk before cooking. As soon as the pudding has thickened, remove from the heat and add the brandy. Turn into custard cups and chill.

CARAMEL PUDDING

SERVINGS: 2

PREPARATION TIME: 15 MINUTES

1 tablespoon water   2 teaspoons potato starch
3 tablespoons sugar   Pinch of salt
¾ cup milk of your choice   ½ teaspoon vanilla extract

Put the water and sugar in a 1-quart saucepan. Bring to a boil and let cook to a dark caramel, stirring constantly. Add ½ cup of the milk and dissolve the caramel in it. Mix the starch with the remainder of the milk and blend into the caramel milk. Thicken on medium heat, stirring constantly. Add the salt and vanilla, then pour into custard cups and chill.

This berry custard laced with kirsch is a favorite dessert in German-speaking countries.

ROTE GRÜTZE

SERVINGS: 6

PREPARATION TIME: 25 MINUTES

3 boxes frozen raspberries, defrosted and well drained
2 cups strawberries, fresh or frozen (without sugar) and defrosted
¼ cup blackcurrant jam

5 teaspoons potato starch
3 tablespoons kirsch
½ cup heavy cream, whipped
1 tablespoon confectioners' sugar or 2 teaspoons honey

Put the raspberries, strawberries, and jam in the blender container and puree. Strain through a sauce strainer to discard the raspberry seeds. Bring all but ¼ cup of the puree to a boil. Mix the potato starch with the remainder of the puree and blend, stirring, into the boiling puree until thickened. Remove from the heat, cool, and add 2 tablespoons kirsch. Pour into custard cups and chill. Beat the heavy cream with the confectioners' sugar and the remaining kirsch until stiff. Spoon an equal amount of the cream on each portion of pudding.

STIRRED CUSTARDS

A stirred custard, made only of egg yolks, sweetener and milk can be used as a quick sauce for fresh fruit or as a base for a foamy Spanish cream.

BASIC PROPORTIONS FOR STIRRED CUSTARD

2 servings	*3–4 servings*	*5–6 servings*
2 egg yolks	3 egg yolks	5 egg yolks
2 T. sugar	3 T. sugar	5 T. sugar
Pinch of salt	Pinch of salt	Pinch of salt
½ cup scalded milk	¾ cup scalded milk	1¼ cups scalded milk
Flavoring of your choice	Flavoring of your choice	Flavoring of your choice

KEY RECIPE: Mix the egg yolks, sugar, and salt and stir together until a foam only starts to build. Gradually add the scalded milk and cook on medium heat, stirring constantly, until the cream coats the spoon or spatula. The custard is done when the foam disappears from the surface of the custard. *Do not boil* or the custard will curdle. Add flavoring and chill in the freezer.

You may use whatever you like as a flavoring for this custard—extract or liqueur. Adapt the flavoring to the fruit served (see page 272).

STRAWBERRIES SAMUEL

SERVINGS: 2

PREPARATION TIME: 10 MINUTES

12 large, ripe strawberries
2 tablespoons kirsch or Curaçao

Stirred custard for 2 (above)

Sprinkle the strawberries with 1 tablespoon of the liqueur. Make the stirred custard according to the key recipe (above), flavoring it with the second tablespoon of liqueur. Chill it in the freezer and pour it over the berries.

This cinnamon-flavored orange custard is a classic dessert from Spain.

NATILLAS Y NARANJAS

SERVINGS: 2

PREPARATION TIME: 10 MINUTES

2 navel oranges, sliced
Ground cinnamon

Stirred custard for 2 (page 291)

Peel the oranges down to the pulp and slice them across in ¼-inch slices. Place the orange slices in a small, deep dish and sprinkle them with a bit of ground cinnamon. Make the custard, following the key recipe (page 291), and flavor it with a bit of cinnamon.

Chill the custard in the freezer, and just before serving pour it over the orange slices.

SPANISH CREAMS A Spanish cream is a cooled custard to which gelatin is added and into which beaten egg whites are folded to obtain a lesser type of Bavarian cream. It is a bit more time consuming than a basic flour-bound pudding, but still an easy and attractive dessert.

BASIC PROPORTIONS FOR SPANISH CREAMS

2 servings	*3–4 servings*	*5–6 servings*
2 egg yolks	3 egg yolks	5 egg yolks
3 T. sugar	¼ cup sugar	½ cup sugar
Pinch of salt	Pinch of salt	Pinch of salt
½ cup scalded milk	¾ cup scalded milk	1¼ cups scalded milk
⅔ tsp. gelatin	1⅛ tsp. gelatin	2 tsp. gelatin
Flavoring of your choice	Flavoring of your choice	Flavoring of your choice
2 egg whites	3 egg whites	4 egg whites

KEY RECIPE: Make a stirred custard as directed in the key recipe (page 291), using the egg yolks, sugar, salt, and scalded milk.

Mix the gelatin with a bit of cold water, add it to the hot custard and stir until well dissolved. Let cool. Add the flavoring, which may be any extract or liqueur of your choice. Whip the egg whites and fold them into the cool custard. Turn into custard cups or a dish.

COCOA SPANISH CREAM

SERVINGS: 2

PREPARATION TIME: 30 MINUTES, INCLUDING
COOLING OF THE CUSTARD

There is one additional tablespoon of sugar to tame the bitter cocoa.

2 egg yolks
¼ cup sugar
¼ teaspoon cinnamon
Pinch of salt
2 tablespoons cocoa

½ cup scalded milk
⅔ teaspoon gelatin
1 tablespoon crème de cacao
2 egg whites, beaten

With the egg yolks, sugar, cinnamon, salt, cocoa and scalded milk, make a stirred custard as directed in the key recipe (page 291). Add the gelatin, softened in a bit of cold water, and stir until dissolved. Cool, then add the crème de cacao. Whip the egg whites and fold into the cooled custard. Pour into custard cups or a serving dish.

This pineapple-rum confection is a favorite dessert in Hawaii.

HAUPIA

SERVINGS: 6

PREPARATION TIME: 35 MINUTES, INCLUDING
COOLING OF THE CUSTARD

6 slices fresh, ripe pineapple
¼ cup rum (light or dark, according to your taste)
1 tablespoon confectioners' sugar
5 egg yolks
⅓ cup granulated sugar

Pinch of salt
1¼ cups scalded milk
2 teaspoons gelatin
1 cup shredded sweetened coconut
4 egg whites, beaten

Marinate the pineapple slices in a mixture of 3 tablespoons of the rum and the confectioners' sugar while you prepare the Spanish cream. Make the stirred custard, according to the key recipe (page 291), with the egg yolks, granulated sugar, salt, and scalded milk. Add the gelatin, softened in a bit of cold water, and stir until dissolved. Add the shredded coconut and the last tablespoon of rum. Cool. Beat the egg whites and fold them into the coconut custard. Spoon the Spanish cream on top of the pineapple slices.

ZABAGLIONE

The great Italian dessert sauce, zabaglione, can be made in a matter of minutes. Although it is really a sauce, it can be eaten as a warm mousse if served as soon as prepared, or as a cold mousse if chilled and mixed with some heavy cream.

BASIC PROPORTIONS FOR WARM ZABAGLIONE

2 servings	*3–4 servings*	*5–6 servings*
2 egg yolks	3 egg yolks	5 egg yolks
¼ cup sugar	⅓ cup sugar	½ cup sugar
¼ cup dry white wine	⅓ cup dry white wine	½ cup dry white wine
2 T. liquor of your choice	2½ T. liquor of your choice	¼ cup liquor of your choice

BASIC PROPORTIONS FOR COLD ZABAGLIONE

Use the same proportions as for warm zabaglione (page 294), plus:

2 *servings*	3–4 *servings*	5–6 *servings*
¼ cup heavy cream	⅓ cup heavy cream	½ cup heavy cream

K E Y   R E C I P E : *For warm zabaglione:* Mix the yolks and sugar in a saucepan and whisk them until they are foamy, thick, almost white, and fall from the whisk in a heavy ribbon that folds upon itself. Place the saucepan on medium-low heat and gradually pour in the white wine, continuing to whisk until the custard feels very warm to the top of the finger and appears homogenous and bound. *Do not boil,* or you will obtain wine-flavored scrambled eggs. Remove the custard from the heat and add the liquor, whisking well to homogenize. Pour into serving cups or glasses and serve warm.

For cold zabaglione: Prepare the warm zabaglione as described above. Pour the cooked custard into the small bowl of the electric mixer and beat on high speed until cold. Whip the heavy cream until it barely holds its shape and fold into the cold zabaglione. Chill in freezer.

Instead of using white wine to make the zabaglione, you may use any fruit juice of your choice and tune the taste of the liquor or liqueur used to the taste of the juice. For example, if you use orange juice, you can also use a bit of very finely grated orange rind and Curaçao, Grand Marnier, or Cognac. Instead of plain white table wine, you can use one of the generous wines like Madeira, port, or Marsala.

SABAYON À LA JULIETTE

SERVINGS: 2

PREPARATION TIME: 10 MINUTES

2 tablespoons candied fruit	2 egg yolks
	3 tablespoons sugar
3 tablespoons rum	¼ cup dry white wine

Let the fruit marinate in 1 tablespoon of the rum from morning to evening. Make the zabaglione according to the key recipe for warm zabaglione (page 295), and when it is cooked add the remaining 2 tablespoons rum. Pour the zabaglione over the candied fruit and mix well. Serve in custard cups or glasses.

Emilio lives in Florence and this is how he prepares peaches.

PESCHE EMILIO

SERVINGS: 6

PREPARATION TIME: 35 MINUTES, INCLUDING COOKING
OF THE ZABAGLIONE

3 white peaches, halved and peeled	5 egg yolks
	½ cup sugar
¼ cup plus 3 tablespoons maraschino	½ cup dry Marsala
	½ cup heavy cream, whipped

Put the peach halves in a serving bowl and sprinkle them with the 3 tablespoons maraschino. Make the zabaglione as described in the key recipe for cold zabaglione (page 295), using the Marsala to cook the custard and the remainder of the maraschino as flavoring. Pour the cold zabaglione over the peaches and keep chilled in freezer until ready to serve.

SOUFFLÉ: A QUICK CLASSIC DESSERT

All instructions given for savory soufflés on pages 52–53 are valid for dessert soufflés. Please read them before proceeding to making one.

Making a soufflé of the type described below represents a time expenditure of 15 minutes for the making and 10 to 14 minutes for the baking, not more; keep portions small. The soufflé is soft at the center and requires no sauce.

BASIC PROPORTIONS FOR SOUFFLÉ

1–3 servings	*4–6 servings*
(3-cup mold)	*(6-cup mold)*
1 T. flour	2 T. flour
2½ T. sugar	⅓ cup sugar
Pinch of salt	Pinch of salt
¼ cup milk	½ cup milk
2 egg yolks	4 egg yolks
3 egg whites	5 egg whites
¼ cup liqueur of	⅓–½ cup liqueur
your choice	of your choice
4 single ladyfingers	6 single ladyfingers

BASIC PROPORTIONS FOR POLYUNSATURATED SOUFFLÉ BATTER

1–3 servings	*4–6 servings*
(3-cup mold)	*(6-cup mold)*
½ tsp. potato starch	1 tsp. potato starch
2½ T. sugar	⅓ cup sugar
Pinch of salt	Pinch of salt
¼ cup skim milk	½ cup skim milk
3 egg whites	5 egg whites
¼ cup liqueur of	⅓–½ cup liqueur of
your choice	your choice
4 single ladyfingers	6 single ladyfingers

KEY RECIPE: This recipe applies to both batters. With flour or starch, sugar, salt, and milk, make a pudding and thicken it on a medium-high flame. Add the egg yolks, if used, and half of the liqueur. Beat the egg whites until they can carry the weight of a raw egg in its shell: mix one quarter of the whites into the custard and fold in the remainder. Butter or grease and lightly sugar the inside of the soufflé mold. Saturate the ladyfingers with the remainder of the liqueur. Spoon half of the soufflé batter into the mold. Add the ladyfingers, top with the remainder of the batter, smooth the soufflé top, and bake, at 400° F., on the lowest rack of the oven, 10 minutes for the 3-cup mold and 14 minutes for the 6-cup mold.

Use any liqueur you like for a flavoring.

Before you start making the soufflé, remember that you may choose to finish it completely but not bake it; wrap it in foil and freeze the uncooked soufflé. When you are ready to bake the soufflé, remove it directly from the freezer to the lowest rack of a 400° F. oven; it will bake in 18 minutes for the 3-cup mold and 25 minutes for the 6-cup mold.

QUICK FRUIT COBBLERS (Clafouti)

To use damaged and old fruit, the French bake them in a crêpe batter. The result is a clafouti, which is nothing more than a fruit cobbler made without baking powder.

BASIC PROPORTIONS FOR CLAFOUTI

2–4 servings	*5–6 servings*
2 T. flour	¼ cup flour
¼ tsp. salt	⅓ tsp. salt
1 egg	2 eggs
1 T. sour cream or yogurt	2 T. sour cream or yogurt
⅓ cup milk	⅓ cup milk
Grated lemon rind or 1 T. liqueur of your choice	Grated lemon rind or 2 T. liqueur of your choice
1 tsp. butter or oil	2 tsp. butter or oil
1½–2 cups cut-up fruit	2½–3 cups cut-up fruit

KEY RECIPE: Put the flour, salt, egg, sour cream, milk, rind or liqueur in the blender container and whirl 1 minute on high speed.

Butter the pan or mold; heat it on a stove burner. Pour one quarter of the batter in the pan and spread it over the whole bottom of the pan, to cook it like a pancake. Put the fruit on top of the cake and spread it well, then pour the remainder of the batter on top. Bake in a preheated 375° F. oven for 35 to 40 minutes.

The following combinations of fruit and liqueurs may be used:
For fall and winter:

> Pears and rum (or ground cloves)
> Apples and applejack (or cinnamon)
> Bananas and rum
> Orange or tangerine slices and orange liqueur

For spring and summer:

> Strawberries and kirsch or Curaçao
> Cherries (any type) and cherry brandy or kirsch
> Peaches and bourbon or brandy
> Apricots with kirsch, cognac or brandy
> Blueberries with lime rind and bourbon
> Italian plums and lemon rind

CRANBERRY-ORANGE CLAFOUTI
SERVINGS: 2 TO 4

PREPARATION TIME: 40 MINUTES, INCLUDING BAKING TIME

Basic clafouti batter for 2 to 4 servings (page 299)
½ eight-ounce jar of cranberry-
orange relish

1 small can tangerine sections or 1
cup fresh tangerine sections

Follow the key recipe (page 299) exactly. Spread the relish on the
bottom layer of the batter, add the tangerine sections, then pour the
remainder of the batter on top and bake.

PEAR CLAFOUTI
SERVINGS: 6

PREPARATION TIME: 50 MINUTES, INCLUDING BAKING TIME

3 ripe pears
Basic clafouti batter for 5 to 6 servings (page 299)

Ground cloves

Peel the pears and slice them into 8 slices each. Follow the key recipe
(page 299), spreading the pears on the bottom layer of the batter and
sprinkling the fruit with a few dashes of cloves. Pour the remainder
of the batter on the fruit and bake.

QUICK TARTS AND TARTLETS

QUICK TART PASTRY
The following recipe will make 5 eight-inch shells ⅛ inch thick, or 4
dozen tartlet shells 3 inches in diameter and of the same thickness.

QUICK TART OR TARTLET PASTRY

With butter or margarine

4 cups sifted all-purpose flour
1½ cups butter or margarine
2 tsp. salt
¾ cup water

With polyunsaturated oil

4 cups sifted all-purpose flour
1 cup sunflower oil
2 tsp. salt
½ cup plus 2 T. water

KEY RECIPE: Proceed for each type of pastry as described in the section on quiches (pages 60–61), then divide each ball of dough into 5 equal parts. Shape each ball into a 3½ × 1-inch cake. Wrap it in freezer paper and freeze. When you want to use one cake of dough, remove it from the freezer and let it defrost: 1 hour at room temperature or from morning to night in the lower part of the refrigerator.

For an 8-inch shell (25 minutes with already defrosted dough): Use a buttered or greased flan ring placed on a buttered or greased unbendable cookie sheet, a dull aluminum pie plate, or a French porcelain fluted plate. (Do not use a detachable-bottomed pan of any kind, or the bottom of the shell will neither brown nor cook properly.) Roll the dough out to a thickness of ⅛ inch and as close as possible to a circle 9½ to 10 inches wide. Fit the dough into the flan ring or plate. Crimp the edge with the tines of a fork, then prick the bottoms and sides of the shell heavily with a fork, so as to obtain row after row of holes ¼ inch apart. Fill the shell with parchment paper or foil and fill the paper to the brim with at least 4 cups dried beans. Let the shell rest 10 minutes, then bake the shell 10 minutes in a 425° F. oven. Remove the beans with a spoon, then remove the foil. Sprinkle with about a teaspoon of sugar and return to the oven for another 3 to 5 minutes, watching carefully so the shell does not brown too much. Remove the shell to a rack and let cool.

For 3½-inch tartlet shells (30 minutes with already defrosted dough): Roll the dough out to a thickness of ⅛ inch and as wide as possible. Cut circles of dough 4 inches wide and fit them into as many buttered 3½-inch pie plates as possible. Prick the dough, line each shell with parchment paper, fill it to the brim with beans and bake 7 to 8 minutes in a 425° F. oven. Remove the beans and papers, sprinkle each of the shells with a pinch of sugar, and return to the oven for 3 to 5 more minutes. Watch carefully so that the shells do not brown too much. Remove to a rack and cool.

Small shells can be stored in tight-fitting cans and kept several weeks; when you have time on a weekend make 3 or 4 dozen shells at once and store them for later use. The shells may also be kept frozen.

QUICK FILLINGS FOR TARTS

The quickest and most delicious filling for a fruit tart is one made of uncooked, sliced fresh fruit set on a bed of stiffly whipped cream flavored with liqueur.

BASIC PROPORTIONS FOR FILLING SHELLS

To fill 1 eight-inch shell

1 cup heavy cream
2 T. sugar
2 T. liqueur of your choice
2 to 3 cups fruit
¼ cup melted apricot jam
    for fruit or currant jelly
    for red and black berries

To fill 1 tartlet

2 T. heavy cream, whipped
½ tsp. sugar
1 tsp. lemon
½ large fruit (pear, nectarine, peach)
    or
¼ to ⅓ cup berries

You may use any of the following fresh fruits, each of which is paired with its most appropriate flavoring and glaze. You can, of course, use any kind of canned or dried stewed fruit you like, using the same flavorings as for the fresh fruit.

Grapes	Flavor the cream with Cognac; use wine jelly as a glaze (no Concord grape jelly, please)
Peaches (peeled)	Flavor the cream with Curaçao; use apricot jam as a glaze
Nectarines (peeled)	Flavor the cream with almond liqueur; use apricot jam as a glaze
Strawberries	Flavor the cream with kirsch or Curaçao; use currant jelly as a glaze
Raspberries	Flavor the cream with kirsch or raspberry brandy and use raspberry jelly as glaze
Blueberries	Flavor the cream with bourbon; use black-currant jam as a glaze
Kiwi berries	Flavor the cream with finely grated lemon rind; use lemon marmalade as a glaze
Apricots (fresh and peeled or dried and stewed)	Flavor the cream with Cognac or kirsch; use apricot jam as a glaze
Cantaloupe	Flavor the cream with port; use peach jam as a glaze
Honeydew melon	Flavor the cream with Marsala; use ginger marmalade as a glaze
Pineapple	Flavor the cream with rum; use pineapple jam as a glaze
Pears (sliced and sautéed in butter)	Use a pinch each of ginger and cloves in the cream, and apricot jam as a glaze
Apples (sliced and sautéed in butter)	Use Calvados or applejack in the cream and apple jelly as a glaze

QUICK TART FILLING FOR POLYUNSATURATED DIETS

To avoid the large amounts of cholesterol-producing butterfat contained in heavy cream, persons on fat-controlled diets can use the following custard to fill 1 eight-inch pie shell or 6 three-and-one-half inch tartlet shells. The custard takes 10 minutes to prepare.

1 teaspoon potato starch
¼ cup sugar
Pinch of salt
1 cup skim milk
1½ teaspoons gelatin

1 teaspoon extract flavoring or 2 tablespoons liqueur of your choice
1 egg white
2 drops yellow food coloring (optional)

Mix together the potato starch, sugar, and salt and dilute with the skim milk. Bring to a boil over a medium flame, stirring to thicken. Add the gelatin, softened in a little bit of cold water, and stir until well dissolved. Add the flavoring. Let cool a bit, then whip the egg white and fold it into the custard. Spoon into baked tart shells. If you allow yourself the use of food coloring, add the 2 drops of coloring —the custard will appear yellow, as if it contained egg yolks.

TARTELETTE AUX RAISINS

SERVINGS: 2

PREPARATION TIME: 10 MINUTES, WITH SHELLS PREBAKED

½ to ⅔ cup grapes of your choice
¼ cup heavy cream
1½ teaspoons confectioners' sugar
1 tablespoon Cognac

2 small tartlet shells (page 302), prebaked
2 teaspoons melted wine jelly

Stem, wash, and dry the grapes. Beat the cream till stiff, adding the sugar and Cognac to it. Fill each shell with half of the cream. Pile half of the grapes into each shell and glaze with the melted jelly.

TARTE AUX POMMES FLAMBÉES

SERVINGS: 6

PREPARATION TIME WITH SHELL PREBAKED: 20 MINUTES

1 eight-inch tart shell (page 301), prebaked
1 cup heavy cream
2 tablespoons confectioners' sugar

¼ cup Calvados or applejack
6 Russet or Golden Grimes apples
¼ cup butter
1 tablespoon granulated sugar

Have the tart shell ready. Whip the cream, with the sugar and 2 tablespoons of Calvados or applejack, till stiff. Fill the shell with the cream. Peel the apples, cut them in 8 slices each. Sauté them in butter to brown and cook them; you may have to cook them in two batches. When all the apples have been browned, sprinkle them with the granulated sugar and flambé them with the remaining Calvados or applejack, and let cool. When cold, arrange the apple slices in concentric circles on the bed of cream.

CHAPTER XV

Quick Bakery

BREAD

The Swiss in their marvelous practicality make one of the best and fastest yeast breads existing—the weggli, that odd-shaped little roll that looks like what in Victorian times would have been unmentionable, a pair of buttocks. For maximum efficiency make the dough early in the morning and put it to rise the whole day in the refrigerator. If you have the time let stand and rise at room temperature for 1½ hours.

WEGGLI

YIELD: 2 DOZEN ROLLS

PREPARATION TIME: 1 HOUR 15 MINUTES, PLUS 3 TO 12 HOURS
RISING TIME

1 cup plus 2 tablespoons lukewarm milk or skim milk

3 tablespoons sugar or 1½ tablespoons honey

1 envelope active dry yeast

¼ cup melted butter or margarine, cooled

1 teaspoon salt

2⅓ cups flour

1 egg yolk

Mix the 1 cup milk and sugar or honey in a large bowl. Sprinkle the yeast over the milk and let stand until the mixture bubbles. Stir in the cooled butter, the salt, and the flour. Knead until smooth and elastic. Let stand 30 minutes at room temperature, then cover and let rise in the refrigerator. Punch the dough down and roll into little balls 2½ inches in diameter. Put the balls on a greased baking sheet. Let them rise until doubled in bulk. Then, just before baking, with the back of a long floured knife blade, cut the dough balls straight down in half, without cutting through at the bottom. Combine the egg yolk with the 2 tablespoons of milk and use the mixture to brush the rolls. Bake for 10 to 12 minutes in a preheated 425° F. oven.

COOKIES

In this author's opinion, cookies are much ado about nothing, but in respect to differing opinions, here are two formulas for fast cookies; one full of dangerous, delicious, fattening heavy cream, the other polyunsaturated.

GRANDMÈRES

YIELD: 3 DOZEN COOKIES

PREPARATION TIME: 20 MINUTES

1 cup heavy cream
1 tablespoon vanilla extract
⅓ cup sugar

Pinch of salt
⅓ cup sifted flour
⅓ cup raisins

Butter a cookie sheet. Whip the cream, vanilla, sugar, and salt, then fold in the flour mixed with the raisins. Spoon teaspoons of batter onto a cookie sheet at 1½-inch intervals and bake for 12 to 14 minutes in a 375° F. oven.

JAPONAIS AUX NOIX

YIELD: 2 DOZEN COOKIES

PREPARATION TIME: 20 MINUTES

3 egg whites
⅓ cup plus 1 tablespoon sugar

1 cup finely ground walnuts,
   almonds, or pecans
¼ teaspoon vanilla extract

Butter or oil and flour 2 cookie sheets. Beat the egg whites with the 1 tablespoon sugar and the vanilla until they can carry the weight of a raw egg in its shell. Fold in the nuts, mixed with the remainder of the sugar. Drop small walnut-sized pieces of the batter onto the cookie sheets and flatten them to the size of a silver dollar with the back of a spoon. Bake 10 to 12 minutes in a 325° F. oven. Remove to a cake rack to cool.

CAKES

If a pie made with polyunsaturated oil or margarine can still taste acceptable, such is not the case for a cake. Make a cake rarely if your diet is strict, but when you make a cake, make a truly good one full of fresh butter, not full of despicably bad-tasting vegetable shortening or noncommittal margarine.

An All-Purpose Cake

The recipe below is for an all-purpose, basic butter cake that is usable for everything from shortcake for berries to batter for an upside-down cake; it is made in 40 minutes from start to finish. The origin is my mother's thrifty French kitchen.

BASIC BUTTER CAKE FOR EVERY DAY

YIELD: 1 NINE-INCH LAYER OR 8 SERVINGS

PREPARATION TIME: 40 MINUTES

10 tablespoons butter
½ cup sugar
¼ teaspoon salt
1 tablespoon vanilla extract

2 eggs
1 cup sifted flour
1 teaspoon baking powder

Cream the butter; add the sugar and salt and vanilla. Beat until white. Add the eggs, one by one, beating hard after each addition. Blend in the flour and baking powder and turn into a buttered and floured 9-inch pan. Bake 30 minutes at 350° F.

STRAWBERRY SHORTCAKE

SERVINGS: 6 TO 8

PREPARATION TIME: 10 MINUTES

1 nine-inch basic butter cake (page above)
⅔ cup kirsch or Grand Marnier
⅓ cup water

3 tablespoons sugar
1 cup heavy cream
1 quart very ripe strawberries, hulled and cleaned

Have the butter cake ready. Mix ½ cup of the liqueur with the water and 1½ tablespoons of the sugar. Stir well to dissolve the sugar. Saturate the cake well with the mixture; this is best done by pouring half of the syrup into a cake platter and setting the cake on it, then spooning the remainder of the syrup over the whole top of the cake.

Whip the cream stiffly with the remainder of the liqueur and sugar. Top the cake with the cream and the berries and serve.

PRUNE UPSIDE-DOWN CAKE

SERVINGS: 6 to 8

PREPARATION TIME: 45 MINUTES, PLUS OVERNIGHT SOAKING TIME FOR THE PRUNES

1 pound soft California prunes, pitted	2 tablespoons butter
	3 tablespoons sugar
⅔ cup water	Basic butter cake batter (page 309)
⅓ cup plus 2 tablespoons rum or slivovitz	1 cup heavy cream

Soak the prunes overnight in a mixture of the water and the ⅓ cup rum or slivovitz.

Melt the butter in a 9-inch cake pan. Add 2 tablespoons of the sugar and the prune soaking liquid. Reduce to 3 tablespoons. Cut the prunes open and flatten them, skin side down, in the cake pan. Keep on a slow burner until the prunes have heated through, then spoon the cake batter over them. Bake for 35 minutes in a preheated 350° oven.

Unmold and serve lukewarm, with the cream whipped with the remaining tablespoon of sugar and the remaining 2 tablespoons of rum or slivovitz.

Two Pretty Cakes for Company Dinners

MOKA

SERVINGS: 12 TO 16

PREPARATION TIME: 1 HOUR

Cake	*Cream*	*Decoration*
4 eggs	6 egg yolks	2 cups sliced, blanched
½ cup granulated	1⅓ cups sifted confec-	almonds
sugar	tioners' sugar	Confectioners' sugar
1 teaspoon salt	5 teaspoons instant	
1 tablespoon rum	coffee powder	
1 cup sifted flour	1 tablespoon rum	
½ cup melted butter	1 cup unsalted butter	

Butter and flour a 9-inch cake pan. Preheat the oven to 325° F. Put the eggs, sugar, salt, and rum into a large bowl and beat with the electric mixer until the mixture is white and thick and spins a very heavy ribbon when falling from the beaters; *fold* in the flour, then *fold* in the melted butter—it is essential *never to stir* to prevent the batter from deflating. Turn into the prepared cake pan and bake 40 minutes on the lowest rack of a 325° F. oven. Invert onto a cake rack, let cool completely, and split horizontally into two layers.

To make the butter cream, put the egg yolks, sugar, and the coffee dissolved in the rum in a large mixing bowl. Beat until very thick, "café au lait" in color, and spinning a heavy ribbon. Cream in the butter, tablespoon by tablespoon, until it has been completely absorbed.

Toast the sliced blanched almonds in a 350° F. oven for 6 to 8 minutes, or until golden. Cool.

Fill the cake with two thirds of the cream. Spread the remainder all around its sides and top; spread the almonds all over the cake and dust lightly with confectioners' sugar.

BÛCHE ARDÉCHOISE

SERVINGS: 8 to 12

PREPARATION TIME: 1 HOUR 15 MINUTES

Roll	*Filling*	*Glaze*
6 eggs	1 can (8¾ ounces)	6 ounces Swiss bitter-
⅔ cup sugar	candied chestnut	sweet chocolate
Pinch of salt	spread	2 tablespoons butter
2 tablespoons rum	3 tablespoons rum	¼ cup warm rum
6 tablespoons bitter	1 cup heavy cream,	¼ cup warm water, if
Dutch cocoa	whipped	necessary

Line a 16 × 12 × 1-inch jelly-roll pan with lightly oiled waxed paper. Preheat the oven to 325° F. Separate the eggs. Whip the egg yolks, sugar, salt, and rum until almost white and until a very heavy ribbon falls from the beaters. Beat the egg whites until they can carry the weight of a raw egg in its shell. Mix one quarter of their volume into the yolk mixture. Slide the remainder of the whites on top of the yolk foam, sift the cocoa over the egg whites, and fold all the ingredients into one another until homogenous. Turn into the prepared jelly-roll pan and bake for 25 minutes. Remove from the oven and let cool completely in the baking pan, covered with slightly damp paper towels.

To make the filling, whip the chestnut spread and rum together, whip the cream two thirds stiff and fold it into the chestnut mixture. Invert the cake on waxed paper, then spread with the cream and roll. Slice the ends off so they look even.

To glaze the cake, melt together the chocolate and butter and gradually blend in the warmed rum. If the icing is too stiff, add as much warm water as will be required to make it workable. Spread the glaze over the cake.

Index

Madeleine Kamman

Madeleine Kamman, born in Paris and educated in languages at the Sorbonne, has, besides a wide culinary experience acquired in the kitchen of a Michelin-starred restaurant, diplomas from several well-known European cooking schools. She is a member of the Escoffier Foundation Society and one of the Eschansons of Châteauneuf du Pape. She has written for Boston Arts, Boston Magazine, Family Health, Farm Journal and other magazines. Mrs. Kamman is food editor-translator of the English edition of La Revue du Vin de France and contributes monthly to the leading French culinary magazine Cuisine et Vins de France. For ten years a food consultant and cooking instructor in Philadelphia, Mrs. Kamman now operates her own school, Modern Gourmet, Inc., in Boston and teaches summer seminars in French cuisine at Luberon College in Aix-en-Provence.